S0-ACB-032

The Process of Competition

The Process of Competition

Edited by

Jackie Krafft

Doctor in Economics
CNRS Research Fellow
IDEFI-LATAPSES, University of Nice–Sophia Antipolis, France

Edward Elgar
Cheltenham, UK • Northampton, MA, USA

Published by
Edward Elgar Publishing Limited
Glensanda House
Montpellier Parade
Cheltenham
Glos GL50 1UA
UK

Edward Elgar Publishing, Inc.
136 West Street
Suite 202
Northampton
Massachusetts 01060
USA

A catalogue record for this book
is available from the British Library

Library of Congress Cataloguing in Publication Data

The process of competition / edited by Jackie Krafft.
A collection of 8 papers by an international group of researchers.
Includes bibliographical references and index.
1. Competition. 2. Competition, International. 3. Industrial efficiency. 4. Industrial organization (Economic theory). 5. Technological innovations—Economic aspects. 6. Evolutionary economics. 7. Industrial policy. I. Krafft, Jackie, 1969–

HB238.P764 2000
338.6'048—dc21 00–020573

ISBN 1 84064 212 2

Printed and bound in Great Britain by Biddles Ltd, *www.biddles.co.uk*

Contents

Figures

Tables

Contributors

Mario Amendola is Professor of Economics at the University of Roma, La Sapienza, Italy.

Kirsten Foss is Associate Professor at the Department of Industrial Economics and Strategy, Copenhagen Business School, Denmark.

Nicolai Foss is Professor of Economic Organization at the Department of Industrial Economics and Strategy, Copenhagen Business School, Denmark, and Director of the 'Learning, Incentives and Knowledge' research program.

Jean-Luc Gaffard is Professor of Economics at the University of Nice–Sophia Antipolis, France, Director of CNRS-IDEFI, and senior member at the Institut Universitaire de France.

Michel Glais is Professor of Economics at the University of Rennes I, and at the ESC Business School of Brest, France.

Israel Kirzner is Professor of Economics at New York University, United States of America.

Jackie Krafft is Doctor in Economics, CNRS Research Fellow at IDEFI-LATAPSES, University of Nice–Sophia Antipolis, France.

Volker Mahnke is Assistant Professor at the Department of Industrial Economics and Strategy, Copenhagen Business School, Denmark.

Patrick Musso is CNRS Research Fellow at IDEFI-LATAPSES, University of Nice–Sophia Antipolis, France.

Michel Quéré is Doctor in Economics, CNRS Research Fellow at IDEFI-LATAPSES, University of Nice–Sophia Antipolis, France.

Jacques-Laurent Ravix is Professor of Economics at the University of Nice–Sophia Antipolis, France, member of CNRS-IDEFI.

1. Introduction

Jackie Krafft

1. THE PROCESS OF COMPETITION: DEFINITION AND OBJECTIVE

This book is dedicated to the analysis of the process of competition. Considering competition as a process implies at first that competition is intrinsically a dynamic and complex phenomenon. In the real world, competition is taken to mean that range of actions aimed at ensuring the realization of the choices of a given firm while restraining at the same time the sphere of actions of its rivals. In the current sense of the word, competition is associated with the verb 'to compete' which involves a process of rivalry between firms for a market or for a productive resource (human, material or financial). This includes rivalry in prices, in improved techniques of production or products, in R&D or in advertising expenses, in the engagement of new productive or distributive activities or in the imitation of existing activities, in the implementation of new forms of organization in which customers, suppliers, partners or even competitors may be involved.

Can this vision of competition be expressed in analytical terms? What are the necessary conditions for it? This book is attempting to answer these questions, using a double point of view. The first crucial point is to assess the different temporal aspects of competition, such as learning, discovery and selection processes, and the connections that can be made between these dimensions which are extensively used in the recent literature. The key element is to determine the evolution of the notion of competition as a process through the emergence of different economic paradigms and to stress what are the basic requirements that allow these different paradigms to deal with the dynamic characteristics of competition. The second crucial point is to analyse the concrete implications of an analysis of the process of competition for public policies, and especially for competition policies. For instance, when competition is analytically considered as a process, pure integration, mergers and acquisitions, cooperation and alliances may become integral parts of the normal functioning of competitive markets. These interfirm relations which are perceived as collusion within the traditional vision of competition can be legitimated for some periods and for specific purposes. Here the key element is to determine the capacity of the analysis of the process of competition to derive operational guidelines for competition policy.

The reader should note the following points. Firstly, the development of an analysis of the process of competition is not dedicated to making existing analytical frameworks more complex by introducing into it numerous characteristics of the concrete functioning of competition. The purpose is rather to elaborate a workable analysis. Secondly, the distinction between 'competition as a state of affairs' and 'competition as a process' is not only a matter of semantics. This distinction conveys alternative frameworks which focus on distinct but sometimes complementary issues. On the one hand, competition as a state of affairs is intrinsically based on the study of equilibrium systems in which the adjustment process is essentially complete. Market clearing is ensured by the fact that agents can have access to information in order to correct their choices through time under perfect rationality. Coordination between agents is then supposed to be perfect and is characterized by a competitive equilibrium or by a Nash equilibrium. Perfect or imperfect competition situations can be described on this basis, each of these situations being analysed as specific equilibria. On the other hand, the process of competition studies situations where market disequilibria prevail. These disequilibria are generated by a constant discovery of new production and market opportunities and, more generally, by the emergence of radical and persistent changes within the economic system. The focus is on the process of adjustment in itself in order to see how interacting firms arrive at any coordination.

For a long time, however, the dynamic and concrete vision of competition has not been at the centre of economic analysis. Even if some authors, such as Hayek (1937, 1946) and Schumpeter (1942) stressed that competition had to be considered as a process, early mainstream economics focused essentially on the negative outcomes of this process. Within this framework, when the process of competition is over, only a few firms remain on the market and the implementation of competitive strategies necessarily implies that some firms acquire or keep a dominant position. The concept of perfect competition in which entry is free, firms are price takers and decisions are independent was dominant in economic analysis and had an important influence on the definition of competition policies. According to the structure–conduct–performance paradigm (Bain, 1956, 1959; Mason, 1957), competition had to be assimilated with a market structure and, consequently, an industry which did not have a competitive structure could not have a competitive behaviour. This idea governed the concrete decisions of antitrust authorities, and markets in which firms were small in number were considered a threat to competition. This vision was significantly weakened during the 1970s (Demsetz, 1973) by the diffusion of the theses of the Chicago School, and the emergence of the analysis of contestable markets (Baumol *et al.*, 1982) which provided a new basis for discussion of this issue during the early 1980s. The Chicago School argued that the methods which were used by the structuralist approach were essentially static in their nature and consequently they were not adequate to analyse intrinsically dynamic competitive phenomena. According to the economists of Chicago, market forces by themselves prevent the existence of dominant firms or monopolistic positions. The authors showed that there is no obvious causality between small number markets and the lack of competition, and no observable tendency to concentration over the long term. The analysis of contestable markets contributed to refining the notion of 'potential competition' which became progressively an analytical reference. As soon as a firm is able to enter a market and to exit without costs according to the 'hit and run' assumption, the market is considered as competitive even if this market is composed of a single firm. In this case, the market structure is naturally composed of this unique firm. This is a 'natural monopoly'. These successive developments show that the conception of competition has evolved in economics. Being considered at first through the comparison of different market structures, competition in the early 1980s was connected to different potentialities of entry and exit. In the mid-1980s the New Industrial Economics emerged as a major framework which soon imposed another vision of competition. Competition was now analysed through the characteristics of different market behaviours where strategic interactions prevailed. Using the apparatus of game theory, this approach was able to describe a complete range of market strategies, from agreements between firms that could be either explicit or tacit, to excessive pricing, price discrimination, predatory pricing or vertical restraints that could deter entry or impose foreclosure (Jacquemin and Slade, 1989; Tirole, 1988; Phlips, 1995).

At that time the deeper understanding of the complexity of competitive phenomena had become a common requirement for economists. However, if we take into account the contributions over the last five years, advances obtained from the 1980s until the early 1990s do not seem sufficient and the 1990s really present a new opportunity to discuss anew the notion and the policy implications of competition as a process. An important feature of these recent developments is that the theme of the process of competition is now studied by economists who belong to different schools of thought. In fact, although this notion was primarily used by heterodox approaches (namely Austrian and evolutionary theories), now it also penetrates more traditional analyses. Moreover, the achievements as well as the limitations of early mainstream analysis are examined and discussed and there is a real attempt to reach a better understanding of the process of competition (Jorde and Teece, 1990; Baumol, 1992; Geroski, 1992; Jacquemin, 1994; Langlois and Robertson, 1995; Machovec, 1995; Vickers, 1995; Blaug, 1997). Competition as a process is a real challenge for all economists and to some extent this challenge calls into question the traditional divisions between existing economic approaches.

The main idea of the recent literature is that the traditional distinction between static and dynamic competition does not contribute at all to the understanding of competitive phenomena. For instance, a study of the works of the founding fathers of the analysis of competition such as Smith, Cournot, Edgeworth and Marshall shows that there was not such a clear divorce between the two notions. It appears that even perfect competition had its roots in the broad concepts of competition as rivalry. Nevertheless, the static analysis was privileged because it allowed the definition of simple criteria for the evaluation of competition, but it was obvious that competitive phenomena were not reducible to these measures. The developments of the 1990s conclude that significant improvements on the debate would be made if we were looking for a more precise definition of the respective domains where these two conceptions apply. Static competition seems extremely useful for analysing all sorts of economic issues such as allocation and price problems, but questions about complex competitive processes and about their effects on productive and innovative phenomena require other approaches.

Within these recent developments, the meeting and the confrontation between alternative approaches on the topic of the process of competition seem to take place progressively. A significant evolution of the different economic paradigms in the last few years was necessary to favour these exchanges. On the one hand, despite considerable advances over the past 15 years on the definition of a wide range of market behaviours and market structures, some ambiguous conclusions remain concerning the effects on economic efficiency within the mainstream framework. For instance, Hay (1993) notes that there is no clear answer whether agreements to exchange information can be considered as competitive or not. Tirole (1988) shows that agreements implying such exchange of information are anti-competitive: overt collusion is not permitted, as well as tacit collusion which may take the form of 'conscious parallelism' with firms making identical price changes more or less at the same time. But Phlips (1995) shows that exchange of information may be needed to facilitate the establishment of non-cooperative equilibria and thus to arrive at the economic efficiency, especially when demands and costs are changing rapidly. The same problem emerges with the issue of vertical integration, which is certainly one of the more difficult to handle within the different market behaviours identified by mainstream economics. Vertical integration solves the double marginalization problem, but may imply at the same time entry deterrence or foreclosure. In this case the condemnation of a vertical integration is not always efficient because the firm can obtain the same results by implementing more flexible vertical restraints, such as exclusivity relationships and franchise fees (Katz, 1989). These ambiguous conclusions emerged when mainstream scholars decided to look progressively beyond the general principle which saw any agreement between firms as a means to simultaneously increase price and decrease output. On the other hand, efforts have been made to analyse the complexity of competitive phenomena and to build a convincing argumentation on specific topics which were not studied by mainstream economics. For instance, as soon as cooperation is not reduced to collusion, it is possible to show that the competitive process works because of and not in spite of the complex network of interfirm arrangements (Penrose, 1959; Richardson, 1960; Loasby, 1991; Foss, 1995).

In the domain of competition policy, different problems are to be solved. Firstly, the problems encountered by economic analysis on the theme of competition have quite naturally penetrated the sphere of competition policy. Apart from the problems we have just mentioned, the notion of workable competition and the analysis of contestable markets which were used to guide competition policy are now described as generating some ambiguities linked especially with the difficulty of defining the sub-additivity of the costs functions of firms in the concrete world. Secondly, and consequently, one may ask whether economic efficiency can still be considered as the main objective of competition policy if we take into account the difficulties of deriving clear conclusions in terms of efficiency from economic models. Thirdly, competitive authorities have to intake their decisions at one moment in time. Nevertheless, from the observation of the concrete functioning of businesses and industries, we know that a given situation can evolve in a way which was not predictable beforehand. These three major difficulties have no obvious or immediate solution. This is presumably why economists are often tempted to suggest a case-by-case study for competition policy. However, the unavailability of a solution should not prevent us thinking hard about a procedure and a global method of evaluation for competitive authorities which could be more reliable, operational and at least able to reduce the effects of these three difficulties.

2. STRUCTURE OF THE BOOK AND PRESENTATION OF THE CONTRIBUTIONS

Three elements are generally presented in order to analyse competition as a process: (a) the distinction between the analysis of the process of competition and the more traditional views of competition; (b) the necessity to characterize the behaviour of firms dedicated to organizing competitive processes; and (c) the evolution of these organizational forms and the role of competition policy. These three elements are key issues in this book and are analysed in turn by the different contributors.

The economic literature on the process of competition is not homogeneous, in the sense that it does not provide a coherent vision of this notion. Different meanings are still competing. Competition is a process of learning and coordination, a process of discovery, a process of trial and error, a process of selection and so on. In Chapter 2, Israel Kirzner, who directly contributed to the development of the analysis of the process of competition, proposes to explain the connections that can be made between these different notions through the study of the evolution of the notion of competition throughout the twentieth century. He shows that the distinction between competition as a state of affairs and competition as a process is not purely semantic, and that it must rather be considered as the basis of two different frameworks. In fact he explains that this distinction, presented by Hayek, has remained neglected for a long time, and this implied that static competition models acquired a dominant position in economic analysis. However, the recent developments on the process of competition show a renewed interest in competition as a dynamic phenomenon and can be interpreted from Kirzner's point of view as a better understanding of the Hayekian distinction.

Kirsten Foss and Nicolai Foss focus in Chapter 3 on recent theories of the firm, trying to relate them to different market process approaches. New developments in industrial organization have analysed as a first priority the nature of the firm by tackling the question of how to distinguish a firm from a market. These analyses significantly improved the understanding of industrial phenomena, but the authors tell us that the time is ripe for an analysis of the vision of the market that these theories of the firm are supposed to convey. In fact, having in mind the advances provided by recent theories of the firm, the authors propose to go back to the analytical notions of competition and market in order to characterize new features of the process of competition.

These two contributions have emphasized that, to analyse properly the process of competition, the adequate framework should be based on a temporal perspective in which disequilibria and discovery phenomena prevail. Austrian approaches have widely discussed the issues of desequilibria and discovery and, as such, these approaches offer a reliable basis to build this kind of framework. However, these questions were also largely debated by other approaches. Marshall and the post-Marshallians such as Penrose, Richardson and Loasby have realized an in-depth analytical work on the articulation between production processes and market processes. Michel Quéré provides, in Chapter 4, a few insights from the Marshallian perspective. He especially emphasizes the ambiguity around the concept of free competition within the *Principles*, due to the conciliation exercise provided by Marshall, and stresses the relevance of complementary attempts like *Industry and Trade,* especially, in order to contribute to the analysis of competition as a process. In Chapter 5, Mario Amendola, Jean-Luc Gaffard and Patrick Musso propose a model that makes it possible to bring into the light the role of competition as a means of realizing increasing returns associated with new and superior technologies. In doing so, they give structure to a conjecture made by Richardson according to which competition is compatible with increasing returns, provided that production takes time.

Assuming the temporality of competitive phenomena involves the analysis of a series of questions about the behaviour of firms. What are the main features of the behaviour of firms within a process of competition framework? The incompatibility between the process of competition and equilibrium analyses implies that it may be difficult to describe this behaviour within a conventional programme of maximization. Other types of behaviour are then to be discovered and described. For instance, adaptation, imitation and routine, but also imagination and innovation, have to be investigated. These types of behaviour were for a long time ignored in the literature because of the dominance of the analysis of rational behaviour. This situation has evolved in a significant manner. The problem now is to determine in which context each type of behaviour is likely to prevail.

Nicolai Foss and Volker Mahnke show, in Chapter 6, that the strategy which implies that firms will acquire and maintain a competitive advantage is essentially a disequilibrium phenomenon linked to discovery, innovation and resource combination. They conclude that strategy cannot be correctly described within traditional analyses of industrial organization and business management because these analyses are based on the study of equilibrium systems. They propose some guidelines for analysing correctly firms' strategies. In Chapter 7, Jackie Krafft and Jacques-Laurent Ravix focus on behaviour of firms in a context where both market knowledge and productive knowledge are considered. They study the conditions of the coordination of different types of investments: the complementary ones which relate to the production process and the competitive ones which relate to the market process. These conditions depend on specific rules of behaviour which require the implementation of different types of business institutions.

Behaviour of firms in the concrete world often implies the elaboration of complex organizational relations between firms, such as alliances, mergers or cooperations, this behaviour being generally implemented by firms in order to organize the process of competition. The role of competition policy is to define some limits when these organizational forms disturb the process of competition. In Chapter 8, Michel Glais focuses on the European merger regulation and stresses that, although the general philosophy of competition policy remains within the conventional vision of competition, the practice of the European Commission relies on broader concepts than economic efficiency to evaluate the nature of the process of competition.

The different chapters of this book give the opportunity to organize economic thinking on the theme of the process of competition and on its implications in terms of competition policy. Of course, a full understanding of the dynamics of competition is far from being accomplished. While some dimensions have been examined in depth, others have to be completed and refined. This attempt will have to be pursued during the next few years.

ACKNOWLEDGEMENTS

Some chapters of this volume have previously been published in French for a book entitled *Le Processus de Concurrence*, edited by Economica, Paris. Permission to reprint an English version of these chapters is gratefully acknowledged:

Kirzner, I. (1999), 'Concurrence et processus de marché: quelques repères doctrinaux', in J. Krafft (ed.), *Le Processus de Concurrence*, Paris: Economica.

Foss, K. and N. Foss (1999), 'Le processus de marché et la firme: vers une perspective en termes de droits de propriété dynamiques', in J. Krafft (ed.), *Le Processus de Concurrence*, Paris: Economica.

Foss, N. and V. Mahnke (1999), 'Recherche en stratégie, processus de marché et avantage concurrentiel', in J. Krafft (ed.), *Le Processus de Concurrence*, Paris: Economica.

REFERENCES

Bain, J. (1956), *Barriers to New Competition*, Cambridge, Mass.: Harvard University Press.

Bain, J. (1959), *Industrial Organization*, New York: Wiley.

Baumol, W. (1992), 'Horizontal Collusion and Innovation', Policy Forum, 'Regulation of Cartels, Dominant Firms and Mergers', *Economic Journal*, **102** (410), 129–37.

Baumol, W., J. Panzar and R. Willig (1982), *Contestable Markets and the Theory of Industry Structure*, New York: Harcourt Brace Jovanovich.

Blaug, M. (1997), 'Competition as an End-State and Competition as a Process', in B.C. Eaton and R.G. Harris (eds), *Trade, Technology and Economics*, Cheltenham, UK and Lyme, US: Edward Elgar.

Demsetz, H. (1973), 'Industry Structure, Market Rivalry and Public Policy', *Journal of Law and Economics*, **16** (1), 1–9.

Foss, N. (1995), 'The Economic Thought of an Austrian Marshallian: George Barclay Richardson', *Journal of Economic Studies*, **22** (1), 23–44.

Geroski, P. (1992), 'Vertical Relations between Firms and Industrial Policy', Policy Forum, 'Regulation of Cartels, Dominant Firms and Mergers', *Economic Journal*, **102** (410), 138–47.

Hay, D. (1993), 'Assessment: Competition Policy', *Oxford Review of Economic Policy*, **9** (2), 1–26.

Hayek, F.A. (1937), 'The Use of Knowledge in Society', *American Economic Review*, **35**, 519–30; reprinted in *Individualism and Economic Order* (1948), Chicago: University of Chicago Press.

Hayek, F.A. (1946), 'The Meaning of Competition', Stafford Little Lecture, Princeton University, May; reprinted in *Individualism and Economic Order* (1948), Chicago: University of Chicago Press.

Jacquemin, A. (1994), 'Capitalisme, Compétition et Coopération', *Revue d'Economie Politique*, **104** (4), 501–15.

Jacquemin, A. and M. Slade (1989), 'Cartels, Collusion and Horizontal Mergers', in R. Schmalensee and T. Willig (eds), *Handbook of Industrial Organisation*, Amsterdam: North Holland.

Jorde, T. and D. Teece (1990), 'Innovation and Cooperation: Innovation for Competition and Antitrust', Symposium 'Collaboration, Innovation and Antitrust', *Journal of Economic Perspectives*, **4** (3), 75–96.

Katz, M. (1989), 'Vertical Contractual Relations', in R. Schmalensee and T. Willig (eds), *Handbook of Industrial Organisation*, Amsterdam: North Holland.

Langlois, R. and P. Robertson (1995), *Firms, Markets and Economic Change*, London and New York: Routledge.

Loasby, B. (1991), *Equilibrium and Evolution*, Manchester: Manchester University Press.

Machovec, F. (1995), *Perfect Competition and the Transformation of Economics*, London and New York: Routledge.

Mason, E. (1957), *Economic Concentration and the Monopoly Problem*, Cambridge, Mass.: Harvard University Press.

Penrose, E. (1959), *The Theory of the Growth of the Firm*, Oxford: Basil Blackwell.

Phlips, L. (1995), *Competition Policy: a Game Theoretic Perspective*, Cambridge, Mass.: Cambridge University Press.

Richardson, G. (1960), *Information and Investment*, 2nd edn (1990), Oxford: Clarendon Press.

Schumpeter, J.A. (1942), *Capitalism, Socialism and Democracy*, New York: Harper.

Tirole, J. (1988), *The Theory of Industrial Organisation*, Cambridge, Mass.: MIT Press.

Vickers, J. (1995), 'Concepts of Competition', *Oxford Economic Papers*, **47** (1), 1–23.

2. Competition and the market process: some doctrinal milestones

Israel Kirzner

1. INTRODUCTION

As the twentieth century nears its conclusion, economic policy-makers, if not the economic theory textbooks, have to a considerable extent come to recognize that the advantages of competition are to be found in the dynamics of the process of competition, rather than in the imagined state of affairs identified in the textbook model of competition. For most of the century, however, the general professional opinion was quite different. Any optimality properties a market system may possess, it was held, are those generated by its approximating the conditions of the perfectly competitive model. And the support for free markets which, it was generally understood, neoclassical economics in its pre-1930 vintage provided, rested (so ran the conventional wisdom during the central decades of this century) upon the dominant role played in neoclassical economics by the model of perfect competition. This chapter offers a brief survey of some significant milestones along the road which have led professional opinion away from these latter positions emphasizing the role of perfect competition in achieving societal economic efficiency towards the current recognition of the greater relevance of the dynamic process of competition for an understanding of the achievements of free markets.

The story to be told is complicated by, and indeed includes, the following circumstance. We wish to provide insight into the gradual dislodgment of the perfectly competitive model from the centre-stage of professional concern, but the story accounting for that earlier centrality of the perfectly competitive (henceforth 'PC') model, is itself a complicated, confusing and controversial one. In fact, we shall argue, an important early step along the road away from the dominance of the PC model consisted in a drastic revision of what had become the orthodox account of the earlier rise of that model. Indeed, as we shall see, the story of the late twentieth century partial decline of the PC model can be construed as being largely the story of continual critical reconsideration of the manner in which that model had, by the 1930s, captured the central attention of the profession. Our story of the decline of the PC model must, then, begin with an outline of the place of that model in the neoclassical world before 1930.

2. NEOCLASSICAL ECONOMICS AND THE PC MODEL

There is no doubt that the economics profession at mid-century believed that the PC model basically captured the way in which neoclassical economics had understood how markets work before Edward Chamberlin and Joan Robinson. 'The perfection of the concept of competition, that is, the emergence of the idea of competition as itself a market structure, was a distinguishing contribution of neoclassical economics' (McNulty, 1968, p.644). Indeed, in 1939 Hicks, deeply engaged in refining and polishing neoclassical economics made an oft-quoted statement to the effect that 'sacrificing the assumption of perfect competition must threaten wreckage of the greater part of general equilibrium theory' (Hicks, 1939, pp.83–4).

It was, in this general view, the work of Chamberlin and Robinson – and nothing else – which challenged this dominance of the PC model, arguing that its lack of realism rendered it incapable of explaining real-world market prices. It was the Chicago School, in its mid-century incarnation, which held on methodological grounds that this lack of realism was unimportant and provided no grounds for questioning the practical usefulness of the PC model.[1]

Yet this orthodox view that the mainstream of neoclassical micro-economics before Chamberlin and Robinson focused primarily on the theory of PC price determination has been riddled with challenges during the past several decades. Brian Loasby (1989, p.62) cites Sraffa's famous 1926 paper as challenging the consistency of Marshall's theory of value because his insistence on increasing returns is incompatible with perfect competition. Clearly Sraffa, like Hicks, understood neoclassical economics, and in particular Marshallian economics, to stand or fall with the PC model. But, Loasby asserts, Sraffa was 'quite wrong to assume that perfect competition was the basis of Marshall's theory of value' (Loasby, 1989). Indeed, Loasby has gone so far as to claim that 'Marshallian competition is a Hayekian discovery process' (ibid., p.55). In a more recent work, Frank Machovec has brilliantly reconstructed the place of competition in the history of economic thought (Machovec, 1995).

The main thrust of Machovec's dogmengeschichtliche revisionism concerns his denial of the view propagated particularly by Stigler (1957) that the classical economists were, in effect, thinking in terms of a crude PC model. But in developing his refutation of this widespread Stiglerian error, Machovec also challenged an equally widespread view concerning the neoclassical mainstream that dominated the profession from the 1880s. Machovec challenged the view that the major neoclassical economists such as Marshall grounded their theory in the PC model or, more precisely, that the development of the neoclassical mainstream from the 1880s onwards, consisted largely in a steady, gradual analytical refinement of the meaning and implications of perfect competition. In Machovec's view, nothing of the sort characterized the neoclassical mainstream before 1920. On the contrary, Machovec maintains, among the neoclassical economists around the turn of the century, Walras was virtually alone in resting his analytical system upon the PC conditions, a step to which he was inexorably pushed by the logic of his general equilibrium system (Machovec, 1995, p.241). It was only during the 1920s, in particular as an outcome of Knight's *Risk, Uncertainty and Profit* (1921), that there occurred a 'Kuhnian revolution that is, a distinct change in concept and analytical apparatus . . . as the model of perfect competition became the keystone of analysis' (Machovec, 1995, p.159). Where conventional wisdom had seen the history of economics since Adam Smith as gradual refinement until the 1920s, of a single conception of competition, that of competition as a completed state of affairs, Machovec maintained that the classical economists and also at least the earlier neoclassical writers saw competition as a dynamic process: 'The process view of the classicists and the early neoclassical writers was purged during the 1920s as the profession adopted an exclusively equilibrium framework for its microeconomic theorizing' (ibid., p.236).

The present writer would, at least in one respect, in fact push Machovec's revisionism even further. The dominance of the PC model in the economics profession of the 1930s, 1940s and 1950s was to a significant extent an outcome of the monopolistic competition revolution of the early 1930s. In contrasting their own static models of monopolistically competitive equilibrium with what they certainly believed to be the dominant earlier models, Chamberlin and Robinson were incidentally formalizing and emphasizing an analytical model of perfect competition which had, for most of the profession, hitherto remained less than precisely articulated. Paradoxically, therefore, it was the very effort to dislodge the PC model in favour of the equally static, but less unrealistic, model of monopolistic competition which thrust that PC model into the analytical limelight. Certainly, Chamberlin and Robinson shared the now conventional view disputed by Machovec that the state of perfect competition was central to the earlier neoclassical theory of value. The efforts to challenge this centrality had the effect, we believe, of focusing more sophisticated analytic attention on the PC model. Their efforts to dislodge the PC model thus had the paradoxical effect of rendering truthful, for the 1940s and 1950s, that dominance in economics of the PC model which they had not quite correctly attributed to pre-1920 economics.

3. FURTHER THOUGHTS ON THE EARLIER NEOCLASSICAL VIEW OF COMPETITION

As we have seen, Machovec has argued that the earlier neoclassicals had shared with the classical economists a process view of competition. It was, he maintained, only Walras's emphasis on the determinateness of general equilibrium which pushed the PC model to the centre of his own system until, under the influence of Knight, the Walrasian centrality for PC came, according to Machovec's reading, to be adopted by the profession in the 1920s in rather revolutionary fashion. But this view that the earlier neoclassical economists thought of competition primarily, if not exclusively, in its dynamic, process sense may be reading a little too much into their work. The circumstance that a writer describes competition in a manner at variance with the fully articulated Knightian version of the PC model does not at all imply that that writer is necessarily thinking in process terms. This point is of some importance and requires some elaboration.

The most significant insight concerning the story of the PC model in the twentieth century is surely the following. Until Hayek's 1946 paper, 'The Meaning of Competition',[2] no one in the profession, it appears, had seen or at least made explicit the crucial difference between competition as a state of affairs and competition as a driving, dynamic process.[3] There is little doubt that Machovec, following McNulty (1967) and others, is correct in reading the classical economists as seeing competition not, as Stigler had believed, as a perfectly competitive state of affairs which they were not quite able to articulate correctly and precisely, but as a rivalrous process. But, astounding as it must appear in retrospect, none of the host of writers before Hayek, during the first half of this century, and including those of the 1930s and later who dwelt on the meaning and implications of the PC model, quite saw with clarity that this model was a strictly equilibrium model, from which all vestiges of process had been completely filtered out.[4]

To see this failure perhaps more clearly one can cite the 1952 work (published after Hayek's paper!) of Fritz Machlup, *The Economics of Sellers' Competition* (1952). This mid-century volume is surely the most careful and complete analysis of the many possible meanings of the term 'competition' of the entire century. There are few aspects of the competitive process and of competitive equilibrium, as they had been treated in a vast literature, which are not carefully and sensitively dissected and labelled, often with newly-coined-labels, in this volume.[5] Yet it becomes clear that Machlup, who incidentally and surprisingly makes no reference whatever to Hayek's 1946 paper (in Hayek, 1949) was, quite amazingly, unaware that the PC model does indeed logically confine one to the equilibrium state. This is apparent in his lengthy discussion of the meanings attached to the term 'perfect market' (Machlup, 1952, pp.117–24). It also emerges almost dramatically in his following statement (ibid., pp.555–6, footnote):

> The disparagers of perfect competition are badly mistaken if they regard perfect competition as inimical to progress. Of course, if they define it as instantaneous entry of newcomers, it is obvious that 'perfect competition is not only impossible but inferior' – as we read in Joseph A. Schumpeter, *Capitalism, Socialism and Democracy* (1942, p.106). But such a model of perfect competition serves no purpose except to confuse the issue. Instantaneous entry of newcomers, instantaneous appearance of imitators, is not only impossible but nonsensical.

One is tempted to surmise that Machlup's 'Austrian' training had such a profound influence on his thinking that, despite the range of nuances which he was able to distinguish in the enormous literature on competition, it somehow became impossible for him to accept that a theorist could seriously think of perfect competition in the way which Schumpeter surely correctly ascribed to mainstream theorists!

Machovec is insightfully correct in attributing Walras's emphasis on perfect competition to his equilibrium perspective. And, as Machovec argues, the dominance within economics which the PC model attained was attained concomitantly with the profession's adoption of the mathematical economist's primary concern with equilibrium conditions. But, at least until Hayek's paper, economists seemed (in retrospect, almost incredibly) entirely unaware of the sharp distinction between the two possible uses of the adjective 'competitive', namely either as describing a process or as describing the equilibrium outcome of some undefined process seen as an already attained and settled state of affairs. Although this failure seems, from today's perspective, to be difficult to comprehend, we will not, I suggest, adequately understand earlier neoclassical writing on competition without recognizing the fact of this failure.

In particular we should therefore avoid the possible error of interpreting references in earlier neoclassical writing to acts of competitive entry as firm evidence of a process view of competition. As a result of the failure to recognize the distinction we have emphasized, such references to acts of competitive entry may have been understood as aspects of a competitive structure rather than as implying any understanding that such competitive acts of entry are strictly and inherently inconsistent with any equilibrium state.

This writer would therefore tend to see the development of neoclassical ideas on competition between the 1880s and 1930s as a more gradual analytical change than Machovec is prepared to accept. In brief it would appear that, under the influence of increasing analytic formalization manifested partly but not exclusively in increased use of geometrical – and eventually more general mathematical – tools, neoclassical economics came to focus more and more on the outcomes of economic processes and less and less on these processes themselves. As part of this change, references to competition came gradually to refer less and less to competitive processes and more and more to the results of such processes. Because the distinction between a competitive process and a 'competitive' state of affairs was as yet entirely unclear, the neoclassical economists such as Knight who engaged in explicit articulation of a precise characterization of competition and were, perhaps unselfconsciously, thinking in equilibrium terms were able to nudge their fellow economists towards thinking within a structural, rather than a process framework. It is, then, not so much that an earlier dominant purely 'process' view of competition succumbed to a revolution in favour of the 'state of affairs' view of competition as that an earlier somewhat nondescript view of competition in which elements of process and of outcomes were rather confusedly jumbled together came gradually to be purged of its process elements. While, from a late twentieth century perspective, this change may appear negative in its extrusion of elements of process understanding, we can at least recognize that the achieved internal consistency attained through exclusively structural understanding of perfect competition may have had much to do with the new dominance of the PC model, and the length of its period of such dominance.

4. HAYEK AND THE MEANING OF COMPETITION

Hayek's 1946 paper was undoubtedly a by-product of his concern in the late 1930s and early 1940s with the role of markets in disseminating mutual knowledge among market participants. The remarkable series of papers which emerged from this concern were published in Hayek's *Individualism and Economic Order* (1949). His paper, 'The Meaning of Competition', is described in that book as reproducing the substance of a lecture delivered at Princeton in May 1946. Hayek begins his paper recognizing that 'some valiant attempts to bring discussion' of the meaning of the term competition 'back to earth' had been made.[6] But he quickly points out that the general view is still that 'the so-called theory of perfect competition provides the appropriate model for judging the effectiveness of competition in real life, and that, to the extent that real competition differs from that model, it is undesirable and even harmful' (Hayek, 1949, p.92).

Hayek vigorously disputed this view. He pointed out in particular that this general view:

> throughout assumes that state of affairs already to exist which, according to the truer view of the older theory, the process of competition tends to bring about . . . and that, if the state of affairs assumed by theory of perfect competition ever existed, it would not only deprive of their scope all the activities which the verb 'to compete' describes but would make them virtually impossible. (Ibid.)

Hayek proceeded to articulate with utmost clarity that:

> Modern theory of competition deals almost exclusively with a state of what is called 'competitive equilibrium' in which it is assumed that the data for the different individuals are fully adjusted to each other, while the problem which requires explanation is the nature of the process by which the data are thus adjusted. (Ibid., p.94)

Hayek's paper reads like a breath of fresh air. Cutting through a veritable forest of confusion in the literature, he was putting his finger on the root difficulty with the profession's preoccupation with the PC model: its being an equilibrium model inherently incapable of offering help in understanding how equilibrium might possible be approached. It should be noted that his approving references to J.M. Clark and to Fritz Machlup[7] do not at all suggest that Hayek's fundamental insight had been anticipated by these writers. Rather, they were being cited as lone writers who at least recognized that real-world competition may have merit that does not depend on its being a close approximation to the PC model.

5. THE SCENE AFTER HAYEK'S 1946 PAPER

Hayek's paper appears to have been virtually ignored in the subsequent literature perhaps, in part, because it was not published in a journal. Mises in his *Human Action* (Mises, 1949, p.278, footnote) approvingly cited Hayek's paper as refuting the doctrines of monopolistic or imperfect competition. Although Hayek did not in fact directly criticize these theories themselves in his paper, Mises obviously recognized the profound implications of Hayek's insights for the way in which Chamberlin's and Robinson's work had been interpreted by the profession. Mises, whose own understanding of competition was, emphatically, steeped in the process mode,[8] instantly appreciated Hayek's contribution. But the present writer has not found other references to Hayek's paper in the literature immediately after 1946.[9]

It was not that the profession failed to see the obvious difference between the term 'competition' as used by businessmen and that term as used by economists.[10] But very few writers recognized that this difference reflected completely different perspectives on the market, each of which might be able to make a separate crucial contribution to economic understanding. Rather, the businessman's perception of active, rivalrous competition was dismissed as a crude expression of the way in which imperfect reality falls short of the sophisticated analytical ideal which the PC model expresses. In other words, the businessman's usage was seen as an uncouth use of language which fails to recognize that the market which he describes as competitive is, in fact, riddled with monopolistic elements – or, more pointedly, that precisely those elements which he sees as competitive are, in fact, more properly to be labelled as monopolistic.

It is true that, when this writer wrote his *Competition and Entrepreneurship*,[11] he was able in 1973 to trace a handful of references in the literature of the 1950s and 1960s to the need to supplement the theory of competitive equilibrium with a process theory, and to recognition that the PC model provides only the former.[12] Yet what were perceived as the most authoritative mainstream voices in those decades continued to articulate the conventional PC doctrine with renewed emphasis. George Stigler's well-known 1957 paper was, indeed, so emphatic in this regard that it may have provoked, precisely as a result of that emphasis, something of a reaction to the orthodoxy which he offered.[13]

Stigler offered a history of the PC model from the time of the classical economists until his own time. He treated Adam Smith's references to rivalrous competition as the early and somewhat crude articulation of a notion of competition which was to receive its refinement and precise formulation only in later generations, specifically in the pioneering mathematical work of Cournot (1838) and, finally, in the careful pronouncements of J.B. Clark and, in particular, of Frank Knight. It was this understanding of the classical economists' notion of competition which was to be challenged in the important and above-cited work of McNulty and, most recently, of Frank Machovec.

One important and fairly prominent contribution, published, as it happens, in the same year as Stigler's paper, challenged key aspects of the mainstream perception of the place of the PC model in early twentieth century neoclassical economics. This was the paper of Shorey Peterson, 'Antitrust and the Classic Model'.[14] In his paper Peterson maintained that it was not the case, as seemed to be argued by the later theories of monopolistic and imperfect competition, that the mainstream economic theory of the 1920s and earlier was one dominated by the PC model. The idea of such a 'classic' model's having dominated 'pre-Chamberlinian thought' seems 'mildly shocking' to Peterson, who described himself as one of the 'economists trained in the 1920s and before' (Peterson, 1957, pp.60–63).

Instead, Peterson insisted, the economics which was learned from the treatises of J.B. Clark and Alfred Marshall understood that the rough-and-ready competition of the real world, particularly when buttressed by the threat of potential competition, sufficed to protect the consumers from the most serious of the distortions with which monopoly elements in the market might menace them. We should notice that, in dwelling on this theme, Peterson does not seem to be disagreeing with the terminology in which all departures from the PC conditions are termed 'monopolistic'. Rather he appears to claim on behalf of the mainstream economics of the 1920s and earlier that the vigorous 'imperfect' competition of the real world, riddled though it may be with such 'monopolistic' elements, may suffice to impose efficiency and 'order' upon market phenomena. It is this which supports Peterson's contention that John Maurice Clark's work on 'workable competition' was not trying to 'close a gap caused by failure of the older theory' (ibid., p.78), but was rather seeking to stem policy misunderstandings likely to be generated by 'recent refinements of the competitive model' (ibid., p.78). And it was this which led Peterson to express surprise that Schumpeter[15] should have read neo-classical doctrine as inconsistent with his own emphasis on the competition of new and better products and on the force of potential competition. Schumpeter's emphasis in these respects was rather to be seen as 'essentially an unfolding of earlier thought' (ibid., p.74).

An intriguing paper of the 1950s by John Maurice Clark which served as the basis for his subsequent book (Clark, 1961) was entitled 'Competition: Static Models and Dynamic Aspects' (Clark, 1955) and was presented at the 1954 American Economic Association meetings. Despite the surprisingly ill-tempered remarks with which Machlup commented on this paper (Machlup, 1955), Clark was clearly groping towards a sound critique of the part which the PC model was playing in mainstream economics at mid-century. It is perhaps relevant to note that, while Clark was certainly thoroughly aware of and indeed insistent upon the distinction between competition as a 'static' state of affairs and competition as a 'dynamic process', his distinction is not quite the same as that which distinguishes between the PC state and the competitive process which might hypothetically produce that PC state. For Clark dynamic competition was not primarily important as a possibly equilibrating force, but rather as a more general force relevant, in particular, for economic progress and growth, as well as for the protection of the consumers against monopolistic exploitation. It should perhaps be emphasized that our observation here is not intended to be in any way critical of Clark. This crusade by Clark, as Machovec points out (Machovec, 1995, p.293), was in reality a 'struggle [that] was hopeless' in the face of the cold reception it received in the profession as it sought to dislodge the dominance of the static PC model. It made no attempt to point out that that model, and the very idea of determinacy in market outcomes – surely the heart of neoclassical theory – acquires relevance only by being supplemented by a theory of competitive process.[16]

6. REFLECTIONS ON MAINSTREAM ECONOMICS IN THE 1940s AND 1950s

Our brief sampling of the literature of the central decades of this century has revealed a certain confusion in regard to the perceived role of the PC model. As has become increasingly apparent since the 1950s, the central body of contemporary neoclassical theory saw and still sees the PC model as its primary tool, and as the main pillar upon which to build a normative case for a free market economy. For a George Stigler, or a Milton Friedman,[17] for example, questions of realism were relatively unimportant. They believed the pragmatic usefulness of the PC model justified its dominant role in economic theory. On the other hand, we have seen that there existed (quite apart from Hayek's completely developed, but virtually ignored, contribution) a definite if rather disorganized set of dissident views, associated with such names as Schumpeter, J.M. Clark and Shorey Peterson. These writers were challenging, not so much the meaningfulness of an economic theory virtually confined, for its central understanding of the workings of a market economy, to the PC models, as the attitude which saw all observed departures from the PC conditions as representing harmfully monopolistic features of reality. Their critiques certainly set their work decisively apart from the extensive literature in the area of industrial organization which explored industries described as oligopolistic, seeing them as variants of monopoly situations (see, for example, Peterson, 1957, p.76). We do not perhaps adequately appreciate how much the very perception of an analytical box labelled 'oligopoly', sprang from the dominance of that orthodoxy in which the word 'competitive' means nothing but one particular market structure, the PC model. Once one refuses to grant use of the adjective 'competitive' to describe any act of entrepreneurial entry aimed at winning pure profit, on the grounds that such acts are, as a matter of definition, 'monopolistic', one has firmly closed one's eyes to the obvious and surely genuinely competitive feature which is common to all situations characterized by freedom of entry. What remains is only the task of classifying different combinations and/or degrees of quasi-monopoly – a task to which so much of oligopoly theory has in fact been devoted.

What distinguishes these dissident views from those that would emerge in the subsequent decades is perhaps their linkages to earlier pre-Chamberlinian conceptions of competition which had not yet been pressed into what would turn out to be the PC mould. They were not Young Turks rebelling at an existing orthodoxy which they found in place; rather, they were expressing dismay at the fashion in which this orthodoxy had displaced a less formal, but more meaningful and useful, earlier orthodoxy. Their work no doubt played a role in keeping alive the notion of active competition in the profession. But a retrospective survey of late twentieth-century economics shows that these voices were drowned out by a textbook literature in which the PC model continued to occupy a more and more central position in economic explanations of market economies.

7. THE LATE TWENTIETH-CENTURY TURN

During the latter several decades of the century, however, new voices have emerged to question the dominance of the PC model. These new voices have not in any sense constituted a unified 'school'; often these voices clashed with each other. Yet the overall outcome achieved by the work expressed in these voices has been to dislodge the PC model, if not from its dominance of the textbooks, yet from its long-established position of almost unchallenged dominance in professional understanding of how the market economy in fact works. In the space available here we certainly cannot adequately describe the way in which these new challenges to the PC model emerged and broadly reinforced each other. What we can attempt to do is to list briefly and identify some of these new voices, so that we can gain appreciation for the way in which, discordant though they may have been, they have nonetheless drilled a certain scepticism into professional consciousness in regard to the relevance of the PC model – a scepticism along an entirely different dimension from that introduced a half-century earlier by Chamberlin and Robinson.

First, there are voices emphasizing the process character of market effectiveness: Here we should include work from the early 1960s onwards by such writers as G.B. Richardson (1960), who was a pioneer in understanding the role of the interactive flow of information in the competitive market process; Murray N. Rothbard (1962), who, although barely mentioning Hayek's work, pursued Austrian ideas on competition with admirable consistency to some of their radical implications; and Paul J. McNulty (1967, 1968), who in the late 1960s articulated the Hayekian insights with great skill and effectiveness and deployed them to offer, as we have already seen, a powerful history of thought critique of George Stigler's views on the history of the PC model.[18]

Second, there are voices emphasizing the powerful effectiveness of freedom of potential entry. Early in the 1960s, Sylos-Labini had published a much-discussed work on oligopoly (Sylos-Labini, 1962),[19] in which the role of entry was extensively explored. Although much of the subsequently inspired work on the role of entry was conducted within the conventional 'structural' framework, this work did focus attention on an aspect of real-world competition which the PC model tended to suppress or at least ignore.[20] A powerful paper by Yale Brozen (1969) sharply criticized the way in which the term 'barriers to entry' had been used, in the conventional literature, to include such dynamically competitive activities (or arenas) as advertising, economies of scale and product differentiation.

Closely related to the foregoing were voices questioning that orthodoxy which defined degrees of monopoly and competition in terms of numbers. Harold Demsetz, in a pioneering paper on the regulation of public utilities (Demsetz, 1968) but one which had far-reaching implications for monopoly theory in general, sharply challenged the standard doctrine on 'natural monopoly'. There is, Demsetz pointed out:

> no clear or necessary reason for production scale economies to decrease the number of bidders. Let prospective buyers call for bids to service their demands. Scale economies in servicing their demands in no way imply that there will be one bidder only. There can be many bidders and the bid that wins will be the lowest. (Demsetz, 1968, p.57)

It was this insight, so strange to conventional wisdom at the time it was introduced, that would subsequently generate the theory of 'contestable' markets (see Baumol *et al.*, 1982). While that theory was largely developed within the mainstream framework on market structures, it did much to widen economists' horizons on the nature and role of competition.

Much in the spirit of the foregoing was the new work of the early 1970s which challenged the then-existing so-called 'structural approach' to the evaluation of oligopoly situations. Some of that work was summarized in a prominent paper by J. Fred Weston (1972). Weston, who himself contributed to this research, was particularly concerned to demonstrate empirically the competitive processes which take place in concentrated markets. Clearly, this line of work, conducted primarily in the 'applied' area of industrial organization and eventually to be dubbed 'the new learning',[21] had important implications for the theory of competition. This line of work has indeed had continual influential impact on industrial organization theory and on antitrust economics during the latter decades of the century.

8. A RETROSPECTIVE REFLECTION

Although it may seem that the contrast emphasized in this chapter between competition as a process or competition as a state of affairs is purely semantic, this is not at all the case. It would be a mistake to understand the shift in recent professional thinking about competition as one primarily concerned with the meaning of the word – or even about the economic policy implications of the use of that word. Rather, the shift we have briefly surveyed constitutes a gradual deepening of professional understanding of the way a market economy works. As long as the PC model dominated microeconomic theory, appreciation for the economic success of the market economy saw that economy as more or less closely approximating the state of perfect competitive equilibrium, with its prices and quantities emerging spontaneously as if from a magic computer. As professional understanding of the dynamic character of the competitive process has deepened, the contributions of the market have come to be glimpsed more profoundly and more accurately. It is the rivalrous competition described by Adam Smith, the entrepreneurial process described by Ludwig von Mises and the knowledge discovery procedure described by Friedrich Hayek which have been 'rediscovered' by a significant proportion of the economics profession as this century reaches its conclusion. This encouraging development should serve as a firm foundation for future research into the competitive process during the decades ahead.

NOTES

1. On this issue see Knight (1946), Stigler (1949) and Chamberlin (1957).
2. This paper was read as a lecture in 1946 and published in Hayek (1949). It is of interest that Hayek, in his *Road to Serfdom* (1944, p.49), had incautiously described as competition the situation in which 'the individual producer has to adapt to price changes and cannot control them'. Galbraith (1948, p.111, n.29) read this as requiring that demand curves facing individual sellers 'be completely elastic at the ruling price'. Certainly this would not be in the spirit of Hayek's 1946 paper. For a looser reading of Hayek than Galbraith's, see Peterson (1957, p.75).
3. The following statement of George Stigler, written 11 years after Hayek's paper which he does not cite, is of interest in this regard. Stigler is referring to Adam Smith's use of the term 'competition' in the rivalrous sense. Stigler comments (1957, p.235) 'Competition is a process of responding to a new force and a method of reaching a new equilibrium'. The fact that, as noted in the text, Stigler saw Adam Smith as something of a crude forerunner of Knight's equilibrium PC model suggests that Stigler was himself perhaps not fully aware of the significance that might be read into his sentence.
4. A careful reading of Schumpeter (1942, pp.77–80, 103–6) may arguably, but not conclusively, suggest an exception to the statement in the text.
5. On the use of new labels to distinguish between subtly different aspects of competition, see Machlup (1952, p.105, n.17).
6. In this regard Hayek cites Clark (1940) and Machlup (1942).

7. See note 6 above.
8. See especially Mises (1949, pp.273–9).
9. Among the earliest references to Hayek's 1946 paper are perhaps the papers by McNulty (1967, 1968).
10. For some references on this point, see Kirzner (1973, p.89, n.).
11. Kirzner (1973). This work cited Hayek's paper as 'penetrating and pioneering' (p.91) in regard to the distinction with which the present chapter is concerned.
12. See Kirzner (1973), especially p.93, n.13, and p.89, n.1.
13. The reference is to Stigler (1957); it was this paper to which McNulty (1967) was primarily responding.
14. The reference is Peterson (1957). This paper was included in the influential AEA-sponsored volume of readings in industrial organization (Heflebower and Stocking, 1958).
15. Peterson was referring to Schumpeter (1942, chaps VII and VIII).
16. It would be a mistake to conclude this section without any reference to a valuable but almost entirely neglected work of the 1950s, which was thoroughly out of step with the static ('state of affairs') notion of competition. This was Lawrence Abbott's *Quality and Competition* (1955). Abbott's emphasis on the dynamics of quality competition differs in spirit, although not perhaps in policy implications, from the work on 'quality as a variable' of E.H. Chamberlin (1957, chap. 6). For an appreciative awareness of Abbott's work, see Rothbard (1962, vol. II, p. 906, n.28).
17. See Friedman (1953).
18. This writer's own book (Kirzner, 1973), was deeply influenced by Hayek and McNulty in this regard.
19. The standard work on barriers to entry had been Bain (1956).
20. For an example of such work, see Needham (1969, chap. 7), reprinted in Breit and Hochman (1971).
21. Important samples of this and related literature were creatively assembled and edited by Yale Brozen (1975).

REFERENCES

Abbott, L. (1955), *Quality and Competition*, New York: Columbia University Press.

Bain, J. (1956), *Barriers to New Competition*, Cambridge, Mass.: Harvard University Press.

Baumol, W.J., J. Panzar and R. Willig (1982), *Contestable Markets and the Theory of Industry Structure*, New York: Harcourt Brace Jovanovich.

Breit, W. and H. Hochman (1971), *Readings in Microeconomics*, 2nd edn, New York: Holt, Rinehart and Winston.

Brozen, Y. (1969), 'Competition, Efficiency, and Antitrust', *Journal of World Trade Law*, **3**; reprinted in Y. Brozen (1975).

Brozen, Y. (ed.) (1975), *The Competitive Economy, Selected Readings*, Morristown, NJ: General Learning Press.

Chamberlin, E. (1957), *Towards a More General Theory of Value*, New York: Oxford University Press.

Clark, J. (1940), 'Toward a Concept of Workable Competition', *American Economic Review*, **30**, June.

Clark, J. (1955), 'Competition: Static Models and Dynamic Aspects', *American Economic Review*, **45**, May.

Clark, J. (1961), *Competition as a Dynamic Process*, Washington, DC: Brookings.

Cournot, A. (1838), *Researches into the Mathematical Principles of the Theory of Wealth*; reprinted (1927), New York: Macmillan.

Demsetz, H. (1968), 'Why Regulate Utilities?', *Journal of Law and Economics*, **11**, April.
Friedman, M. (1953), *Essays in Positive Economics*, Chicago: University of Chicago Press.
Galbraith, J. (1948), 'Monopoly and the Concentration of Economic Power', in H.S. Ellis (ed.), *A Survey of Contemporary Economics*, Homewood, IL: Irwin.
Hayek, F.A. (1944), *The Road to Serfdom*, Chicago: University of Chicago Press.
Hayek, F.A. (1949), *Individualism and Economic Order*, London: Routledge and Kegan Paul.
Heflebower, R. and G. Stocking (eds) (1958), *Readings in Industrial Organization and Public Policy*, published for the American Economic Association, Homewood, IL: Irwin.
Hicks, J. R. (1939), *Value and Capital*, 2nd edn (1946), Oxford: Clarendon Press.
Kirzner, I. (1973), *Competition and Entrepreneurship*, Chicago: University of Chicago Press.
Knight, F. (1946), 'Immutable Law in Economics: Its Reality and Limitations', *American Economic Review*, May.
Loasby, B. (1989), *The Mind and Method of the Economist*, Aldershot, UK and Brookfield, US: Edward Elgar.
Machlup, F. (1942), 'Competition, Pliopoly and Profit', *Economica*, **9**, February and May.
Machlup, F. (1952), *The Economics of Sellers' Competition, Model Analysis of Sellers' Conduct*, Baltimore: The Johns Hopkins Press.
Machlup, F. (1955), 'Discussion', *American Economic Review*, **45**, May, 480–83.
Machovec, F. (1995), *Perfect Competition and the Transformation of Economics*, London and New York: Routledge.
McNulty, P. (1967), 'A Note on the History of Perfect Competition', *Journal of Political Economy*, **75**, August.
McNulty, P. (1968), 'Economic Theory and the Meaning of Competition', *Quarterly Journal of Economics*, **82**, November.
Mises, L. (1949), *Human Action*, New Haven: Yale University Press.
Needham, D. (1969), *Economic Analysis and Industrial Structure*, New York Holt, Rinehart and Winston; reprinted in Breit and Hochman (1971).
Peterson, S. (1957), 'Antitrust and the Classic Model', *American Economic Review*, **47**, March.
Richardson, G.B. (1960), *Information and Investment*, Oxford: Oxford University Press.
Rothbard, M. (1962), *Man, Economy and State: A Treatise on Economic Principles*, Princeton: Van Nostrand.
Schumpeter, J.A. (1942), *Capitalism, Socialism and Democracy*, 3rd edn (1950), New York: Harper.
Stigler, G. (1949), *Five Lectures on Economic Problems*, London: Macmillan.
Stigler, G. (1957), 'Perfect Competition, Historically Contemplated', *Journal of Political Economy*, **65** (5).
Stigler, G. (1965), *Essays in the History of Economics*, Chicago and London: University of Chicago Press.
Sylos-Labini, P. (1962), *Oligopoly and Technical Progress*, Cambridge, Mass.: Harvard University Press.
Weston, J.F. (1972), 'Implications of Recent Research for the Structural Approach to Oligopoly', *Antitrust Law Journal*, **41**.

3. Economic organization in a process perspective

Kirsten Foss and Nicolai Foss

1. INTRODUCTION

During the last two decades, the study of contracting and organization has emerged as a central field of research in economics (notably Alchian and Demsetz, 1972; Williamson, 1985, 1996; Hart and Holmström, 1987; Grossman and Hart, 1986; Coase, 1991; Holmström and Milgrom, 1991; Milgrom and Roberts, 1992; Hart, 1995). Much of this work, usually called 'the economics of organization', has consisted in slicing up and analysing islands of small-numbers interaction (in fact, usually bilateral monopolies) in a sea of competitive market relations.[1] More specifically, analysis has usually started out from an ex ante competitive equilibrium setting, for the reason that this reduces 'market forces to simple constraints on expected utilities [which] greatly facilitates equilibrium analysis' (Hart and Holmström, 1987, p.74) of the contracting problem. Thus contracting can be reduced to an 'optimization' problem, whereas the introduction of imperfect competition broadens the problem to one of 'equilibrium' analysis; that is, many more interdependent variables now have to be taken into account. To the formalist, the latter option is an unnecessary complication.

In much of recent theory, there is an implicit two-step procedure. First, all economic activity is assumed to be representable 'as if' clearing in competitive equilibrium. Second, taking this as given, the analyst then proceeds to analyse the small-scale contracting process. This suggests at least one observation and one question. The observation is that there is an intimate connection between the market process and the contracting process. The question concerns what happens to our understanding of contract choice, and economic organization more broadly, if we broaden our view of the market process from the competitive equilibrium to a more dynamic – Austrian, evolutionary or radical subjectivist – conception (Hayek, 1937, 1968; Kirzner, 1973, 1992, 1997; O'Driscoll and Rizzo, 1985; Littlechild, 1986; Nelson and Winter, 1982;

Shackle, 1972). The formalist will of course respond that incorporating processual, dynamic elements simply introduces unnecessary and ill-understood phenomena into the analysis. 'Tractability' is lost, for example, because reservation utilities may become endogenous.

While we agree that some formal tractability is easily lost, there are many other advantages of introducing more dynamic views of the market process in the analysis not only of the contracting process but also, and more generally, of economic organization. For example, we may conceptualize the firm as an agent in the process of equilibration (Kirzner, 1973) and thus separate the contribution to equilibration provided by markets and prices (Hayek, 1945) and by firms (Coase, 1937), respectively. Furthermore, because of its equilibrium starting point, the modern economics of organization essentially assumes that the knowledge problem (Hayek, 1937, 1945) – that is, the problem of how to make best use of dispersed knowledge – has been solved already.[2] For example, the optimal uses of assets are fully known to agents; it is reaching this already discovered optimal use that may be problematic, for example, because of the 'hold-up problem'. Thus firms are not seen as solutions to the more general, Hayekian problem of the dispersion of knowledge (Minkler, 1993; Foss, 1999; Sautet and Foss, 1999). Because of its competitive equilibrium starting point, such fundamental issues relating to discovery and the dispersion of knowledge are out of reach for the modern economics of organization.

In this explorative chapter we approach such issues, beginning from a market process perspective. We begin by arguing that alternative theories of the *market* process (neoclassical, Austrian and radical subjectivist theories) imply different, but possibly complementary, requirements with respect to the way we should think about the nature of the *firm* as a crucial agent in the market process. For example, Austrian and radical subjectivist perspectives imply a view of the firm that stresses entrepreneurship, novelty, learning and other manifestations of endogenous change. However, we argue that such a perspective is non-existent in the economics of organization.

The question then arises of what a theory of the firm inspired by Austrian and radical subjectivist views of the market process may look like. We try to develop one such story, using not only market process theory but also the economics of property rights (Alchian, 1965; Alchian and Demsetz, 1972; Cheung, 1983; Barzel, 1997). On this basis, we address issues in the theory of economic organization by looking more closely into those mechanisms inside firms that endogenously produce change, such as learning, experimenting and increasing division of labour, and tie this to the issue of coordination by managerial allocation of property rights inside the firm. We argue that the firm arises as an institution that coordinates a complex system of activities characterized by such endogenous change. Thus we contribute both to the theory of market processes and to the theory of economic organization.

2. THEORIES OF THE MARKET PROCESS

Although Williamson (1988, p.94) observed that the 'proposition that process matters is widely resisted and has attracted little concerted research attention from economists', not everybody has resisted this 'proposition' and there has been ample 'concerted' research effort, taking place under the banner of market process economics.[3] This is a broad line of thought that includes the Austrian school of economics (for example, Mises, 1936, 1949; Hayek, 1937, 1945, 1968; Kirzner, 1973, 1992; Lachmann, 1986), evolutionary (Nelson and Winter, 1982), Schumpeterian (Schumpeter, 1934), radical subjectivist (Shackle, 1972) and post-Marshallian economics (Richardson, 1960; Loasby, 1976, 1991), as well as some contributions with a more formal, neoclassical character, such as stability analysis (for example, Fisher, 1983), learning theory (Frydman, 1982) and some instances of cooperative game theory (Boettke and Prychitko, 1998). This is a confusing set of diverse perspectives; how do we make sense of all this diversity?

A discussion that comes handy in this context is that of Littlechild (1986). Specifically, he suggests that we focus on the level of individual agents, and inquire into the way 'the decision makers perceive of the world, how these perceptions change over time, how additional information may be sought, and how the decision maker can limit his exposure to uncertainty' (ibid., p.27). Evidently, this is based on the presumption that the *differentia* between alternative theories of the market process are based on different assumptions as to the epistemic and cognitive powers of agents. Littlechild then argues that it is possible to make an overall distinction between three ideal typical models of the market process,[4] namely the *neoclassical model* (for example, Arrow, 1959; Frydman, 1982); the *Austrian model* (for example, Hayek, 1937, 1968; Kirzner, 1973, 1992) and the *radical subjectivist model* (for example, Shackle, 1972; Lachmann, 1986, O'Driscoll and Rizzo, 1985).

In the following we briefly explicate Littlechild's distinction and add some of our own thoughts on the subject.

2.1. The Neoclassical Model

As Littlechild explains, what is primarily characteristic of the neoclassical model is that 'the form the future can take is known in advance' (Littlechild, 1986, p.8). Specifically, agents can fully characterize the vector of variables that is relevant for his actions and can fully characterize the probability distributions of these variables. Thus the neoclassical agent lives in a world characterized by Knightian risk. As Littlechild explains, the agent 'is unsure what the price of honey will be tomorrow, but he knows that honey will be traded. Conversely, he never finds honey in the shops if he had not previously expected it to be there' (ibid., p.28).

Understood as a model of learning, the neoclassical model thus primarily deals with the question of how agents react when known data are changed; it does not deal with the unexpected and agents do not have to discover anything. Bayesian updating of priors into posteriors is one mode of learning that is consistent with the neoclassical model, but not the only one; one can also have agents that use various forecasting techniques (Frydman and Phelps, 1984). In this context the analyst is concerned with, for example, how rapidly subjectively held distributions of prices may converge to the objective ones. This reflects a view that the primary rationale of markets is to secure the efficient allocation of given resources.

2.2. The Austrian Model

The Austrian model, particularly as developed in Kirzner's work (1973, 1992, 1997), posits that 'a consumer may discover honey for the first time' (Littlechild, 1986); the discovery of hitherto unnoticed opportunities is centre stage in this model. Epistemically, we may say that 'Tomorrow is a vector of which the agent knows some components but not others; he or she knows that there will be other components, but not what they will be' (ibid., p.29). An implication of this is that the agent cannot construct probability measures over these 'other components'. How do agents act, given such ignorance?

The answer developed by Kirzner (1973, 1992, 1997) is that agents spontaneously tend to discover hitherto unnoticed opportunities and that pure profit incentives play a key role here. Central to Kirzner's argument is the point that, what he calls 'Robbinsian maximizing' (after Lionel Robbins), is inadequate to form the basis for a theory of the market as a dynamic process. This is because, in the conventional conceptualization of the problem confronting the individual decision maker, the whole decision structure is given. What should be included in the behavioural make-up of agents is what Kirzner calls 'alertness', that is, the ability to recognize and act on new opportunities for profit. Given this view of the agent, the market process is seen as one of continuous entrepreneurial discovery of hitherto unnoticed profit opportunities, and the role of the market is to allow for the effective use of local knowledge (Hayek, 1937, 1945), as reflected in profit-motivated entrepreneurship.

2.3. The Radical Subjectivist Model

Finally, in the radical subjectivist model, 'the future is not so much unknown as it is non-existent or indeterminate at the time of decision. The agent's task is not to estimate or discover, but to create' (Littlechild, 1986, p.29). Thus the issue concerns the creation of the opportunity set. For example, the radical subjectivist agent may be seen as creating the change in data to which the Kirznerian entrepreneur reacts. In a string of publications over many years, George Shackle (for example, 1972) grappled with the issue of how agents exercise their creative imagination, and he strongly criticized the maximizing model of rationality. His work has conventionally been seen as critical rather than constructive. There is an element of truth to this, however, for Shackle never tells us much about what bounds choice and its consequences, so that one may easily jump to the conclusion that, in the radical subjectivist view, anything goes.

However, Shackle's (and other radical subjectivists') primary aim was simply to stress the creative aspects of action; there is no denial that choice and its consequences are constrained. For example, there are constraints on the level of the agent (for example, heuristics, rules-of-thumb, moral norms) and there are (system) constraints that work on an aggregate level, such as industry-level selection forces (Alchian, 1950). While the former category of constraints are ex ante, that is, works on the imagination and the consequent decisions themselves, the latter category of constraints are more of an ex post character. Thus we are led rather naturally to an evolutionary or Schumpeterian interpretation of the radical subjectivist view of the market process, in which the market stimulates the generation of novelty on an ex ante basis and selects among alternative imaginative entrepreneurial offerings ex post.

2.4. The Market Process and the Firm

As this section has briefly clarified, there are different, albeit arguably complementary, views of the nature and role of the market process, namely as allocating given resources (neoclassical), as prompting the discovery of hitherto unnoticed opportunities (Austrian), and as stimulating the emergence of (and selection from) novelty (radical subjectivist). The question now is how this connects to economic organization.

We can begin by asking what the three respective views of the market process may imply with respect to the way we conceptualize the firm. Table 3.1 provides one interpretation of this. Without further argument at this stage, we note that the neoclassical model relates rather directly to the modern economics of organization: there is the same emphasis on the efficient allocation of *given* resources. (We develop this argument in more detail in the next section.) However, the Austrian and the radical subjectivist models imply views of the firm that differ from this 'Robbinsian' (Kirzner, 1973) perspective, since they would seem to lead to more entrepreneurial and dynamic conceptions of the firm (Cowen and Parker, 1997; Sautet and Foss, 1999).

Table 3.1 The market and the firm

	The role of markets	The role of firms
Neoclassical model	Ensure efficient allocation of given resources through the provision of the 'right' price incentives	Firms arise as efficient responses to market failure, and as alternative means of allocating given resources through incentive and property rights systems that differ from those characteristic of markets
Austrian model	Promote the discovery of hitherto unnoticed opportunities for profit and thus stimulate plan consistency	Firms are embodiments of entrepreneurial plans
Radical subjectivist model	Generate novelty (and select among the resulting variation)	Firms are important sources of novelty (through innovative activity) in the economy

However, note that it is necessary to tease out, as it were, various views of the firm from Austrian and radical subjectivist models of the market process. In these theories there is very little explicit analysis of the contracting process, or of the various types of contracts and institutions within which the market process takes place. Moreover, there is no explicit attempt to discriminate between different types of economic organization. Thus these theories of the market process are paradoxically and remarkably silent about perhaps the main actor in the market process, namely the firm.

We shall take it as a working hypotheses that underlying views of the market process are bound to influence the analyst's view of the nature of economic organization. Intuitively, an Austrian or radical subjectivist will tend to see, for example, the rationales of contractual forms and economic organization in a different light from that of the neoclassical economist. Thus, whereas the neoclassical economist may view, say, the incompleteness of the employment contract as a matter of economizing with given contract drafting costs, the Austrian or radical subjectivist may stress that incompleteness confers the flexibility needed for experimental activity inside the firm (a view that we develop later at greater length). This suggests that it does make a difference for the way economic organization is conceptualized and analysed whether one begins from a neoclassical or an Austrian or radical subjectivist view of the market process. As we explain in more detail in the following section, this difference has to do with whether and how change is included and conceptualized.

3. ECONOMIC ORGANIZATION, CHANGE AND THE MARKET PROCESS

The recognition that change and economic organization are related phenomena does not seem to appear in economics until the debates of the 1920s and 1930s on the economic feasibility of socialism.[5] During this debate, the Austrians (Mises, 1936; Hayek, 1945) argued that it is only when change enters into consideration that it is possible to discriminate among alternative types of economic organization in terms of allocation and optimality. Hayek (1945, p.82) pointed out: 'It is . . . worth stressing . . . that economic problems arise always and only in consequence of change. As long as things continue as before, or at least as they were expected to, there arise no new problems requiring a decision'.[6]

Basing their schemes on the economics of the stationary state allowed the market socialists to suppress most relevant questions of economic organization and to portray market socialism in a much too positive light. The other side of the coin is, of course, that non-trivial problems of economic organization derive from change, and particularly unanticipated or at least surprising change. In such a view, the economic problem of society – or indeed of any kind of economic organization – is not so much a matter of the allocative problem of making best use of 'given' resources; rather, it is a matter of which type of institution will most efficiently cope with the calculation, incentive and coordination problems introduced by economic change.

3.1. Process and Economic Organization

Although the socialist calculation debate was a debate in comparative systems theory, the overall insight that there is a relation between change and economic organization is applicable (*mutatis mutandis*) to the analysis of economic organization in a market economy. Thus, in a stationary state, there would be no repeated transaction costs, once the initial search costs, contract drafting costs, monitoring costs and so on had been expended at date 0. There would be no further 'costs of discovering what the relevant prices are' (Coase, 1937). There might still be information asymmetries, monitoring problems, shirking and so on but, since these problems would not change in extent and character, all relevant contingencies could be contracted over. Thus contracts would be complete, and all rights could be fully specified in these contracts. This changeless world is the world of a substantial part of the modern economics of organization. It is also a world in which it is hard to find a role for firms (Hart, 1995; Langlois and Robertson, 1995). Change would thus seem to be necessary to understand the rationale of firm organization.

Now, this linking of firms and change might seem to clash with Hayek's emphasis on the superiority of adaptation to changes by means of the price mechanism (Hayek, 1945). According to Hayek, the advantage of the price mechanism lies in its role as an economizer with information and bounded rationality. It is because it operates with an informational minimum that the price mechanism is a superior institution for adapting to change. If one pushes this logic, it is easy to be led to the conclusion that, from a Hayekian point of view, there is no need for firm organization (Jensen and Meckling, 1992). However, as any economist knows today, the existence of the firm must be rationalized in terms of failures of Hayek's 'telecommunications system' of prices.

In turn, many of these failures arise precisely because of the kind of unanticipated or at least surprising economic change that the Austrians emphasized. Such change gives rise to various types of 'costs of using the price mechanism' that in turn help explain why firms exist (Coase, 1937). Thus the Coasian emphasis on planned coordination and the Hayekian emphasis on spontaneous coordination are not mutually exclusive. Moreover, both focused on unanticipated change as the sort of change that is primarily important when it comes to identifying the relative advantages of firms and markets. Thus Hayek is quite clear that the institution he focuses on derives its primary efficiency properties from its ability to handle unanticipated change, and Coase makes essentially the same point about the institution that concerns him: the rationale of the firm is to provide managed coordination in the face of indescribable future contingencies; hence the emphasis on the incomplete employment contract in Coase (1937). In other words, flexibility is a main message of the analyses of both Coase and Hayek.

The emphasis on flexibility in the face of the possibility of unanticipated change would seem to be a distinctly non-neoclassical aspect of Coase's analysis (Foss, 1994), and one that is much closer to the Austrian or even radical subjectivist/evolutionary theories of the market process. However, Coase's basic analysis is formulated in such broad terms that many other interpretations, including neoclassical interpretations, are perfectly possible. We next consider alternative contributions to the theory of economic organization and discuss how these link up with Austrian and radical subjectivist theories of the market process.

3.2. The Economics of Organization and Theories of the Market Process

As suggested earlier, the modern economics of organization embraces a broad spectrum of theories about different sources of the costs of transacting and this is reflected in the many different explanations of firms as solutions to contractual problems. Common to at least the formal manifestations of these theories – namely incomplete contract theory (Grossman and Hart, 1986; Hart, 1995) and principal-agent theory (Hart and Holmström, 1987; Holmström and Milgrom, 1991) – is that they are partial equilibrium models, examine small-scale interaction, focus on (explicit and implicit) contracting relations, use non-cooperative game theory, assume Bayesian behaviour, and use perfect Bayesian equilibria as the relevant solution concepts. On the more verbal side, one may distinguish between the nexus of contract and measurement cost approaches (Alchian and Demsetz, 1972; Jensen and Meckling, 1976; Fama, 1980; Cheung, 1983; Barzel, 1982, 1997) on the one hand, and the kind of transaction cost economics associated with, particularly, Williamson's work (Williamson, 1985, 1996) on the other.

A distinction that has become crucial in recent work is the one between 'complete contracting' and 'incomplete contracting' theories. The former category, which includes principal-agent, nexus of contracts and perhaps also measurement cost theories, belong squarely in the camp based on an (implicit) assumption of a neoclassical type of market process. This is because complete contracting essentially implies 'that the form the future can take is known in advance' (Littlechild, 1986, p.28). Not all relevant information may be available to the economic agents; indeed, what drives these models is the assertion that some information is privately held. Information may, for example, be lacking on valued attributes of assets or, in the case of humans, the effort they exert. Prices may therefore not perfectly reflect marginal value. This may create problems of excessive sorting (Barzel, 1982), inefficient levels of performance (Alchian and Demsetz, 1972) and underinvestment in durable production assets (Grossman and Hart, 1986). Different types of economic organization are argued to exist as efficient responses to such problems.[7] All of this is perfectly consistent with the neoclassical model of the market process.

In contrast, incomplete contracting theories, such as Williamson's transaction cost approach, may in some respects seem closer to the Austrian market process model. Here, recall, the problem is neither uncertainty nor risk, but ignorance. In such a world, 'tomorrow' may bring about discoveries of improved materials or techniques (for example, Hart, 1995), and contracting will necessarily be incomplete. Such discoveries may influence the value of property rights over assets in ways that were not foreseen at the time of contracting. The allocation of rights to determine the use of the assets thus becomes important. In the work of Williamson (1985, 1996), it is the authority granted by the legal status of the employment contracts that provides the manager with the rights to determine (within the boundary of the contract) how assets should be used. In the work of Hart and his colleagues (Grossman and Hart, 1986; Hart, 1995), it is the allocation of ownership rights which provides agents with the power to decide about non-contractually specified uses of assets. In both cases the organization of transactions within firms is the best way of securing against hold-up where transactions involve specific assets.

However, in these models, agents are assumed to be able to comprehend and take measures against contracting hazards on an ex ante basis. This may be seen as a problem, for the basic notion of incomplete contracts may be interpreted as involving the notion of unanticipated change. In spite of this, it portrays agents as so clever that they are able to choose those governance structures (and allocation of ownership) that can most efficiently handle 'unanticipated' future change; that is, those institutions that minimize the loss from incentive conflicts of various kinds.[8] Thus, in the work of, for example, Hart (1995), the joint surplus from a contractual relation is assumed to be known (at least probabilistically), and ignorance is only present as an assumed lack of ability to specify the exact nature of the object over which one contracts. However, this is perceived of as sufficient to produce contracting hazards and to provide a rationale for the firm.[9]

3.3. The Neglect of Process in the Economics of Organization

Although it is possible, as we have seen, to ascribe certain elements of the Austrian view of the market process to some theorizing within the modern economics of organization, it is fair to say that the latter body of theory, taken as a whole, is a static affair. For example, principal-agent theories assume that all contracting action can be compressed into one initial grand contract and that principals know all the possible actions that are open to agents; agents, for example division managers in a firm, are assumed to hold the same model of reality; all uses of assets (including optimal ones), present and future, are assumed to be fully known to the actors and so on.

Thus the role of firm organization in the economics of organization is purely a matter of efficiently allocating given resources to given means; there is little or no notion of learning, entrepreneurship and discovery. There is, in short, no notion of process – at least in the Austrian and radical subjectivist understanding of this. The roles that can be ascribed to firms in the modern economics of organization are narrowly circumscribed, being limited to providing contractually embodied structures of property rights and incentives that make joint surplus as large as possible, given constraints (such as asymmetric information and risk preferences).

However, a perspective on economic organization informed by market process theories surely cannot neglect other roles of the firm. Thus market process theories suggest that we might also see the firm as an embodiment of entrepreneurship or as an innovating entity (cf. Table 3.1), in addition to, for example, a nexus of employment contracts and property rights. The question then arises how such a view should be expressed. Evidently, there are many possibilities (see, for example, Langlois and Robertson, 1995) and we shall only pursue one of these, one that takes its starting point from the changing division of labour. It is surely one of economics' oldest empirical truths that the menu of inputs and outputs and corresponding markets have continuously expanded, through the growing 'extent of the market', the continuously increasing division of labour, and process and product innovations introduced by entrepreneurs. Thus the changing division of labour is an important mechanism, endogenously injecting change in an economy.

In the following section, we shall provide a sketch of what a theory of the firm that is informed by these insights might look like.[10] Like Coase (1937) and Williamson (1996), we stress the importance of the incomplete employment contract. And like Hart (1995), we stress the importance of the discretion provided by ownership. However, we, unlike these contributions, do not focus on how authority and ownership may solve incentive conflicts but on the flexibility it provides for solving coordination problems caused by a changing division of labour inside the firm.

4. WHAT A PROCESS THEORY OF THE FIRM MAY LOOK LIKE

4.1. Change and the Division of Labour

As Adam Smith (1776, chap.1) pointed out, the division of labour and specialization in production are main sources of productivity improvements. Specifically, he ascribes productivity gains to improvements in a worker's ability to perform a task as it is repeated more often, the time that is saved from avoiding having to switch from one task to another, and an improved ability of workers to identity labour saving innovations. Many of the labour saving innovations envisaged by Smith are the results of experimentation (and are seen by him as such). In the words of Leijonhufvud (1986, p.215), 'The mental task of analyzing the production process so as to carry through the division of labor leads to the *discovery* of these opportunities for mechanization'. In other words, the division of labour is a Hayekian (Hayek, 1968) discovery procedure (Loasby, 1991).

Many of the advantages of the division of labour can be attributed to the replacement of craft production by the serial production of the factory system (Leijonhufvud, 1986). This saves on capital costs, since tools are used more fully and inventory costs are reduced. Thus the division of labour introduces change in more than one dimension. It gives rise to increased marginal productivity of workers and it introduces changes in the methods of production. We shall argue that these types of endogenous changes are relevant for understanding firm organization, since they continuously introduce new coordination problems. For example, serial production required a much more precise time phasing of the inputs of individual workers than the artisan production it replaced (Leijonhufvud, 1986). Moreover, as part of the increased mechanization of production, new machines were introduced that integrated tasks hitherto performed by many workers. It changed labour tasks from direct transformation to the more human capital-demanding task of tending machines (Ames and Rosenberg, 1965).[11]

While the degree of specialization is indeed limited by the extent of the market (as pointed out by Smith), it may certainly also be limited by increased coordination costs. More specifically, it also depends on the marginal costs of coordinating increasingly specialized tasks and the marginal benefits from greater division of labour. The question then is which institutions will reduce coordination costs. In the following sections we argue that firm coordination can reduce some of those costs of coordination that are caused by increasing division of labour. In particular, we focus on the costs of coordinating complex and interdependent technologies. In order to develop this argument, we utilize basic Coasian arguments. First, in order to state more precisely the link between the division of labour, learning in production and coordination, we draw on the property rights approach, initiated in Coase (1960) and developed by, among others, Alchian (1965), Demsetz (1967), Cheung (1983) and Barzel (1997). An emphasis on property rights has always been central to the Austrian tradition (for example, Mises, 1936), so a combined process-property rights approach is very much in line with Austrian thinking (see also Foss and Foss, 2000b). Second, we elaborate the basic idea in Coase (1937) that the firm's rationale lies in its ability to resolve coordination problems that are caused by change, rather than in its ability to align incentive conflicts.

4.2. The Division of Labour as a Division of Property Rights

Mises (1936, p.27) pointed out that ownership refers to 'the power to use economic goods', and Barzel (1994, p.394) provides a convenient summing-up of the economic concept of property rights as:

> an individual's net valuation, in expected terms, of the ability to directly consume the services of the asset, or to consume it indirectly through exchange. A key word is *ability*: The definition is concerned not with what people are legally entitled to do but with what they believe they can do.

In short, property rights are the economic rights agents hold over assets. Assets may be physical assets, such as tools, buildings and other equipment, or they may be human assets, such as the effort and work time provided by an agent. It is customary to distinguish between three different categories of property rights, namely 'use rights', which define the potential uses of an asset; 'income rights', or the right to consume an asset; and 'rights to transfer' permanently to another party ownership rights over an asset – that is, to alienate or sell an asset.

Often physical and human assets have different properties each of which can be specified and be subject to negotiations between parties to a transaction. Moreover, user rights over different attributes of assets may be shared between individuals. For example, a copying machine can be used in different time periods and for many different types of copy work, different individuals may have different rights to use a computer in different time periods and for different purposes and so on.

Thus the division of labour can be tied to the possession of use rights if it is interpreted as a subdivision of user rights over assets, so that each individual holds rights over a more narrow set of assets or holds a more narrow set of rights over the same assets. There is a connection between the division of labour, learning (by doing) and the allocation of use rights that is central to our argument. This connection is a consequence of the fact that learning by doing usually requires the exercise of use rights over some assets. This implies that patterns of learning by doing in production depends on allocation of use rights between different individuals over time, and the division of labour may be one reason for reallocation of user rights.

Thus experimentation (as envisaged by Smith) depends on the allocation of use rights over assets. However, the extent of experimentation depends on how well-specified and easily monitored use rights are, since the more well-specified these rights are, the less able are those who use assets to experiment and the more constrained will be their learning and experimentation. If, for example, the manner in which a computer operator runs a program is pre-specified in a contract and easily monitored, his learning by doing may be limited to improving the speed with which he activates the keyboard. If he has greater discretion in deciding how to operate the program, he might have a greater opportunity for learning by experimenting.[12] Discretion enables individuals to learn a broader set of skills. It also enables them to conduct experiments that may result in innovations.

4.3. The Division of Labour and Coordination Problems

However, discretionary behaviour need not always result in productivity gains. This may, for example, be the case if there are strong technological interdependencies, so that the functional performance of a technology is greatly influenced by the fit between parts and between activities. In such a case, discretionary behaviour may result in, for example, bottlenecks or in uneven development of components.[13] From a property rights perspective, these problems can be ascribed to imperfectly specified rights over assets as production tasks are subdivided. This is because it is difficult to specify all valued dimensions of assets prior to specialization, since many of the valued dimensions of assets only become apparent from experimenting with the use of assets. Even if important dimensions can be specified, it may be difficult to allocate these rights in ways that ensure the best use of assets. This may, for example, be the case with the time and place dimension of assets, where misallocations result in excess stocks of intermediate products or in idle assets. In fact, with a great deal of interdependence in a complex system, the best time and place to use an asset depend on the specification of the uses of all other assets that are needed in the production.

This kind of uncertainty creates costs of (labour) specialization that are due to economic agents' lack of ability to specify a completely comprehensive plan of production. For example, bottlenecks may appear where the complexity and interdependent activities make it difficult to specify how best to sequence various activities and where the introduction of more specialized tools and equipment creates capacity utilization problems due to technical indivisibilities. Moreover, if interface specifications are imperfect, labour-saving innovations may result in an uneven development of tools, equipment and components. Basically, these problems arise when those who deliver parts or carry out activities are not aware of the need for mutual adjustment. Solving problems that arise from technological interdependencies is an important source of innovative improvements[14] (as pointed out by Rosenberg, 1976; Sahal, 1981). However, such innovations do not emerge because of increased (labour) specialization, but because of learning in coordination. The question then arises: what institutional set-up best provides for experimentation and accumulation of experience in coordination?

4.4. The Coordination of Complex Systems and the Existence of the Firm

Our answer is that one of the reasons why managed coordination may be advantageous relative to coordination by the price mechanism is that the former reduces costs of learning about the coordination of technologically interdependent tasks. Thus the existence of the firm is explicitly seen in a dynamic context, where dynamics is introduced by continuing experimentation to solve problems, which arise from an increased division of labour. In contrast, virtually all other contributions to the economics of organization take the costs of coordinating various tasks as well as the extent of specialization in the economy as given, and proceed to analyse why all transactions among specialized agents are not coordinated either in firms or in open markets.

From the literature on incremental innovations, it is apparent that the solution to problems of bottlenecks and uneven development in components is based on learning by doing in production and development (Rosenberg, 1976; Sahal, 1981). The firm may provide a low-cost way of discovering solutions to coordination problems of bottlenecks and uneven development of components relative to pure market transactions. It is in the handling of some of the coordination problems associated with interdependence between tasks that we find the rationale of the firm. Specifically, firms can be viewed as solutions to problems of coordination in situations where user rights over assets cannot be perfectly specified and allocated in ways which ensure the functionality of complex technologies. These coordination problems produce a need for experiments. In the context of firm activity, experiments take place in the form of the many trials and errors involved with setting up a smoothly running production system which consists of many interdependent specialized tasks. Of course, such experimentation is only needed if there is uncertainty with respect to the best way of operating technically interdependent production systems. As a result of such technological uncertainty, firms may start different kinds of experiments and follow different paths of learning.

However, for managed direction of resources to be efficient, it is required that managers are at least as qualified in discovering the relevant prices (that is, finding the highest valued uses of assets) as independent contractors would be. Otherwise, costs of transacting may be saved at the expense of efficiency in the use of resources. If managers are better able to determine the valuable uses of resources compared to other agents, managers have a natural ownership advantage over resources. Such an advantage explains the single-person firm, but not necessarily why managers hire employees who are prepared to take orders within certain limits in order to take advantage of this knowledge. 'Managers' could as well rent the labour time of an agent to perform a certain well-specified task.

In actuality, managers stand a good chance of acquiring superior knowledge about the relevant (shadow) prices of rights over assets that make up a complex technology. One of the reasons why one might expect the discovery of opportunities for productivity improvements to be less costly within the boundaries of firms is that managers hold control rights over assets, including rights to redefine and reallocate specific rights. They are thus able to conduct experiments without continually having to renegotiate contracts which have more or less unforeseen outcomes. This saves time, as well as ink costs.[15]

Managers are then able to create controlled experiments in which they only change some aspects of the tasks in order to trace the effects of some specific rearrangements of rights. Setting up a controlled experiment may be more difficult across boundaries of firms and in particular if interdependencies exist between many different firms and if, owing to high information costs, it is difficult to specify all the tasks which must not be changed during the experiment. Coordinating interdependent tasks within the boundaries of a firm may provide managers with a more complete picture of the nature of interdependencies – information which is important not only in relation to eliminating bottlenecks, but also in relation to avoiding problems of uneven development of components by setting up interface standards and other more permanent solutions.

4.5. The Evolving Firm

So far, the argument has been that, relative to markets, firms may economize on the transaction costs of learning the best way of coordinating technological interdependent systems. Now, once a firm has discovered how to coordinate some specialized tasks, there may be little advantage from managed direction relative to market transacting, and coordination by order contracts could replace coordination by management.[16] However, such specialization between firms would give way to economic gains from further division of labour in tasks, and this in turn would create new uncertainty and new opportunities for reducing coordination costs by experimenting. In other words, there will be continuing *processes* of specialization in tasks, learning in coordination and specialization between firms, and new ways of coordination will continuously be imagined by managers/entrepreneurs, much like the process of cumulative causation envisaged by Allyn Young (1928). Thus firms contain many mechanisms that *endogenously* produce change, such as the changing division of labour inside firms.

5. CONCLUSION

This chapter has been wide-ranging and explorative. The primary aim of the discussion has been to define and discuss an agenda, namely that of bringing issues of process issues more closely together with issues of economic organization. While we possess some insight into the market process, the prevailing economics of organization is a largely static affair, in spite of lip service being paid to process issues, such as unforeseen contingencies (Kreps, 1996). However, we have suggested that non-standard ideas on experimentation, complexity, entrepreneurship and endogenous change may be used to construct a story of, for example, why there should be firms in a market economy. Specifically, our story involved the idea that firms exist because they provide superior mechanisms for experimenting with complex production technologies. However, this is only one out of many, many ways in which issues of economic organization may be brought into contact with process issues. We look forward to more work on the subject.

NOTES

1. This is true even of Williamson's (1985, 1996) work. See Holmström and Roberts (1998).
2. This is also the case for agency problems, involving asymmetric information, since the principal always knows what he himself does not know (Foss, 1999; Foss and Foss, 2000a). For example, he knows the range of actions that are open to the agent but not which particular action the agent chose.
3. It should be noted that this is a potentially confusing label. Thus one might be led to the conclusion that 'market process economics' only deals with allocation by means of exchange of property rights in the setting of the market institution. Such is not the case. Market process economics also deals with non-market modes of allocation, such as centrally planned economies, government institutions and firms. Thus, when market process economists talk about the 'market process', what they really mean is 'the economic process'.
4. However, Littlechild's classification is not entirely uncontroversial. For example, some may argue that there really is not such a thing as a 'neoclassical model of the market process', since neoclassical economics is equilibrium economics, and therefore per definition not process economics. However, see Koppl (1992) for an argument that much of basic neoclassical price theory may be thought of in terms of process.
5. Lavoie (1985) provides a classic overview and interpretation of the debate. In general, it is hard to underestimate the importance of this debate for the theory of economic organization (broadly conceived). Thus many modern insights in agency theory, the theory of mechanism design, property rights theory and, of course, in the informational role of the price system hark back to this important episode in the development of economics. One of the less appreciated insights that emerged from this debate is the one being developed in this section.
6. Hayek (1945) and Mises (1936) even suggested that, in a stationary state, the choice between central planning or private property market organization cannot be made on grounds of economic efficiency.
7. For example, in order to realize economies of scale many individuals may be needed to work on the same piece of equipment. However, high information costs make it difficult to determine in advance how much the operation of each individual contributes to the wear and tear of the equipment. This creates a situation where there will be insufficient incentives to invest in maintenance. According to Barzel (1997), one way of controlling such problems is to use a fixed wage contract in which workers are remunerated for their time rather than their output. But since a worker who receives a fixed wage for a fixed period of time has no incentive to identify the tasks needed for an effective operation of equipment, managers have to specify and monitor the task to be performed. A similar problem arises when team production is involved, as in the well-known Alchian and Demsetz (1972) paper. In both of these cases, the solution is to set up an organization in which a specialized monitor is given the rights to meter effort, receive the residual income from these activities, to alter membership of the team and to sell all these rights.
8. Technically, agents can perform 'dynamic programming'. See Kreps (1996) for a discussion of this.
9. The story is this: an agent will have greater incentives to undertake a transaction-specific investment in his human capital if he also has residual user rights over complementary physical assets. This is because he then avoids the threat of hold-up by an owner of complementary physical asset, for a share of the residual income his investment can produce.

Firms are thus defined by the physical assets over which a legitimate owner has formal residual user rights. Firms reduce uncertainty in only one dimension: they provide a guarantee for a certain share of the residual income of investments in human capital. Firms do not enable the discovery of the nature of the object over which one contract; such discoveries take place independently of whether or not firms exist.

10. In the last few years, an increasing number of authors have argued that the theory of economic organization stands to gain from being infused with Austrian ideas. Thus some have argued that Austrian insights into the necessity of pricing for efficient resource allocation provide a unique perspective on the boundaries of the firm (Klein, 1996), while others have argued that firms are also (like markets) characterized by a dispersal of knowledge (Jensen and Meckling, 1992; Minkler, 1993; Cowen and Parker, 1997; Foss, 1999; Sautet and Foss, 1999). While all these contributions differ from the modern economics of organization in the emphasis they place on dispersed knowledge, they, too, are characterized by a somewhat static character: they are concerned with the firm's role as a coordinator of existing, dispersed knowledge. In contrast we want to develop a more process-oriented approach, one that puts more of an emphasis on learning and discovery.
11. For example, machines that replace labour often organize work in different sequences and have a different minimum efficient scale of production compared to workers. Therefore increased division of labour and mechanization (which follows from labour specialization) requires coordination of the time phasing, as well as of the capacities of the different machines to take advantage of economies of throughput and parallel scale economies.
12. High information costs and ignorance often imply that transacting parties voluntarily leave rights over certain properties of an asset unspecified. For example, to specify completely all rights to use a computer requires full knowledge of all possible uses and all the different ways in which the computer may be operated, as well as a detailed listing of these uses. In addition, one would need to perform a tight surveillance of the users of the computer in order to enforce one's rights. Many rights over a computer are therefore left unspecified, and these rights may be captured by the user of the computer, who is then capable of exercising some discretion in his decisions on how to use or operate the computer.
13. Of course, with higher degrees of discretion individuals also have more room for shirking or otherwise appropriate a greater part of the value from the use of an asset. However, we neglect shirking here, because we want to focus on the pure coordination aspects of the problem.
14. Problems of bottlenecks and uneven development of components exist even with self-sufficiency, since individuals producing for their own needs may be unaware of how best to carry out an activity or to develop the technologies they use. Specialization in production, however, is likely to magnify the problems.
15. In this connection, wage contracts may also be an efficient way of sharing risks from experimenting.
16. Managed direction could still be advantageous in cases where adaptation of interdependent production systems to unforeseen exogenous contingencies is called for.

REFERENCES

Alchian, A. (1950), 'Uncertainty, Evolution and Economic Theory', reprinted in *Economic Forces at Work* (1977), Indianapolis: Liberty Press.

Alchian, A. (1965), 'Some Economics of Property Rights', reprinted in *Economic Forces at Work* (1977), Indianapolis: Liberty Press.

Alchian, A. and H. Demsetz (1972), 'Production, Information Costs and Economic Organization', *American Economic Review*, **62**, 772–95.

Ames, E. and N. Rosenberg (1965), 'The Progressive Division and Specialization of Industries', *Journal of Development Studies*, **1**, 363–83.

Arrow, K. (1959), 'Towards a Theory of Price Adjustment', in M. Abramowitz (ed.), *The Allocation of Economic Resources,* Stanford: Stanford University Press.

Barzel, Y. (1982), 'Measurement Costs and the Organization of Markets', *Journal of Law and Economics,* **25**, 27–48.

Barzel, Y. (1994), 'The Capture of Wealth by Monopolists and the Protection of Property Rights', *International Review of Law and Economics,* **14**, 393–409.

Barzel, Y. (1997), *Economic Analysis of Property Rights*, 2nd edn, Cambridge: Cambridge University Press.

Boettke, P. and D. Prychitko (eds) (1998), *Market Process Economics,* 2 vols, Cheltenham, UK and Lyme, US: Edward Elgar.

Cheung, S. (1983), 'The Contractual Nature of the Firm', *Journal of Law and Economics*, **26**, 1–22.

Coase, R. (1937), 'The Nature of the Firm', *Economica,* **4**, 386–405; reprinted in O. Williamson and S. Winter (eds) (1991), *The Nature of the Firm*, Oxford: Oxford University Press.

Coase, R. (1960), 'The Problem of Social Cost', *Journal of Law and Economics,* **3**, 1–44.

Coase, R. (1991), 'The Nature of the Firm: Origin, Meaning, Influence', in O. Williamson and S. Winter (eds), *The Nature of the Firm*, Oxford: Oxford University Press.

Cowen, T. and D. Parker (1997), *Markets in the Firm: A Market Process Approach to Management*, London: The Institute of Economic Affairs.

Demsetz, H. (1967), 'Toward a Theory of Property Rights', reprinted in *Ownership, Control and the Firm* (1988), Oxford: Basil Blackwell.

Fama, E. (1980), 'Agency Problems and the Theory of the Firm', *Journal of Political Economy*, **88**, 288–307.

Fisher, F. (1983), *Disequilibrium Foundations of Equilibrium Economics,* Cambridge: Cambridge University Press.

Foss, N. (1994), 'The Two Coasian Traditions', *Review of Political Economy,* **6**, 37–61.

Foss, N. (1999), 'The Use of Knowledge in Firms', *Journal of Institutional and Theoretical Economics*, **155**, 458–486.

Foss, K. and N. Foss (2000a), 'Competence and Governance Perspectives: How Do They Differ? How Does It Matter?', in N. Foss and V. Mahnke (eds.), *Competence, Governance and Entrepreneurship*, Oxford: Oxford University Press.

Foss, K. and N. Foss (2000b), 'An Experimental View of the Firm', forthcoming in *Review of Austrian Economics*.

Frydman, R. (1982), 'Towards an Understanding of Market Processes', *American Economic Review,* **72**, 652–68.

Frydman, R. and E. Phelps (1984), *Individual Forecasting and Aggregate Outcomes*, Cambridge: Cambridge University Press.

Grossman, S. and O. Hart (1986), 'The Costs and Benefits of Ownership: A Theory of Vertical and Lateral Integration', *Journal of Political Economy,* **94**, 691–719.

Hart, O. (1995), *Firms, Contracts and Financial Structure*, Oxford: Clarendon Press.

Hart, O. and B. Holmström (1987), 'The Theory of Contracts', in T. Bewley (ed.), *Advances in Economic Theory: Fifth World Congress*, Cambridge: Cambridge University Press.

Hayek, F. (1937), 'Economics and Knowledge', reprinted in *Individualism and Economic Order* (1948), Chicago: University of Chicago Press.

Hayek, F. (1945), 'The Use of Knowledge in Society', reprinted in *Individualism and Economic Order* (1948), Chicago: University of Chicago Press.

Hayek, F. (1968), 'Competition as a Discovery Procedure', reprinted in *New Studies in Philosophy, Politics, Economics and the History of Ideas* (1978), London: Routledge and Kegan Paul.

Holmström, B. and P. Milgrom (1991), 'Multitask Principal-Agent Analyses: Incentive Contracts, Asset Ownership and Job Design', *Journal of Law, Economics and Organization,* **7**, 24–52.

Holmström, B. and J. Roberts (1998), 'The Boundaries of the Firm Revisited', *Journal of Economic Perspectives,* **12**, 73–94.

Ikeda, S. (1990), 'Market Process Theory and ''Dynamic'' Theories of the Market', *Southern Economic Journal,* **57**, 75–92.

Jensen, M. and W. Meckling (1976), 'The Theory of the Firms: Managerial, Agency Cost and Ownership Structure', reprinted in J. Barney and W. Ouchi (eds) (1988), *Organizational Economics,* San Fancisco: Jossey-Bass.

Jensen, M. and W. Meckling (1992), 'Specific and General Knowledge and Organizational Structure', in L. Werin and H. Wijkander (eds), *Contract Economics,* Oxford: Blackwell.

Kirzner, I. (1973), *Entrepreneurship and Competition*, Chicago: University of Chicago Press.

Kirzner, I. (1992), *The Meaning of the Market Process,* London: Routledge.

Kirzner, I. (1997), 'Entrepreneurial Discovery and the Competitive Market Process: An Austrian Approach', *Journal of Economic Literature,* **35**, 60–85.

Klein, P. (1996), 'Economic Calculation and the Limits of Organization', *Review of Austrian Economics,* **9**, 3–28.

Koppl, R. (1992), 'Invisible Hand Explanations and Neoclassical Economics: Towards a Post-Marginalist Economics', *Journal of Institutional and Theoretical Economics,* **184**, 292–313.

Kreps, D. (1996), 'Markets and Hierarchies and (Mathematical) Economic Theory', *Industrial and Corporate Change,* **5**, 561–95.

Lachmann, L. (1986), *The Market as an Economic Process*, Oxford: Blackwell.

Langlois, R. (ed.) (1986), *Economics as a Process: Essays in the New Institutional Economics*, Cambridge: Cambridge University Press.

Langlois, R. and P. Robertson. (1995), *Firms, Markets and Economic Change*, London: Routledge.

Lavoie, D. (1985), *Rivalry and Central Planning*, Cambridge: Cambridge University Press.

Leijonhufvud, A. (1986), 'Capitalism and the Factory System', in R. Langlois (ed.), *Economics as a Process: Essays in the New Institutional Economics*, Cambridge: Cambridge University Press.

Littlechild, S. (1986), 'Three Types of Market Process', in R. Langlois (ed.), *Economics as a Process*: *Essays in the Institutional Economics*, Cambridge: Cambridge University Press.

Loasby, B. (1976), *Choice, Complexity and Ignorance*, Cambridge: Cambridge University Press.

Loasby, B. (1991), *Equilibrium and Evolution*, Manchester: Manchester University Press.

Milgrom, P. and J. Roberts (1992), *Economics, Organization and Management*, Englewood Cliffs: Prentice-Hall.

Minkler, A. (1993), 'The Problem with Dispersed Knowledge: Firms in Theory and Practice', *Kyklos*, **46**, 569–87.

Mises, L. (1936), *Socialism*; reprinted (1981), Indianapolis: Liberty Press.

Mises, L. (1949), *Human Action*, London: William Hodge.

Nelson, R. and S. Winter (1982), *An Evolutionary Theory of Economic Change*, Cambridge, Mass.: Belknap Press.
O'Driscoll, G. and M. Rizzo (1985), *The Economics of Time and Ignorance*, Oxford: Basil Blackwell.
Richardson, G. (1960), *Information and Investment*, Oxford: Oxford University Press.
Rosenberg, N. (1976), *Perspectives on Technology*, Cambridge: Cambridge University Press.
Sahal, D. (1981), *Patterns of Technological Innovation*, Reading, Mass.: Addison-Wesley.
Sautet, F. and N. Foss (1999), 'The Organization of Large, Complex Firms: an Austrian View', unpublished manuscript.
Schumpeter, J. (1934), *The Theory of Economic Development*, Cambridge, Mass.: Harvard University Press.
Shackle, G. (1972), *Epistemics and Economics*, Cambridge: Cambridge University Press.
Smith, A. (1776), *An Inquiry into the Nature and Causes of the Wealth of Nations*; reprinted (1981), Indianapolis: Liberty Press.
Williamson, O. (1985), *The Economic Institutions of Capitalism*, New York: Free Press.
Williamson, O. (1988), 'The Economics of Governance: Framework and Applications', in R. Langlois (ed.), *Economics as a Process: Essays in the New Institutional Economics*, Cambridge: Cambridge University Press.
Williamson, O. (1996), *The Mechanisms of Governance*, Oxford: Oxford University Press.
Young, A. (1928), 'Increasing Returns and Economic Progress', *Economic Journal,* **38**, 527–42.

4. Competition as a process: insights from the Marshallian perspective

Michel Quéré

1. INTRODUCTION

There are at least three main reasons to revisit the analytical place and role of competition from the Marshallian economic framework and discuss its current relevance for present-day discussions about competition as a process. One is the methodological choice of Marshall to keep a relative distance from excessive formalism in economic theory (Keynes, 1925). The second is that we need to keep in mind the fact that Marshallian analysis has been built on ethical foundations (Coase, 1975; Reisman, 1986). The third is that the Marshallian conception of competition is empirically-based and, as such, has to be thought of as contingent upon the dominant characteristics of economic systems (Marshall, 1920).

The first dimension essentially refers to the ambiguous balance between a normative and a historical approach to economic phenomena. As noticed by J.M. Keynes, Marshall found in a historical approach a too weak analytical rigour, that is an inability to 'justify their confidence that the causes which they assigned to economic events were the true causes' (Keynes, 1925, p.20). But, at the same time, Marshall was also reluctant to favour completely a mathematical approach to economic phenomena, essentially because he was convinced that mathematical formulations were also leading to potential sources of errors. This is why he always reduces formal developments to footnotes or annexes in the successive editions of the *Principles*. What is the originality of Marshallian analysis lies in the attempt to reconcile the two types of approach, which is a main feature of the *Principles*. However, he never found sufficient analytical grounds for historical approaches that could satisfy his very perfectionist mind and, as indicated by M. Paley Marshall, he himself ends up considering these historical attempts as a 'white elephant'. This leads him to publish the latter in the form of more theme-oriented contributions like *Industry and Trade* (1919) or *Money, Credit and*

Commerce (1923). However, according to competition, the views expressed in the latter contributions will appear of crucial relevance to qualifying the role and place of competition in Marshallian analysis.

As pointed out by Coase (1975, p.28), the second reason is that we do not forget that 'Marshall himself had come to economics because he wanted to help in eliminating poverty and in enhancing the quality of man and man's life'. As such, the rules conducting society dynamics are ethically-based and notions like duty, tolerance and 'noblesse oblige' are examples of ethical obligations that take an important place in directing those dynamics. However, one needs to add that those ethical foundations are expressed much more in the first edition of the *Principles* and that they largely disappeared in the following successive editions (cf. Reisman, 1986, pp.160–61). Thus the Marshallian conception of competition has much to do with ethical issues. Competition is a sort of necessary problem that public authorities need to organize and control with the aim of securing an acceptable level of social cohesion among the individual components of a society. Indeed, the key word for public authorities is 'compensation', in the sense that they mainly aim at maintaining a market economy within an acceptable range of economic functioning that avoids the 'natural danger' (in terms of individual poverty) that can result from excessive competition (Stigler, Lecture 3 on Progress and Poverty, 1969, in Wood, 1982, p.171):

> Competition is a monster now grown of overwhelming strength. If we were perfectly virtuous, he would feel himself out of place and shrink away. As it is, if we resist him by violence, his convulsions will reduce society to anarchy. But if he can be guided so as to work on our side, then even the removal of poverty will not be too great a task.

The third dimension refers to the lack of a general or stable theory on what competition should be about and how it should be managed. In contrast to Cournot, Marshall rejected 'any simple and uniform doctrine on the relationships among production costs, demand and value' (*Principles*, 1920, p.57). This is the price to be paid for promoting an empirically-based conception of competition which varies from one system to another and also changes over time in the required regulation mechanisms to ensure a satisfactory level of welfare within a specific economy. As a result, this empirically-based conception of competition is the essential reason why we can draw upon some interesting features of the Marshallian analysis and contribute to the current debate on competition as a process.

However, each of these reasons is also a source of confusion, in the sense it does not allow for an explicit doctrine on what competition requires to be, first, understood and, second, suitably managed. Even for his contemporary contradictors, the Marshall's conception of competition was confused, as

Hyndman points out in reporting on the lecture on this subject given by Marshall in 1890 (Groenewegen, 1995, p.460):

> Competition was good, co-operation was good, free trade was good, protection was good; there was trouble between capital and labour which ought not to exist, etc., etc., but not one word did Professor Marshall vouchsafe as to the solution of the problems which he did not even state correctly.

However, we wish here to argue that, more than confusion, this is an original way of thinking about competition. In fact, what appears very relevant is, first, to discuss the ambiguity of the Marshallian definition of free competition which is developed in the *Principles,* as noticed by a few scholars, and, as a consequence, to bring to light the major reasons for such ambiguity; second, to express the original character of the Marshallian conception of competition which lies mainly in the aim of linking in a systematic way the characteristics of production mechanisms with those of the related markets' functioning; and third, to draw some insights from the Marshallian framework to discuss its current relevance for the analysis of competition as a process.

2. AN AMBIGUOUS CONCEPTION OF COMPETITION WITHIN THE MARSHALLIAN ANALYSIS

In fact, the Marshallian conception of competition can be expressed and commented upon from three different but complementary sources. Of course, one is that of the *Principles* and we will see that the structure and aim of the book confines the Marshallian conception of competition to a very specific meaning or, as pointed out by Pursell (1958), to an '(uncomfortable) niche'. Second, we can learn from two complementary contributions more directly coping with economic problems derived from competition: 'Lectures on progress and poverty', given in Bristol in 1883, and 'Some aspects of competition', given in 1890. Third, we can finally learn from the last two books published by Marshall (and from *Industry and Trade*, especially) because they express in more detail his empirically-based conception of the process of competition, even if the latter is actually not directly thought of as a simple and single doctrine in those books.

In this first section, we will essentially consider the reasons why competition has an ambiguous analytical role in the *Principles*. We will follow in that respect two basic arguments: one is to make explicit the methodological difficulties faced in the *Principles* and the reasons why they induce a confusing content for the concept of competition; the other is the ambiguous character of the concept of free competition which is at the core of the Marshallian conception of competition within the *Principles*.

As pointed out by Thomas (1991), a dominant characteristic of the *Principles* lies in the conciliation problem that Marshall tried to face. To a large extent, Book IV of the *Principles* is the opposite of Book V: on the one hand, Marshall attempts to understand the mechanisms that conduct industrial dynamics; on the other hand, he provides us with a static conception of short-term equilibrium between the normal supply and demand of an economy. In fact, this conciliation attempt fails because of the methodological difficulty it induces (see Hart, 1996; Quéré and Ravix, 1998). In the background of this conciliation problem arises the relative importance of biological versus mechanical analogies in economic analysis. Marshall aims at rendering compatible both types of approach in a single framework of analysis within the *Principles*. But if Thomas has convincingly argued that Marshall does not succeed in making the two approaches compatible, it is still interesting to learn from the conceptual construction that he promotes in order to make the resolution of this conciliation problem the best that he could devise.

According to this methodological issue, it is interesting to note how it influences the role of competition within the Marshallian framework. In fact, the originality of competition within the Marshallian analysis lies in the complexity of defining and understanding the concept of free competition. The distinction between pure and perfect competition and free competition has been underlined by Stigler (1957, 1968) and perfectly expressed by Shirai (1968) when he quotes the successive evolutions of the definition given by Marshall to competition within the first, second and eighth editions of the *Principles*. To some extent, the evolution in Marshall's mind with respect to competition has been to reject the analytical interest of pure and perfect competition and to promote a more pragmatic concept of free competition which has to be more compatible with an empirically-based approach.

Marshall progressively rejects a conception of pure and perfect competition because of its weak relevance to empirical observation and especially because of his belief that a perfect market does not exist. In Marshallian terms, a perfect market is 'a district, small or large, in which there are many buyers and many sellers all so keenly on the alert and so well acquainted with one another's affairs that the price of a commodity is always practically the same for the whole of the district'. Such a definition is not thought to be feasible by Marshall, for at least two complementary reasons. One is that it implies that consumers only buy commodities for their own use and not for any trade transaction; the other is that it is always impossible to have exact information on the best price for a particular commodity. If Marshall believed that some specific markets, financial markets for instance, tend towards a situation where pure and perfect competition can prevail, these are only thought of as an exception as regards the general functioning of the economy. And, even in that case, perfect knowledge regarding the functioning of such markets is still impossible. Basically, Marshall rejected the concept of pure and perfect competition because he was persuaded of the impossibility of separating the nature of competition from its effects. This is certainly the essential reason for the major change in the definitions given in the first and second editions of the *Principles*.

In fact, the nature of competition means that competition cannot be analysed without considering the very nature of production. In other words, the organization of production comes first and contributes to influencing any process of competition. That means that estimating a commodity price first depends on the determination of its production cost. But, here, what prevails in the production system is a huge diversity and difficulty of correlating the cost of a commodity to its market price because 'even in the same place and the same trade no two persons pursuing the same aims will adopt exactly the same routes. The tendency to variation is a chief cause of progress; and the abler are the undertakers in any trade, the greater will this tendency be' (*Principles*, 1920, p.295). So competition appears as a result and a guarantee of the diversity of production, in the sense that it contributes to defining an acceptable range of competing production organizations.

Referring to a concept of free competition is therefore associated with the necessity to cope with markets' imperfections. Free competition becomes an acceptable device to assume an equilibrium between normal supply and normal demand in the short run and, nevertheless, to take care of the need for a more realistic representation of competition where market imperfections appeared as a necessary condition for long run industrial evolution (ibid., p.289): 'Of course, normal does not mean competitive. Market prices and normal prices are alike brought about by a multitude of influences, of which some rest on a moral basis and some on a physical; of which some are competitive and some are not'. This quotation makes very explicit this mixture of analytical and methodological problems that Marshall wanted to reconcile when considering the actual working of an economic system. As a consequence, the concept of free competition appears very ambiguous. In other words, the transition from pure and perfect competition to free competition induces a few problems for the analysis.

Within the introductory part of the *Principles*, Marshall makes the aim of his concept of free competition more explicit. He does not share completely the view of competition as a fight among rivals about commodities' supply or demand mediated by the price system. He relates to competition as a sort of civilian type of relationships within an economic system. Modern economic actions should be directed by intelligence much more than by egoism and this evolution justifies more loyalty and trust in the economic transactions. As a consequence, this leads to a conception of individuals' actions which implies a higher importance of cooperative and collective agreements, and a decline in a conflictual representation of competition. Here we find, in the concept of free competition, this methodological insistence on the ethical foundations of economic activity. Competition is not a means of confrontation of separate individuals or companies on a market, it is a process by which economic activity is organized and evolves over time. In that respect, in 'modern' economies, competition is not simply a devastating force, it is a major source of progress that nevertheless needs to be guided by public authorities. In some sense, it is because of this liberty in a context of loyalty and trust that it becomes possible to give up this liberty. In that respect, individual work contracts are the most explicit examples. This abandonment is the basis of modern functioning for economic systems and paves the way for justifying the concept of free competition. Indeed, a major characteristic of free competition lies in this need for a context of 'liberty of industry and labour'.

But, as a consequence, the concept of free competition becomes ambiguous, in the sense that it requires a subtle interaction between competition and cooperation. As such, the concept of free competition is not unique and it has to be empirically-based, especially in accordance with the production characteristics. This is especially pinpointed by Marshall in a well known letter sent to J.B. Clark in November 1902, in which he comments on his own theory of value as developed within the *Principles* (cf. Shirai, 1968, p.10; Thomas, 1991, p.10; Foster, 1993, pp.980–81):

> I then (pre-1870) believed it was possible to have a coherent though abstract doctrine of economics in which competition was the only dominant force; and I then defined 'normal' as that which the undisturbed play of competition would bring about: and now I regard that position as untenable from an abstract as well as from a practical point of view.

Thus Marshall does not believe that competition should be driven by some general laws or mechanisms, nor does he consider the existence of a general continuity among markets' structures, from perfect competition to monopoly, for instance. What he essentially called for is to cope with the specific character of competition which requires an understanding based on empirical observation. This willingness to cope with the diversity of competition is the result of that of industrial production. It is because productive constraints, productive organizations, and industries more largely, differ that there is a need to face the corresponding diversity of competition. It is interesting to note here that the existence of the representative firm as an analytical device for dealing with this diversity of the production system has to some extent an analytical correspondance on the demand side of the economy, which is the concept of a special (or particular) market. If different companies produce the same commodity with different means of organizing production, the feasible ways of producing (that is, those allowing for a reasonable production cost as regards the equilibrium price) are largely dependent on the functioning of the related markets. In fact, firms are not confronting each other on a common general market. On the contrary, they are acting on differentiated markets, depending on their own history and especially their customer relations. Particular markets are a means of securing companies because of the guaranteed selling of commodities to a specific set of customers whose relationships are based on trust and long-term commitments. As such, particular markets expressed the existence and the importance of market imperfections in order to create a context where competition can prevail.

Thus, as regards these different types of problem, free competition becomes a sort of weakly normative concept expressing this double diversity related, on the one hand, to the functioning of the production system and the diversity related to the different ways compatible with the suitable production of the same commodity and, on the other hand, to the specificity of markets' functioning which are not at all reduced to spot markets but imply taking account of the historical structuring of relations between a producer and its main customers. And, as a consequence, the representative firm and the existence of particular markets then appear as a sort of heuristic device aimed at coping with this more realistically-based conception of economic functioning.

Finally, the ambiguous conception of competition underlined through the concept of free competition is a derivative of the methodological aim of Marshall, who wanted to set up his analytical framework in line with the actual economic working of society. Now, derived from this specific choice, it is possible to express the originality of competition in this specific framework, that is, to cope in greater detail with this diversity attached to the concept of free competition.

3. THE ORIGINALITY OF THE MARSHALLIAN CONCEPTION OF FREE COMPETITION

Because the concept of the representative firm has a distinctive purpose in the *Principles* which is to make compatible a static view and a dynamic view of economic activity, the originality of the concept of free competition is not fully expressed in the successive editions of that book. Therefore it is interesting to take into account the different complementary attempts provided by Marshall to make more precise the role and characteristics of competition. This essentially means referring to *Industry and Trade,* which appears as one of the results arising from his 'white elephant', that is the failure to achieve a major contribution coping with the dynamics of economic activity.

The complexity of the competition process is, first, particularly expressed in the 1890 address, where Marshall largely insists on the necessity of taking account of the obvious diversity of competition mechanisms. In that respect, the puzzling issue lies in the definition of what exactly a market means.

In fact, at the core of the Marshallian problem of qualifying an empirically-based understanding of competitive contexts is that difficulty of dealing with the definition of a market. More precisely, that difficulty lies in the symbiotic relation existing between production constraints and market functioning. The insistence of Marshall on the definition of particular markets expresses this and the originality of the Marshallian conception of competition is based on this rejection of a strict dichotomy between the firm as a producer and the market as a regulation mechanism of commodities produced by firms. In the Marshallian analysis, the firm is not an alternative mode of coordination with the market: the two are intrinsically linked, and this motivates Marshall in a search for an analytical framework able to deal with a concept of free competition that makes it possible to understand price and non-price competition among economic agents.

Thus the understanding of the law of supply and demand is empirically-based in the Marshallian framework. On the demand side, there prevails a conception of markets based on the actual functioning of the economic system and, as a consequence, the importance of particular markets allows for coping with the diversity of markets' size, characteristics and regulation mechanisms: 'the market may be a district of any size; it may be the whole of a country' (*Industry and Trade*, p.182).

Here, on the demand side, two extreme contexts structure the Marshallian reasoning; on the one hand, a few world markets exist in which competition is global, fairly perfect and the tendency 'for the same price to be paid for the same thing at the same time in all parts of the market' applies (*Principles*, 1920, p.270); on the other hand, secluded markets exist too, where competition is practically non-existent, and where 'lie the great majority of the markets which the economist and the business man have to study' (ibid., p.274). Markets also change with regard to the time period and the physical area that they cover. Depending on those two characteristics (time and space), the forces of demand and supply will act differently to determine an equilibrium.

On the supply side, the main difficulty lies in the ambiguous influence of the laws of returns. Developing an empirically-based conception of production means coping with the fact that returns are not constant and that they can vary over time, increasing or decreasing. As a consequence, an empirical observation of production shows that 'the law which governs the shape of this curve (supply curve) is not so simple as the corresponding law for the demand curve'. Owing to this search for pragmatism, this hypothesis induces a complex interaction between the laws directing the production costs of the firm and those directing the related market functioning. In fact, quantitative fluctuations in the production of firms are not only a source of disturbance for production costs; they also disturb the market functioning. As a consequence, the mechanisms regulating the market are very diverse, vary from one to the other and reveal a corresponding variety in the competition characteristics.

In fact, production characteristics largely influence the conditions of market functioning (and reciprocally), partly because production costs include the distribution and trade costs of a specific commodity, and partly because the market functioning also contributes to determining the most suitable mode of organizing production processes. As a consequence, the way in which competition occurs depends as much on productive characteristics as on market functioning and price mechanisms. This intrinsic link between production and exchange justifies the use of both concepts: that of the representative firm on the supply side and that of a particular market on the demand side (ibid., p.380): 'We must take account of the fact that very few firms have a long-continued life of active progress and of the fact that the relations between the individual producer and his special market differ in important respects from those between the whole body of producers and the general market'. If such a situation is due to the need to understand the diversity of competition processes from empirical observation, nevertheless it does not allow Marshall to make this objective compatible with the coherent theory of equilibrium between normal supply and normal demand as expressed in Book V of the *Principles*, as we have already argued.

However, to consider in more detail the Marshallian empirically-based conception of the articulation between production and exchange and, as a consequence, the place and role of competition in industrial dynamics implies starting again from the importance of special or particular markets. Even if Schumpeter himself considered that 'there are positive suggestions in the *Principles*, in particular the comments on special markets of individual firms' (Schumpeter, 1941, p.242), we nevertheless consider that there are limitations due to the conciliation exercise of the *Principles* and that it is preferable to deal with a few later attempts provided by Marshall.

More especially, this need for a better understanding of the empirical forces that direct the competition process is more clearly expressed in one of the late Marshallian contributions, *Industry and Trade*. Usually, one considers that the two main purposes of Marshall in this book were, on the one hand, to demonstrate the existence of a continuity between a monopoly and a free competition context (Liebhafsky, 1955) and, on the other hand, to show how seminal Marshall was in the emergence of the theory of imperfect competition: 'Marshall was the father of the idea of imperfect competition' (Whitaker, 1975, p.6). However, we consider that there is more in *Industry and Trade* and we want especially to emphasize two aspects: one is the typology of competitive contexts provided by Marshall and which is not very often mentioned; the other is the characteristics of special and particular markets as well as their influence on the competition process.

In *Industry and Trade*, Marshall provides us with a typology of competitive contexts, differentiated as regards the coordination mechanisms that prevail between the production and the market sides for those economic activities. In other words, Marshall tries to organize the puzzling diversity of competitive contexts (see *Industry and Trade*, pp.653–54). He does so by suggesting the existence of three dominant categories of competitive contexts: 'friendly emulation' where the major purpose is to share resources, with the aim of organizing cooperative agreements among companies in order to make feasible the common discovery of new productive opportunities; 'ordinary business competition', which corresponds to a context where the usual mechanisms of price competition prevail; and 'competition with destructive aims', a situation where the explicit purpose of companies is to establish a monopoly and to force the other incumbents from the market. Interestingly, Marshall associated with these three dominant contexts a corresponding type of coordination mechanism as regards cooperative agreements: 'constructive associations', 'joint action for the regulation of prices', and 'deliberate destructive agreements' are the natural associates for determining those three major types of competitive contexts. As a consequence, the predominance of one mode of competition over the others largely depends on the characteristics of policy intervention, their aims and related effectiveness in favouring one dominant mode of regulation.

According to the characteristics of particular markets, the arguments developed in *Industry and Trade* are interesting because they aim to characterize the intrinsic complementarity existing between production and market. What Marshall especially develops is the need to understand the diversity of complementary mechanisms between production and exchange. A firm is, according to Marshall, facing the impossibility of determining exactly its production costs because the production resources have already been acquired with a different aim (whether they are human resources or machines). As such, the way of combining and organizing production is a source of difficulty in identifying the actual production costs. So, within many industries, the identification of a supply price is only partially the result of a rational and technical calculation of the companies. Even if a firm is only more or less able to identify a reasonable supply price, a supplementary difficulty appears, which is to include in this technical calculation the subjective perception that an entrepreneur has from his (or her) market, from both quantitative and qualitative viewpoints.

Here the characteristics of particular markets appear especially relevant, for two main reasons. One is the fact that a company is acting, not in a general market but in a particular 'market space'. That means that spot markets are not the usual mode of coordinating exchange. On the contrary, relationships among producers and customers are fairly particular in the sense that they require specific and mutual knowledge between the partners involved. Marshall insists on trust as a necessary condition to qualify market mechanisms and to complement the usual price regulation. Also, it is difficult to identify the size and the frontiers of a particular market. Markets are not restricted to the simple act of selling commodities at a moment in time; they need to be thought of as a long-term and interactive process of relationships among a set of partners. In that respect, Marshall refers more especially to such a 'market space' by including the complementarity existing among different types of partners over time (*Industry and Trade*, p.182):

> Everyone buys, and nearly every producer sells, to some extent in a 'general' market, in which he is on about the same footing with others around him. But nearly everyone has also some 'particular' market; that is, some people or groups of people with whom he is in somewhat close touch: mutual knowledge and trust lead him to approach them, and them to approach him, in preference to strangers.

Consequently, it is impossible to isolate one particular exchange in time, and competition becomes a much more fuzzy concept because it cannot be reduced to a price competition that prevails for the exchange of a specific commodity at a moment of time. Because of the specific characters of particular markets, competition becomes a process that intrinsically associates production and exchange characteristics.

As a consequence, a particular market induces the existence of productive and trade connections among producers and their customers, connections that are relatively stable over time. This is thought of as a necessary condition in order to make feasible an evolution of productive activities. It is because of this mixture of cooperation and competition that producers can invest, develop new productive opportunities and markets, and become a source of economic progress. What is usually thought of as the reverse of competition becomes in the Marshallian analysis a necessary condition to establish a suitable context of free competition. However, particular markets are also dangerous, for two essential reasons. One is the risk of being isolated through these specific and durable relationships with a few customers. It can appear that external forces in the environment (such as newly differentiated commodities, technological innovation, and the like) are not sufficiently taken into account within particular markets and that they become a source of a major shock that endangers the viability of those particular relationships. The other is the differentiation that can occur among particular markets. As they are necessarily interdependent, companies can develop opportunistic behaviours consisting in maintaining a high level of profits within their particular markets and selling at a very much lower price the same commodities on other markets.

A complementary reason makes the concept of a particular market very interesting: it is the influence that production constraints have on the characteristics of a particular market. Here, Marshall insists that the frontiers of a particular market are very relative and that, under certain circumstances, a producer can sell his or her production out of his or her particular market, even if he (or she) does not sell it at a profitable price. In a context of increasing returns that implies an important level of irreversible investments, if the production is not immediately sold on its particular market, a producer will try to extend the frontiers of the latter because of the need to fully employ its production resources and capacity. Therefore a risk exists of extending the frontiers of its particular market and this can succeed or fail in the sense that a destructive process of competition can prevail and ruin every company involved, even on their initial particular markets. Again price competition is just one part of a competitive process and the latter requires a larger understanding including the complex coordination mechanisms existing between production and exchange as well as the necessity of facing the evolution of productive characteristics in time by considering the change of the frontiers of particular markets.

On the basis of these comments, we may emphasize that competition is not associated with a market structure depending on price conditions for specific commodities. Competition needs to be understood as a 'market space' where a subtle relationship between cooperation and competition determines a concept of competition which is intrinsically linked to the dynamics of industrial activities. As such, competition is a means of progress and requires public intervention in order to favour a suitable context encouraging industrial progress and economic growth.

4. THE CURRENT RELEVANCE OF THE MARSHALLIAN CONCEPTION OF FREE COMPETITION

From this discussion about the Marshallian implications of the concept of competition, two main issues need to be underlined in the current debate related to competition as a dynamic process. One is the use of the Marshallian framework to contribute to this debate and the second is the incidence of the Marshallian framework in terms of policy issues and implications.

Marshall is usually associated with the foundation of the neo-classical paradigm. What we discussed previously also shows that the Marshallian aim was much more complex than to simply focus on the determination of the equilibrium of normal supply and demand. Beyong the reconciliation attempt of a static and a dynamic understanding of economic systems which remains the dominant aim of the *Principles*, Marshall tries to promote an empirically-based conception of economic evolution. This is particularly sensitive when considering the dynamics of industrial activities. Therefore one can argue that a sort of second Marshallian tradition also exists whose objectives and purposes are to qualify the growth of the economy according to the production characteristics and constraints faced by economic agents.

Consequently, it is difficult to consider Marshall strictly as the father of a neo-classical paradigm that cannot fit the understanding of knowledge-building as opposed to evolutionary or resource-based approaches of the firm (see Nonaka and Takeuchi, 1995, p.33). On the contrary, our argument is that Marshall is of a certain relevance for some modern attempts at understanding the firm as a depository of knowledge. In that respect, it is interesting to note that, for instance, the Marshallian analysis of competition as a process has largely inspired authors such as Penrose (1959) and Richardson (1975) respectively, regarding the importance of the subjective perception entrepreneurs have on the characteristics of their markets and regarding the possible compatibility between increasing returns and a competitive context because of the temporal dimension of production processes (Fazio and Quéré, 1999).

More broadly, in a recent contribution, Fransman (1994) opposes two traditions in the theory of the firm, the one considering the firm as an organization treating information, the other as an organization which is knowledge-specific. It is possible to find in the Marshallian analysis some elements that cast light on this second tradition. In particular, the most important insight is the fact that considering the codependence of production and market characteristics implies a conception of competition that enlarges the scale of the analysis from the firm itself to a more systemic set of partners, including customers or other similar producers. The argument that competition needs to be understood as a 'market space' implies abandoning consideration of a theory of the firm per se and enlarging the analysis to a concept of industry. In that respect, if there are some proximities between those Marshallian insights and the Penrosian conception of the theory of the growth of the firm, Marshall is still very interesting in that he stresses the necessity of coping with a more aggregate frame of analysis than the firm itself by emphasizing an ambiguous concept of industry. In that regard, the need to consider, not the firm by itself, but a more aggregate level of analysis (even if he refers to a fuzzy concept of industry) is still of evident relevance and a source of reflection still to be developed today.

To take account of this change in the scale of analysis appears a necessary condition of understanding how the existence of increasing returns in production can be compatible with the working of a context of free competition. The elements qualifying the industrial dynamics developed in the Marshallian analysis have obviously been extended by authors like Young (1928), Penrose (1959) and Richardson (1960). Such contributions still today appear a very stimulating way to cope with the complexity of industrial dynamics as well as the role of competition in that process (see Quéré *et al.*, 1997). Indeed, the main message delivered by Marshall is the necessity to cope with the diversity of the competition process resulting from the complexity of production constraints and market mechanisms. It is the specific character of markets (the existence of particular markets especially) and the existence of increasing returns that allow for the continuous discovery of new industrial activities and markets, and guarantee the feasibility of new productive investments. As a consequence, this intrinsic evolutive character of competition justifies the need for policy interventionism.

The puzzling issues opened by the diversity of competition effects are of a crucial relevance and importance which require full attention from public policies and a subtle determination of public interventionism. This is due to structural differences among economic systems which justify a need for specific public policies; 'the problem of the relations between competition and combination is one for which differences of national character and conditions show themselves strongly' (Marshall, in Pigou, 1925, p.266).

Paradoxically, the need to secure new productive investments and new markets can require restraints from policy-making. In some contexts, it is necessary to restrain competition in order to avoid a too destructive process. One needs to recall here the importance that Marshall accorded to some ethical arguments as justifications and guidelines for public intervention. In some cases, policy restraints appear as the best guarantee for maintaining economic progress (*Principles*, 1920, pp.621–2):

> In particular, this increased prosperity has made us rich and strong enough to impose new restraints on free enterprise; some temporary material loss being submitted to for the sake of a higher and ultimate greater gain . . . The aim is to devise, deliberately and promptly, remedies adapted to the quickly changing circumstances of modern industry; and thus to obtain the good, without the evil, of the old defence of the weak that in other ages was gradually evolved by custom.

In that respect, market imperfections are a necessary guarantee of economic progress, and policy-making must intervene in a subtle way to maintain a paradigm of free competition where 'competition with all its imperfections remained the best foundation for effectively organising economic society' (Groenewegen, 1995, p.457) but, at the same time, to avoid an economic context where destructive competition will prevail. This explains the initial ambiguity of the Marshallian analysis as regards the place and role of competition: 'Economic progress requires as a condition free individual responsibility but not the maintenance of those rights of property that lead to extreme inequalities of wealth' (Marshall, in Pigou, 1925, p.282). This is why a stable doctrine cannot exist and why the regulation of competition by public intervention is necessary and necessarily based on empirical observation. As such, no stable rule can be established over time and there is a need to continuously redefine the characteristics of public intervention in accordance with learning from empirical observation.

The search for an empirically-based analysis of competition explains why Marshall has tried to cope with the diversity of complementary coordination between production and exchange conditions. At least one can finally consider that the continuous insistence of Marshall on industrial districts when he tried to define and characterize a market functioning expresses this complex and evolutive intermediation between production and market characteristics that determines the guidance of the competition process through a suitable intervention of policy-makers.

REFERENCES

Coase, R. (1975), 'Marshall on Method', *Journal of Law and Economics*, **18** (1), 25–31.

Fazio, G. and M. Quéré (1999), 'E.T. Penrose ou la 22ième Conception d'une Théorie de la Firme', *Oeconomia*, **33** (8), 187–205.

Foster, J. (1993), 'Economics and the Self-Organisation Approach: Alfred Marshall Revisited', *Economic Journal*, **103** (419), 975–91.

Fransman, M. (1994), 'Information, Knowledge, Vision and Theory of the Firm', *Industrial and Corporate Change*, **3** (3), 713–58.

Groenewegen, P. (1995), *A Soaring Eagle: Alfred Marshall, 1842–1924*, Aldershot, UK and Brookfield, US: Edward Elgar.

Hart, N. (1996), 'Marshall's Theory of Value: the Role of External Economies', *Cambridge Journal of Economics*, **20** (3), 353–70.

Keynes, J.M. (1925), 'Alfred Marshall, 1842–1924', reprinted in A.C. Pigou (ed.), *Memorials of Alfred Marshall*, London: Macmillan.

Liebhafsky, H.H. (1955), 'A Curious Case of Neglect: Marshall's Industry and Trade', *Canadian Journal of Economics*, **21**, 339–53.

Marshall, A. (1890), 'Some Aspects of Competition', reprinted in A.C. Pigou (ed.) (1925), *Memorials of Alfred Marshall*, London: Macmillan.

Marshall, A. (1919), *Industry and Trade*, London: Macmillan.
Marshall, A. (1920), *Principles of Economics*, 8th edn, London: Macmillan.
Marshall, A. (1923), *Money, Credit and Commerce*, London: Macmillan.
Marshall, A. and M. Paley Marshall (1879), *The Economics of Industry*, 2nd edn, London: Macmillan.
Nonaka, I. and H. Takeuchi (1995), *The Knowledge-Creating Company*, Oxford: Oxford University Press.
Penrose, E.T. (1959), *The Theory of the Growth of the Firm*, Oxford: Oxford University Press.
Pigou, A.C. (1925), *Memorials of Alfred Marshall*, London: Macmillan.
Pursell, G. (1958), 'Unity in the Thought of Alfred Marshall', *Quarterly Journal of Economics*, **72**, 588–600.
Quéré, M., J.L. Ravix, J.T. Ravix and P.M. Romani (1997), 'Frontières de la Firme, Division Institutionnelle du Travail et Processus de Concurrence', in P. Garrouste (ed.), *Les Frontières de la Firme*, Paris: Economica.
Quéré, M. and J.T. Ravix (1998), 'Alfred Marshall and Territorial Organization of Industry', in M. Bellet and C. L'Harmet (eds), *Industry, Space and Competition*, Cheltenham, UK and Lyme, US: Edward Elgar.
Reisman, D. (1986), *The Economics of Alfred Marshall*, London: Macmillan.
Richardson, G.B. (1960), *Information and Investment*, Oxford: Clarendon Press.
Richardson, G.B. (1975), 'Adam Smith on Competition and Increasing Returns', in A. Skinner and T. Wilson (eds), *Essays on Adam Smith*, Oxford: Clarendon Press.
Schumpeter, J.A. (1941), 'Alfred Marshall's Principles: A Semi-Centennial Appraisal', *American Economic Review*, **51** (2), 236–48.
Shirai, T. (1968), 'Alfred Marshall on Free Competition', *Ozaka Economic Papers*, **16** (2), 11–5.
Stigler, G.J. (1957), 'Perfect Competition, Historically Contemplated', *Journal of Political Economy*, **65** (5).
Stigler, G.J. (1968), *The Organization of Industry*, Chicago: The University of Chicago Press.
Thomas, B. (1991), 'Alfred Marshall on Economic Biology', *Review of Political Economy*, **3** (1), 1–14.
Whitaker, J.K. (1975), *The Early Economic Writings of Alfred Marshall, 1867–1890*, 2 vols, London: Macmillan.
Wood, J.C. (1982), *Alfred Marshall – Critical Assessments*, 4 vols, London: Croom Helm.
Young, A. (1928), 'Increasing Returns and Economic Progress', *Economic Journal*, **38**, 527–42.

5. Innovative choice and competition process

Mario Amendola, Jean-Luc Gaffard and Patrick Musso

1. INTRODUCTION

Joseph A. Schumpeter sees the essence of the process of competition in the development of a new technology, a new source of supply and a new type of organization. But what does it exactly mean when we say that competition operates through innovation? Of course that innovation is a means of reducing production costs or for capturing new markets. But also and mainly, as we intend to demonstrate, that innovation cannot be successful unless competition takes place in such a way as to allow firms to be well coordinated with each other and with respect to what happens to the market demand.

Innovative choices do not consist in the instantaneous development and adoption of new technologies and/or new products. They are rather decisions to carry out structural changes which imply that new production processes must be substituted for the old ones (section 2). As this kind of substitution takes time, coordination problems necessarily emerge along the way, the solution of which depends on how competition actually operates (section 3). A specific analytical framework aimed at giving structure to this conception of the role of competition is presented (section 4). It will make possible a simulation analysis, which casts light on the competition conditions under which innovative choices are successful (section 5).

2. INNOVATION PROCESSES

The process of innovation is, at the same time, one of development of the technology and of transformation of the productive structures of the economy, and it is characterized by a continuous feedback between technology and the environment (Amendola and Gaffard, 1988). An innovative choice in fact implies the breaking up of the existing industrial structure and a modification of the market conditions, followed by a gradual reshaping which reflects the changes in cost conditions, in profitability and in relative prices, the modifications of the consumers' preference system, and all the other events that represent the specific episodes that mark the actual profile of the process of innovation. The latter thus appears as a process of research and learning which results in the appearance of new productive options that bring about a modification of the environment itself. Technology is then the result of the process of innovation, and not a precondition for it. The process of innovation is seen as a process of 'creation of technology' which, when successfully brought about, makes it possible to obtain increasing returns.

Thus defined, innovation is an essentially sequential process which takes (and can change) form, content and direction at each successive step.

The problem of technological change thus consists, not so much in the choice between given alternatives (whether based on complete or incomplete information), as in a search for coordinating as well as possible the innovation process. Accordingly, the economic aspect of this problem is no longer represented by the 'rationality' of the choice between known alternatives, but by the 'viability' of the process through which a different alternative is brought about: a viability that depends in turn on how coordination problems are dealt with step by step, that is, on how the process of competition takes place.

3. COMPETITION PROCESSES

There are three ways in which economic activity can be coordinated: conscious planning within firms, cooperation agreements and price mechanisms regulating the relations between firms and between firms and their customers on the market (see Richardson, 1972). In this perspective, the competition process appears as a complex process which is a blend of market and organizational forces whereby market and organization, looked at as institutional structures which channel processes of change, must be considered as complements rather than as substitutes. Market forces (price mechanisms) have an impact on technical and organizational changes within firms. Organizational and technical choices in turn influence market conditions.

Traditionally, the conception of competition has taken two basic forms. On the one hand, it has been the force which, by equating prices and marginal costs, assures an efficient allocation of scarce resources.

According to McNulty (1968, p.643):

> Competition in this sense is somewhat analogous to the force of gravitation in physical science; through competition, resources gravitate toward their most productive uses, and, through competition, price is forced to the lowest level which is sustainable over the long run. Thus viewed, competition assures order and stability in the economic world much as does gravitation in the physical world.

On the other hand, competition is a descriptive term which defines an idealized state of affairs: 'The concept of perfect competition ... is analogous not to the principle of gravitation but rather to the idea of a perfect vacuum; it is not an ordering force but rather an assumed state of affairs' (ibid.). Similarly, oligopolistic (or monopolistic) competition must be considered as a descriptive term: that of an 'imperfect' state of affairs corresponding to given costs conditions and given 'imperfect' information structures.

Oligopoly competition seems to be more than a descriptive term. It is concerned with a dynamic process of rivalry. Generally speaking, this process will be destructive or creative. It can result in a waste of productive resources and no real advantage for the customers or, alternatively, it can allow firms (and customers) to benefit from increasing returns. Nevertheless, the models of oligopoly competition, including models of continuing rivalry to reduce costs and improve quality, do not usually address this problem. They rather deal with the intensity of competition and the characteristics of industrial structures as determined by given information and cost conditions. They are not equipped for exploring in what conditions the competition process is destructive or creative.

The idea of competition as an ordering force, that dominates classical economics, is a disequilibrium concept of market activity. It is, therefore, the concept of competition best suited to be associated with an innovation process portrayed as a qualitative change: that is, with a change which takes place through distortions of productive capacity that imply the appearance of problems of coordination between supply and demand, step by step. On the other hand, an orderly competition should be an equilibrating process in the sense that it makes innovative choices viable. Competition is really successful when price and quantity adjustments are carried out which make it possible to obtain normal profits, that is when these adjustments do not result in waste of productive resources. Thus viewed, competition not only coexists with increasing returns but helps firms to capture them (Amendola *et al.*, 1999).

In order to explore how competition operates as an ordering force, it is not appropriate to consider a number of competing firms which are making similar products in given and unchanged cost conditions. Instead, it is worth envisaging firms which undertake innovative activities, as in Richardson

(1975, p.355; 1998, p.162): 'These activities having to do with the discovery and estimation of future wants, with research, development, and design, with the execution and co-ordination of processes of physical transformation, with the marketing of goods and so on'. We may therefore stress that the real problem that the firms have to deal with is how to make the best use of what resources they have, including productive capacity. As a matter of fact, at any given moment, the productive capacity of a firm cannot be chosen but is inherited from past decisions, so that the problem which it actually faces is how to make the best use of this capacity and not 'what it should do if it were given unlimited time to adjust itself to constant conditions' (Hayek, 1948, p.102).

The time dimension of production, together with the time dimension of decision processes, is the main problem concerning a firm which decides to set up a new productive capacity. As a matter of fact, productive capacities must be built before they can be utilized. During the period of construction of an entirely new productive capacity, the innovative firm has to bear sunk costs that result in a temporary competitive disadvantage. But after that, after the end of the phase of construction, there will be a period, which has been called 'the close period' (Hicks, 1954, p.164), during which the first mover will take advantage of its innovative choice as it will be alone in possessing the new superior capacity operative. The existence and the interaction of these different periods and of the lags associated with them, which are the expression of the time dimension of the production process and of the decision processes, are the main aspect of the process of change. In this process the end of the road is never reached, the market is never in 'perfect competition', but a strong competition may obtain that results in increasing returns.

A neo-Austrian representation of the production process (Hicks, 1973; Amendola and Gaffard, 1988, 1998) is suited to dealing with the above time articulation of events. Production appears as a scheme for transforming in time a sequence of primary labour inputs into a sequence of final output. The production process is fully vertically integrated: this makes it possible both to exhibit explicitly the phase of construction of productive capacity by bringing it inside the production process and to stress that it must necessarily come before the phase of utilization of the same capacity. This representation of the production process must be coupled with a representation of the decision process that focuses on its sequential character, that is on the fact that it is essentially based on trial and error algorithms, where prices and quantities partially reflect reaction to market disequilibria.

The competition process is thus associated with an innovation process portrayed as a qualitative change which takes place through distortions of productive capacity that imply the appearance of problems of coordination of economic activity.

4. THE ANALYTICAL FRAMEWORK

The model we present here is derived from Amendola and Gaffard (1998). It makes it possible to exhibit the time structure of production processes and to analyse the sequential interaction of competing firms ($i = 1,2$) in a process of restructuring of productive capacities (Amendola *et al.*, 1999).

In each firm i production is carried out by means of processes of a neo-Austrian type. An elementary process of production, which embodies the technology j, is defined by the input vector:

$$\mathbf{a}_j^i = \left[a_{jk}^i\right]; \qquad k = 1 \ldots n^c + n^u$$

whose elements represent the quantities of labour required in the successive periods of the phase of construction c (from 1 to n^c) and, following it, of the phase of utilization u (from n^c+1 to n^c+n^u) of the productive capacity, so that:

$$\mathbf{a}_j^i = \left[\mathbf{a}_j^{ic}, \mathbf{a}_j^{iu}\right]$$

and by the output vector:

$$\mathbf{b}_j^i = \left[b_{jk}^i\right]$$

with $b_{jk}^i = 0 \quad \forall\, k = 1,\ldots,n^c$

At each given moment t the productive capacity of a firm i is represented by the intensity vector:

$$\mathbf{x}^i(t) = \left[\mathbf{x}^{ic}(t), \mathbf{x}^{iu}(t)\right]$$

each element of which is a number of elementary production processes of a particular age, still in the construction phase or already in the utilization phase.

In each period the level of activity of the firms is constrained by available financial resources or, alternatively, by available human resources.

The available financial resources $F^i(t)$ are:

$$F^i(t) = m^i(t-1) + h^i(t-1) + f^i(t)$$

where the internal financial resources are given by $m^i(t-1)$, the money proceeds from the sales of final output, and $h^i(t-1)$ the idle money balances involuntarily accumulated in the past and ready for use, and the external financial resources by $f^i(t)$.

The available human resources are:

$$\psi^i(t) = (1+g)^t L(0)\, w^i(t)^{\vartheta}$$

where g is the natural growth rate and ϑ the wage elasticity of the labour supply.

When the human constraint is more stringent than the financial constraint, money balances are involuntarily accumulated:

$$h^i(t) = \max\left[0, m^i(t-1) + h^i(t-1) - \omega^i(t)\right]$$

where $\omega^i(t)$ is the actual wage fund, which is defined below.

Within the sequential setting considered prices are fixed within each given period and can only change at the junction of one period to the next one. As a consequence we have:

$$m^i(t) = \min\left[p^i(t)d^i(t), p^i(t)s^i(t)\right]$$

Real stock changes are substitutes for the price changes, which cannot take place within the period. Excess supply results in an accumulation of undesired stocks for the firm:

$$o^i(t) = \max\left[0, s^i(t) - d^i(t)\right]$$

where $s^i(t)$ and $d^i(t)$ are current real supply and real demand for the firm i, respectively.

Current final production of the firm i will then be:

$$q^i(t) = s^i(t) - \eta o^i(t-1); \qquad 0 \le \eta \le 1$$

which can also be written in the following form:

$$q^i(t) = \tau^i(t) \sum_{k=n^c+1}^{n^c+n^u} B_k^i(t) x_k^i(t)$$

with τ^i being the rate of utilization of the productive capacity inherited from the past. The coefficients $B_k^i(t)$ stand for the output coefficients of elementary process of production of age k at period t.

The aggregate market demand, $D(t)$, is determined as follows:

$$D(t) = (1 + \hat{g}) D(t-1) p^{\theta}, \quad \theta \le 0$$

that is, it depends on the average market price, given an exogenously determined growth rate $\hat{g}$.

The market shares are:

$$d^i(t) = \delta^i(t) D(t)$$

with:

$$\delta^i(t) = \frac{\dfrac{\delta^i(t-1)}{p^i(t-1)}}{\sum_i \dfrac{\delta^i(t-1)}{p^i(t-1)}}$$

that is, a firm's market share depends on the dynamics of its price in relation to the dynamics of the average market price.

The evolution path followed by each firm is actually determined by the behaviour of the decision variables, namely, the rate of starts of new production processes $x_1^i(t)$, the rate of utilization of productive capacity τ^i, the price of final output $p^i(t)$, the wage rate $w^i(t)$, the ratio k^i of the external financial resources $f^i(t)$ to the money proceeds from the sales of final output $m^i(t)$ and the rate of scrapping $u_k^i(t)$.

Each firm determines the rate of starts of production processes in such a way that the productive capacity available n^c+1 periods later will match a final demand which is expected to be equal to the current one multiplied by a growth factor $1 + \gamma$:

$$x_1^i(t) = \max\left[0, \frac{d^i(t-1)(1+\gamma^i(t-1))^{n^c+1} - \overline{\tau}^i \sum_{k=2}^{n^u} B_{k+n^c}^i(t+n^c)x_{k+n^c}^i(t+n^c)}{\overline{\tau}^i B_{n^c+1}^i(t+n^c)}\right]$$

with $\gamma^i(t-1) = \dfrac{d^i(t-1) - d^i(t-2)}{d^i(t-2)}$ and where $\overline{\tau}^i$ is the desired rate of utilization of productive capacity.

Different investment behaviours may be considered by introducing more or less stringent limits to the variations of the *desired* rate of starts from one period to the next: limits which represent more or less aggressive investment behaviours.

Each firm determines current production by fixing the current rate of utilization of its productive capacity, $\tau^i(t)$, so as to adjust its current supply to the expected final demand $\hat{d}^i$:

$$\tau^i(t) = \min\left[1, \frac{\hat{d}^i(t) - \left(o^i(t-1) - o_d^i(t)\right)}{\sum_{k=1}^{n^c+n^u} B_k^i(t)x_k^i(t)}\right]$$

where $\hat{d}^i$ is such that:

$$\hat{d}^i(t) = \frac{m^i(t-1)^2}{p^i(t)\, m^i(t-2)}$$

As the result of the production and investment decisions the actual wage fund is given by:

$$\omega^i(t) = w^i(t) \sum_{k=1}^{n^c+n^u} A_k^i(t)x_k^i(t)\rho_k^i$$

where $A_k^i(t)$ are the labour coefficients of elementary process of production of age k at period t and ρ_k^i stand for the elements of the vector ρ^i which allows us to take into account what are the consequences on the labour demand of a variation in the rate of utilization of the productive capacity:

$$\rho^i = \left[\rho_1^i, \ldots, \rho_{n^c}^i, \ldots, \rho_{n^c+n^u}^i\right]$$

with: $\rho_k^i = 1$ for all $1 \le k \le n^c$ and $\rho_k^i = \tau^i(t) + \zeta^i(1 - \tau^i(t))$ for all $n^c + 1 \le k \le n^c + n^u$, where ζ^i stands for the labour required to maintain a process of production idle.

The price charged by each firm is determined as follows:

$$p^i(t) = \frac{w^i(t) \sum_{k=1}^{n^c+n^u} a_{jk}^i \rho_k^i}{\bar{\tau}^i \sum_{k=n^c+1}^{n^c+n^u} b_{jk}^i}$$

that is, in such a way as to cover the cost of production when using the productive capacity which is the expression of the up-to-date technology adopted, at the desired rate of utilization of this productive capacity.

This price can be adjusted in reaction to the market disequilibrium perceived in the previous period:

$$\breve{p}^i(t) = p^i(t)\left[1 + \chi^i \frac{d^i(t-1) - s^i(t-1)}{s^i(t-1)}\right]; \qquad 0 \le \chi^i \le 1$$

Moreover, changes in price from one period to the next are both upward and downward bounded.

Changes in the wage rate paid by each firm reflect the disequilibria arising on its labour market, that is:

$$w^i(t) = \left(1 + \upsilon^i \frac{\left(\sum_{k=1}^{n^c+n^u} A_k^i(t-1) x_k^i(t-1) \rho_k^i(t-1)\right) - \psi^i(t-1)}{\psi^i(t-1)}\right) w^i(t-1)$$

where υ^i is a reaction coefficient.

External financial resources are such that:

$$f^i(t) = \min\left[k^i m^i(t), f_d^i(t)\right]$$

where k^i stands for the borrowing power of each firm, and $f_d^i(t)$ is the demand for external financing resulting from the production and investment decisions actually taken.

Finally, the prevailing resource constraints determine the rate of scrapping of production processes.

The performance of each firm is measured by its unit margins, whereby a unit margin is defined, in each period, as the ratio of the difference between the price (calculated as mentioned above) and the current unit cost of output – obtained by dividing the total cost of production of the amount of output obtained in that period by the same amount – to the price itself:

$$um^i(t) = \frac{p^i(t) - c^i(t)}{p^i(t)}$$

where

$$c^i(t) = \frac{w^i(t) \sum_{k=1}^{n^c + n^u} A_k^i(t) x_k^i(t) \rho_k^i(t)}{q^i(t)}$$

Unit margins on average equal to zero mean that firms realize normal profits. Unit margins will be instead necessarily negative at the beginning of any innovation process characterized by higher construction costs. This reveals the initial competitive disadvantage suffered by the innovative firm. On the other hand, negative unit margins may also reveal the existence of excess capacities, that is, of a lower degree of utilization of productive capacity with respect to the desired level and vice versa.

5. INNOVATION AND PRICE COMPETITION

Let us consider an economy in a steady state. Innovative choices carried out in a context of incomplete information result in a breaking of this steady state. Coordination problems necessarily arise.

The above model is used to simulate the impact on the innovation process of a price competition here defined as the choice by the firms to change the price they charge in reaction to the appearance of a disequilibrium in their markets. The innovative choices consist in introducing successive technological improvements. These improvements are forward biased: increasing construction costs are more than compensated by increasing rates of output. See Appendix I.

In a first simulation (which will be taken as a reference in what follows) the two firms innovate one after the other, but with the same (and constant) frequency. With no financial resource constraints and fixed (constant) nominal wages, both firms remain on the market. There are not too strong fluctuations in the market shares. Both firms realize positive unit margins. They are able to exploit the increasing returns associated with the introduction of new technologies (simulation 1). As a matter of fact, constant nominal wages and prices rigidities make it possible for competition, normal profits and increasing returns to be compatible (see Amendola *et al.*, 1999).

Now if firm 1 (that is, the first mover) innovates more frequently than firm 2, the latter exits from the market. As a matter of fact, firm 1 takes advantage of systematically longer close periods (simulation 2). If firm 2 gets involved in a price competition, which consists in fixing its price in reaction to perceived market disequilibria (with prices more downward than upward flexible), then it remains on the market despite the disadvantage created by a lower innovation frequency (simulation 3a). There is a range of values of key parameters (price reaction coefficient, degree of asymmetry in price reaction, relative innovation frequency) that allows the competition to be maintained under conditions in which both firms obtain normal profits (average unit margins are equal to zero). A larger asymmetry in innovation frequencies, which allows firm 1 to re-establish a definitive competitive advantage (simulation 3b), will be compensated by a larger asymmetry in price reaction by firm 2 (simulation 3c). However, with respect to the simulation taken as reference, there are larger fluctuations in market shares, and hence larger fluctuations in unit margins, which become negative on average. Average unit margins are reduced as the result of lower price in the case of firm 2, and as the result of lower rate of utilization of productive capacity in the case of firm 1. A sustained price competition allows the less innovative firm to stay on the market. Thus any first mover expecting to be confronted by a too strong price competition has no real incentives to innovate. In other words, some restraints on price competition may appear as a condition for making innovation processes viable.

A more stringent financial constraint makes it possible to re-establish the incentives required by a pure innovation strategy (simulation 4).

Summing up, price rigidities seem to be a condition for allowing firms to capture the benefits of their innovative choices and, in fact, for making them credible.

REFERENCES

Amendola, M. and J.L. Gaffard (1988), *The Innovative Choice: an Economic Analysis of the Dynamics of Technology*, Oxford: Basil Blackwell.

Amendola, M. and J.L. Gaffard (1998), *Out of Equilibrium*, Oxford: Clarendon Press.

Amendola M., J.L. Gaffard and P. Musso (2000), 'Competition, Innovation and Increasing Returns', forthcoming in *Economics of Innovation and New Technology*.

Hayek, F.A. (1948), *Individualism and Economic Order*; reprinted (1980), Chicago: University of Chicago Press.

Hicks, J.R. (1954), 'Stickers and Snatchers', *Oxford Economic Papers*; reprinted in J.R. Hicks (1983), *Classics and Moderns*, Collected Essays on Economic Theory, vol. III, Oxford: Blackwell.

Hicks, J.R. (1973), *Capital and Time,* Oxford: Clarendon Press.

McNulty, P.J. (1968), 'Economic Theory and the Meaning of Competition', *Quarterly Journal of Economics*, **82**, 639–56.

Richardson, G.B. (1972), 'The Organisation of Industry', *Economic Journal*, **82**, 883–96.

Richardson, G.B. (1975), 'Adam Smith on Competition and Increasing Returns', in A. Skinner and T. Wilson (eds), *Essays on Adam Smith,* Oxford: Oxford University Press.

Richardson, G.B. (1998), 'Competition, Innovation and Increasing Returns', *The Economics of Imperfect Knowledge*, Cheltenham, UK and Lyme, US: Edward Elgar.

APPENDIX I

Figures 5.1 Simulations

Simulation 1: Price and Average Price

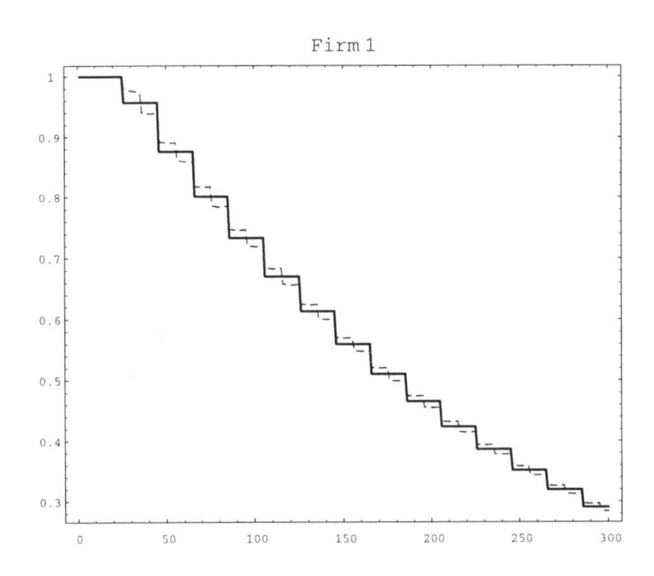

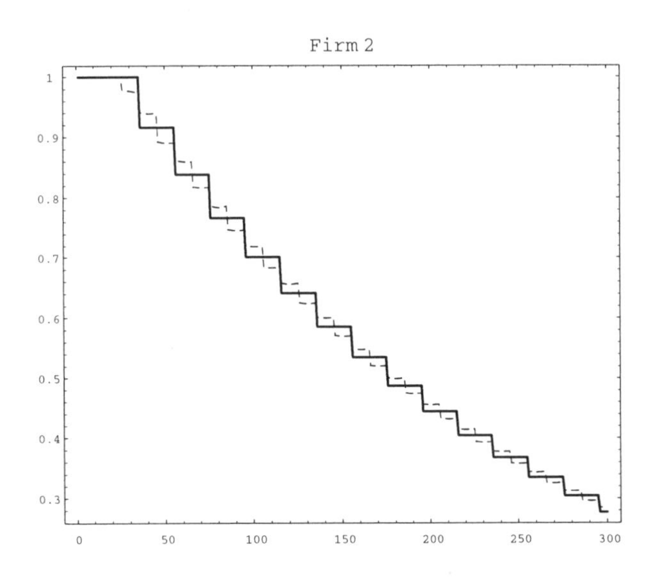

Simulation 1 (cont.): Market Shares

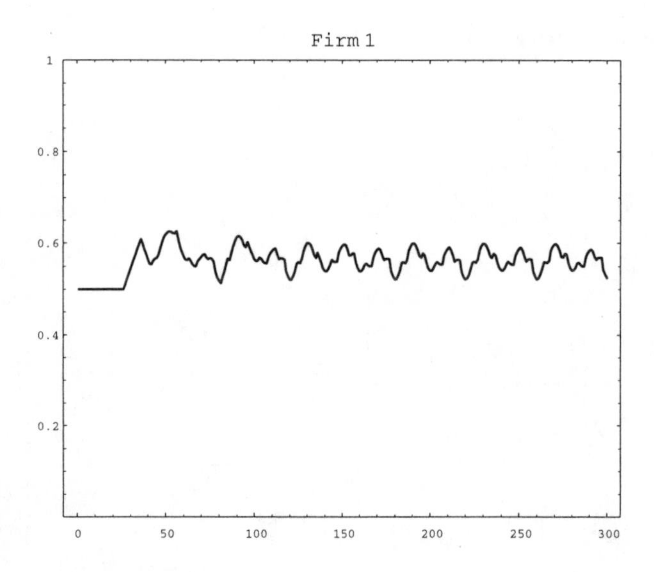

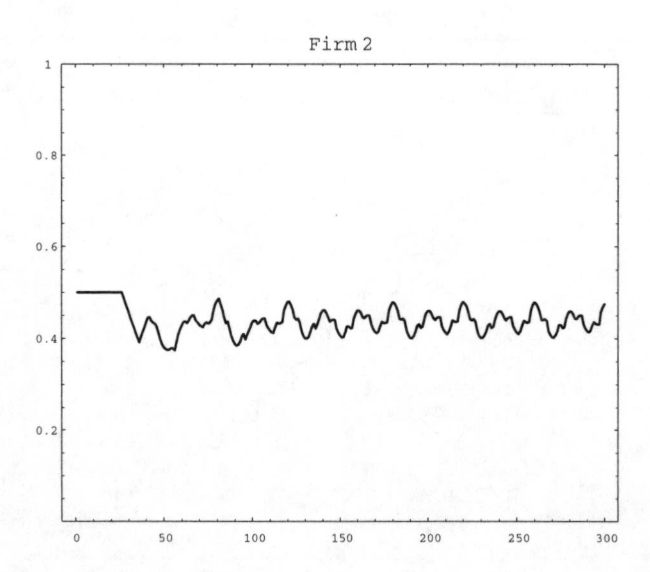

Simulation 1 (cont.): Rate of Capacity Utilization

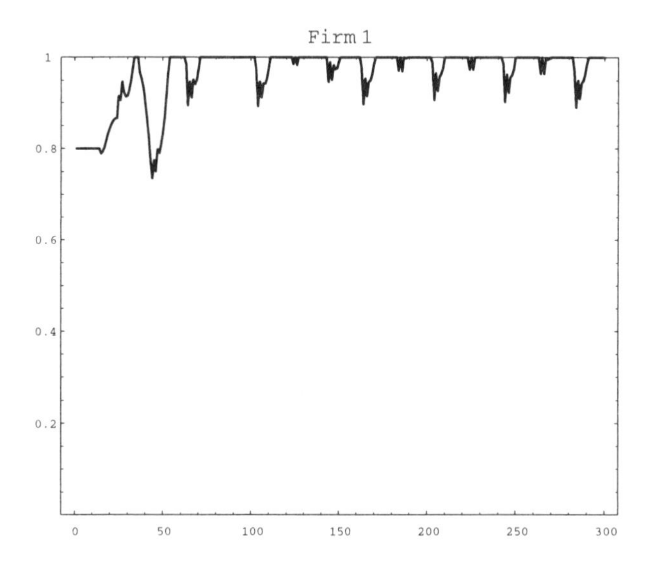

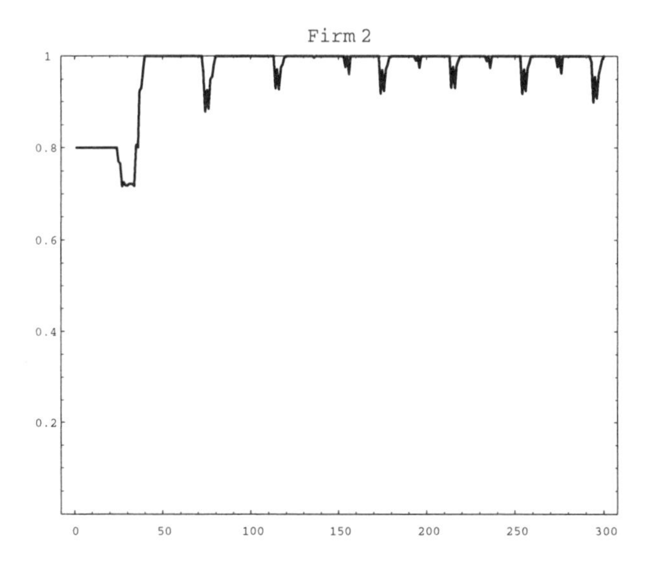

Simulation 1 (cont.): Unit Cost

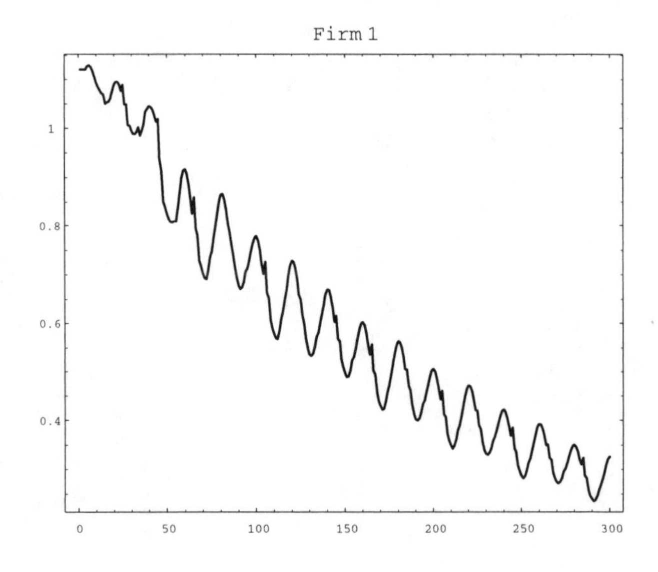

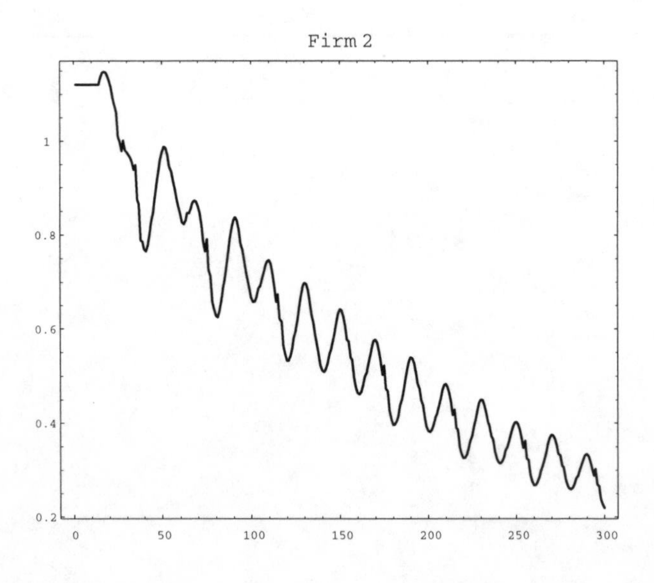

Simulation 1 (cont.): Unit Margin

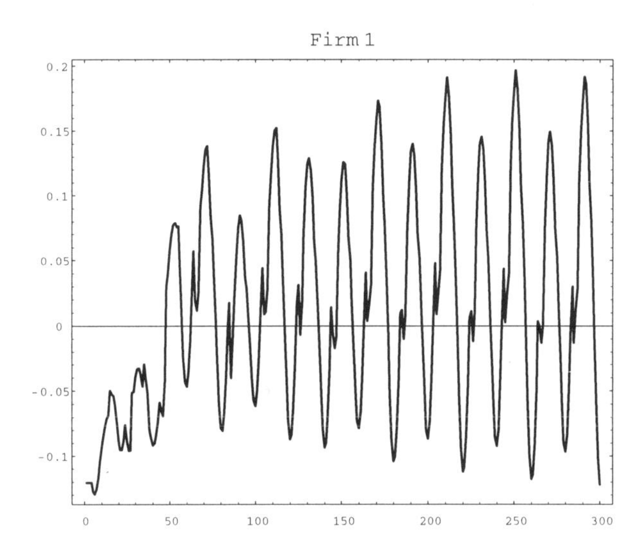

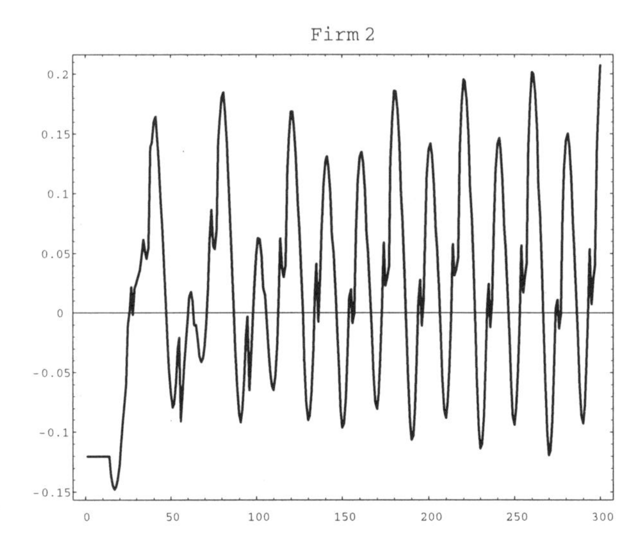

Simulation 1 (cont.): Unit Margin (Moving Average)

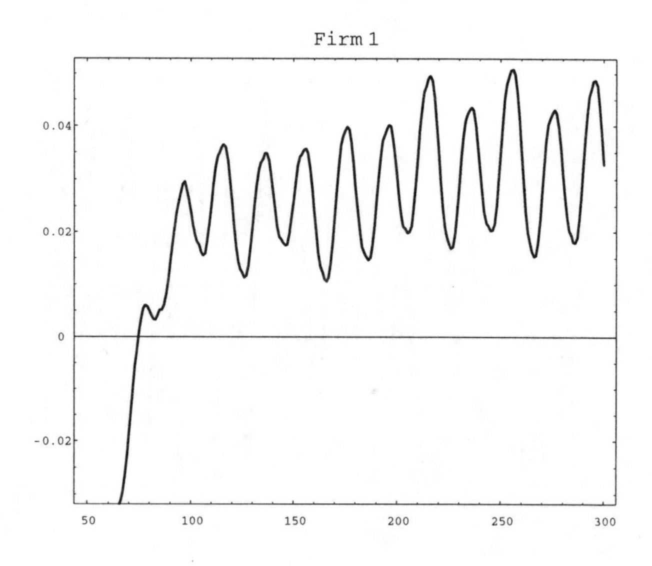

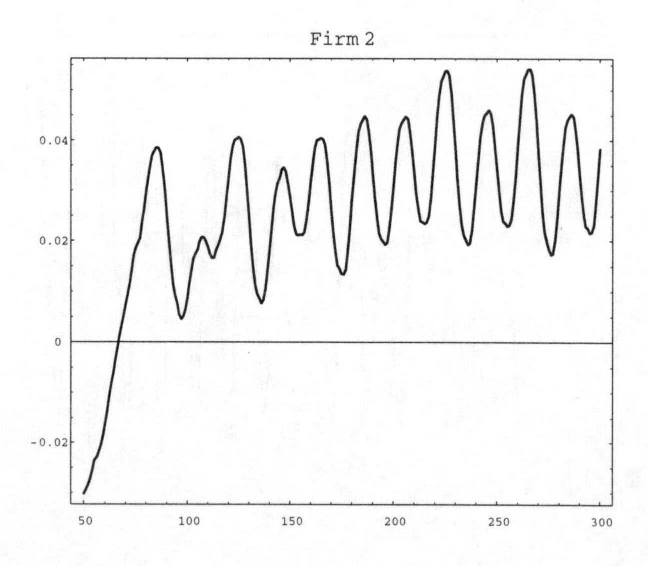

Simulation 2: Price and Average Price

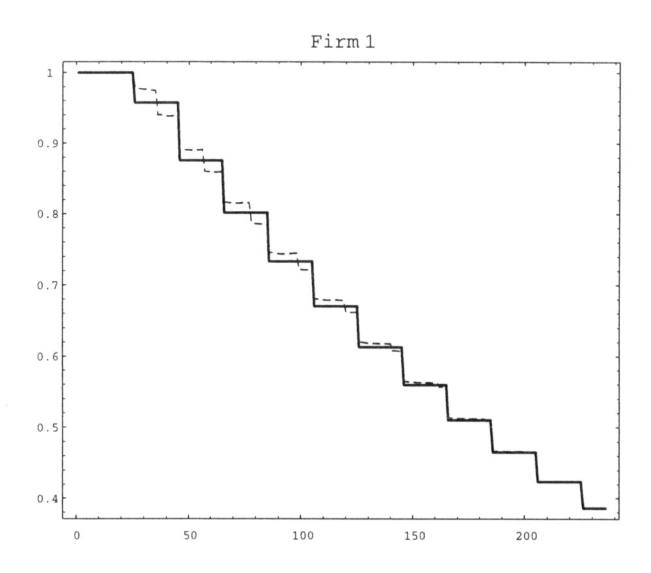

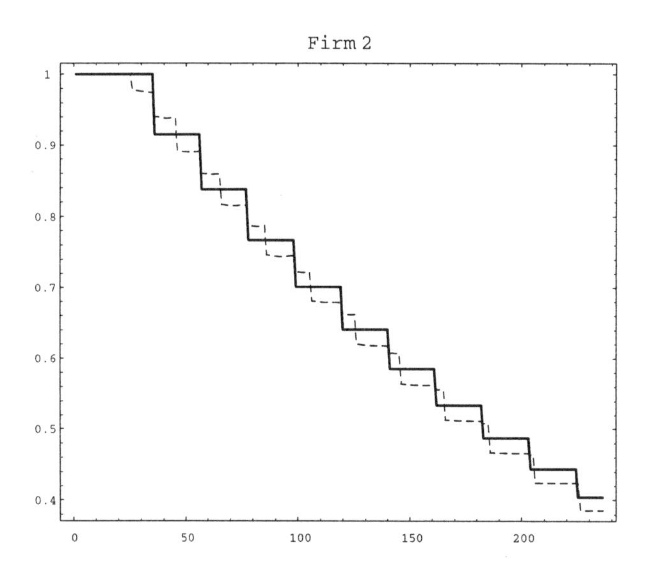

Simulation 2 (cont.): Market Shares

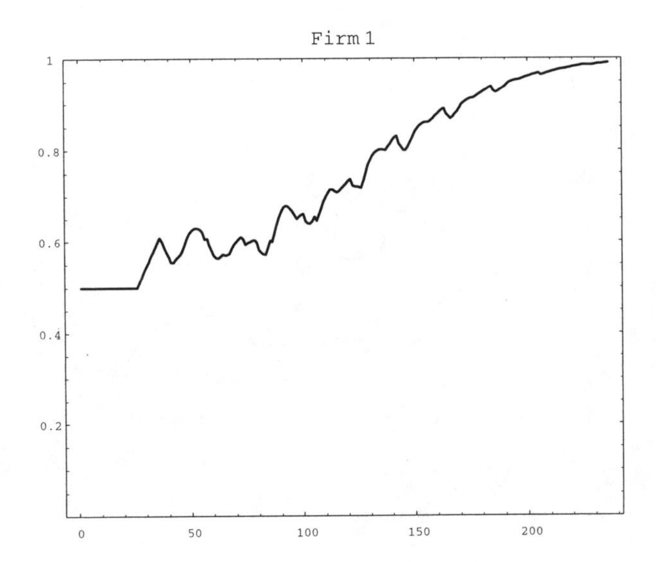

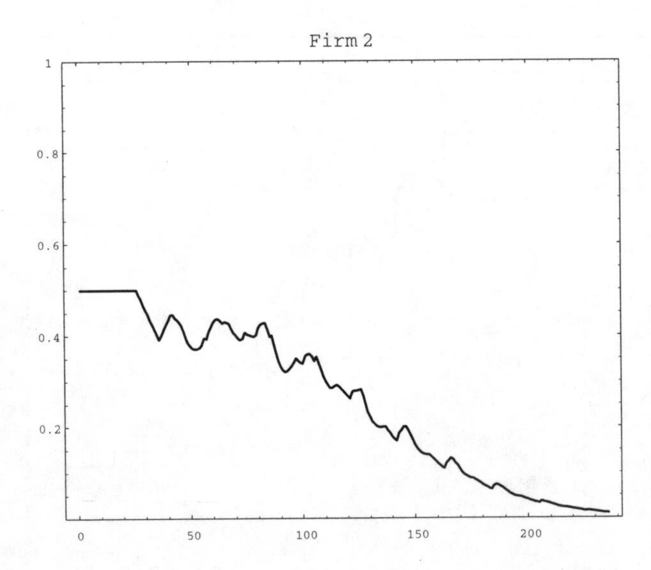

Simulation 2 (cont.): Rate of Capacity Utilization

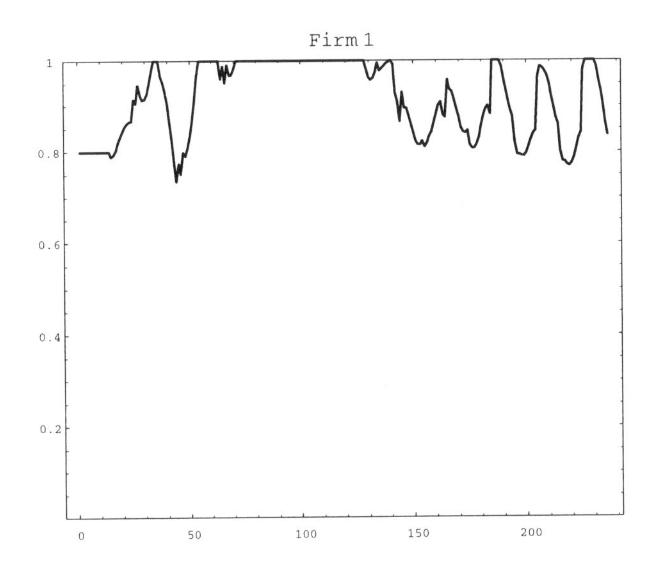

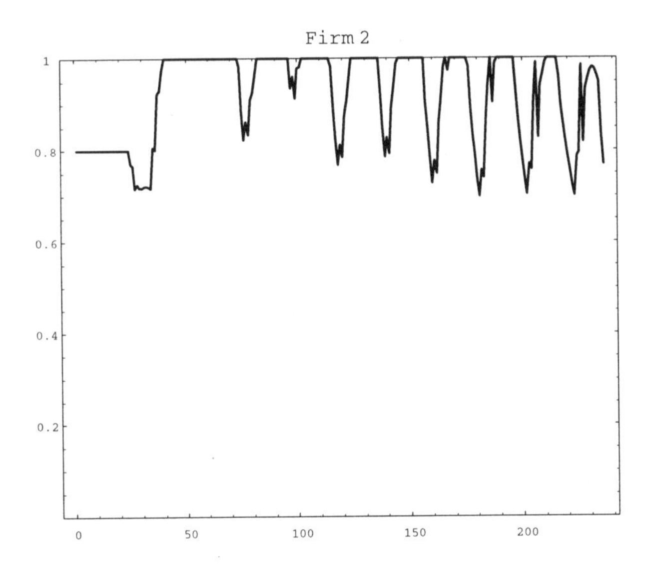

Simulation 2 (cont.): Unit Cost

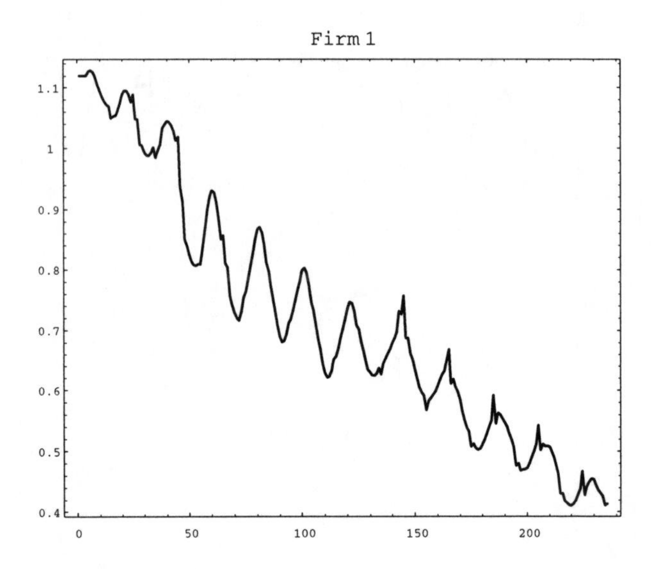

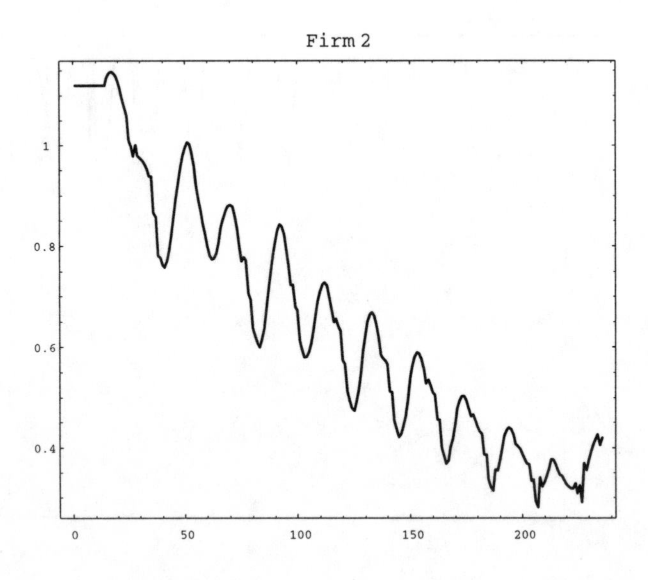

Simulation 2 (cont.): Unit Margin

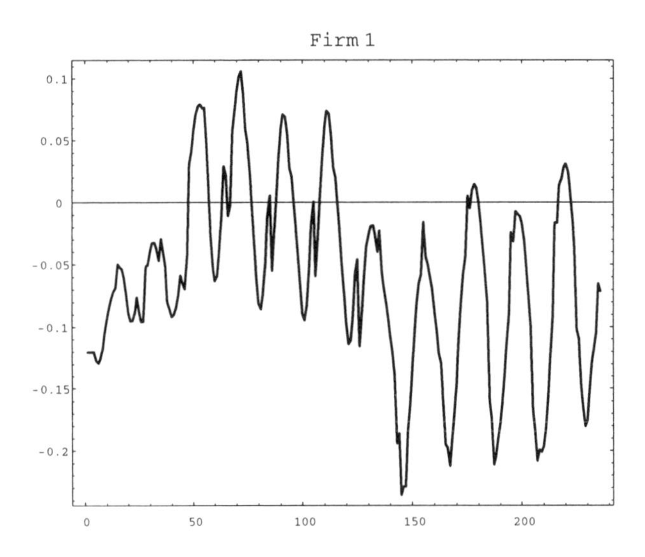

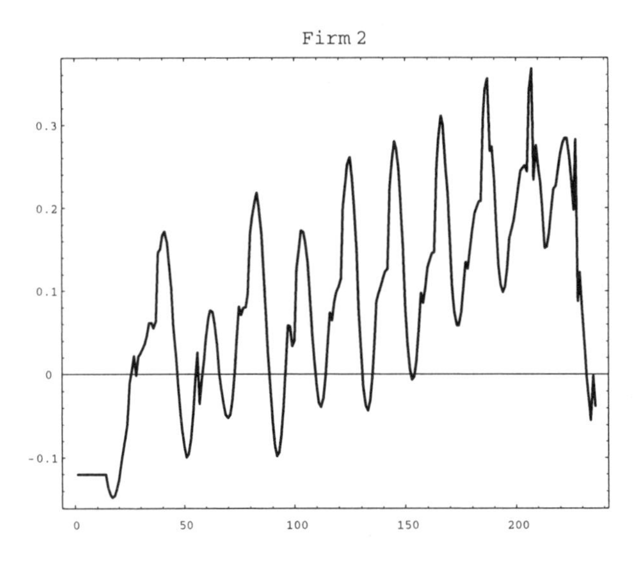

Simulation 2 (cont.): Unit Margin (Moving Average)

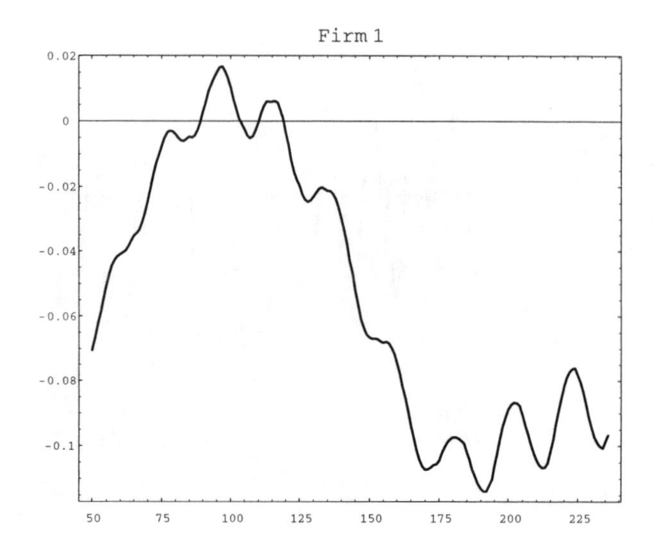

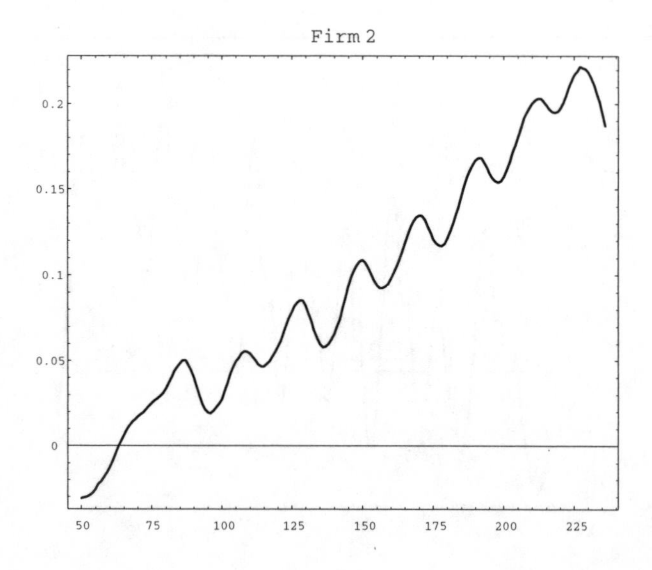

Simulation 3a: Price and Average Price

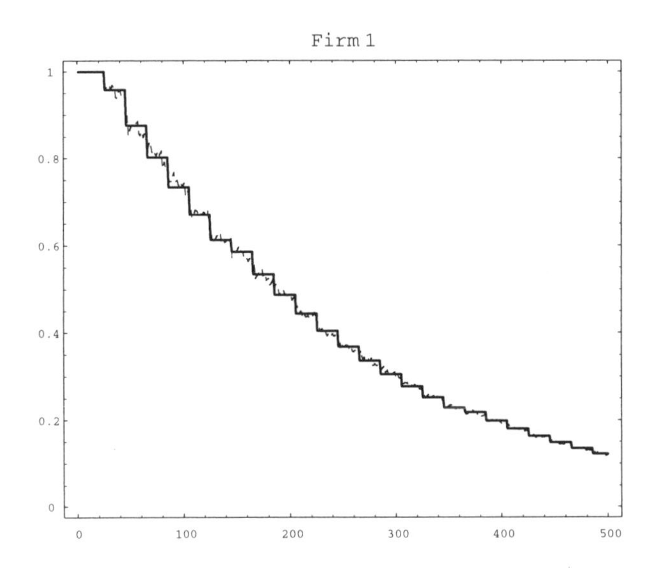

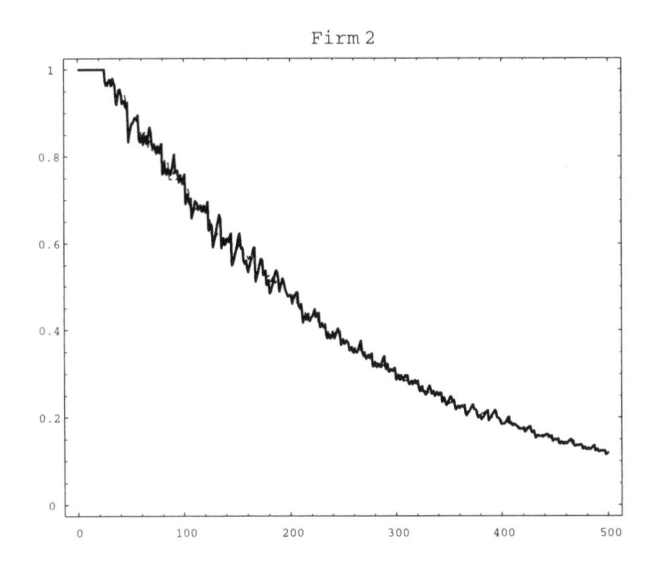

Simulation 3a (cont.): Market Shares

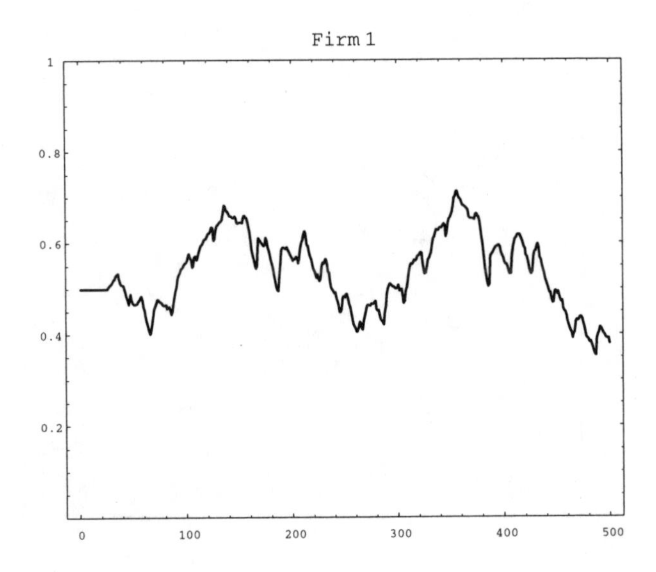

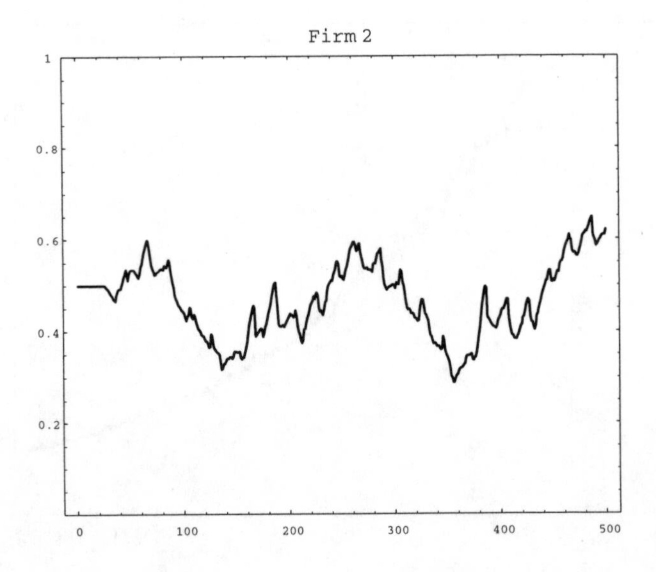

Simulation 3a (cont.): Rate of Capacity Utilization

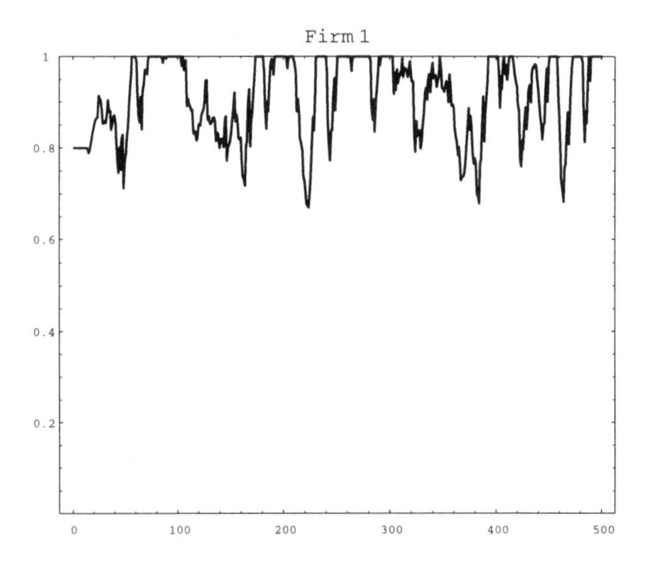

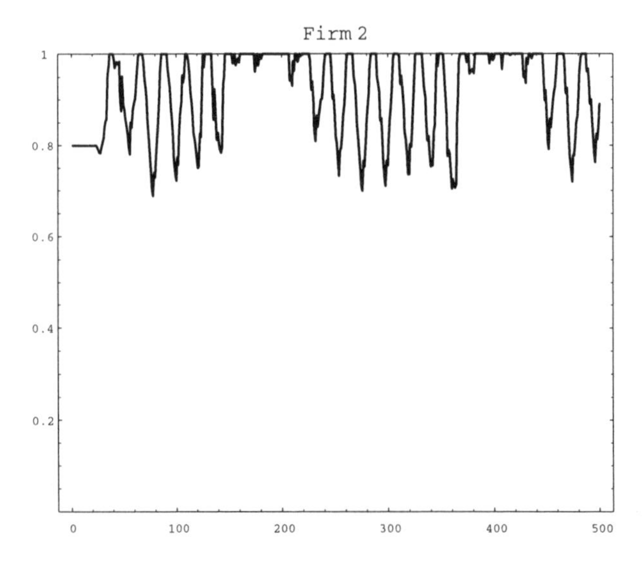

Simulation 3a (cont.): Unit Cost

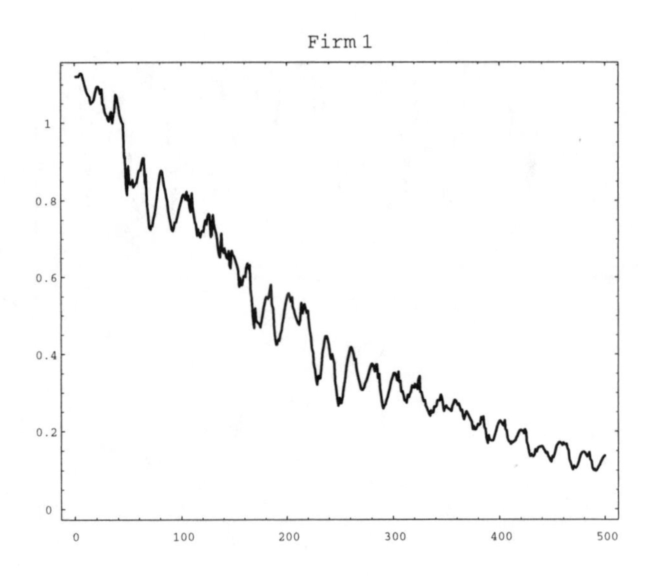

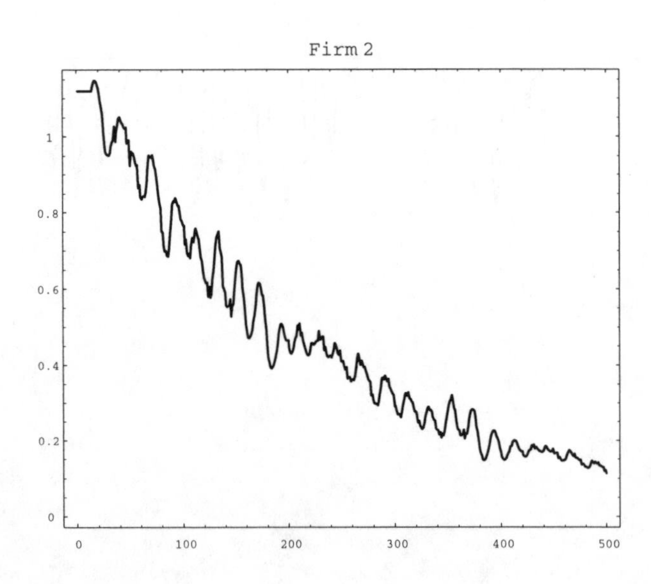

Simulation 3a (cont.): Unit Margin

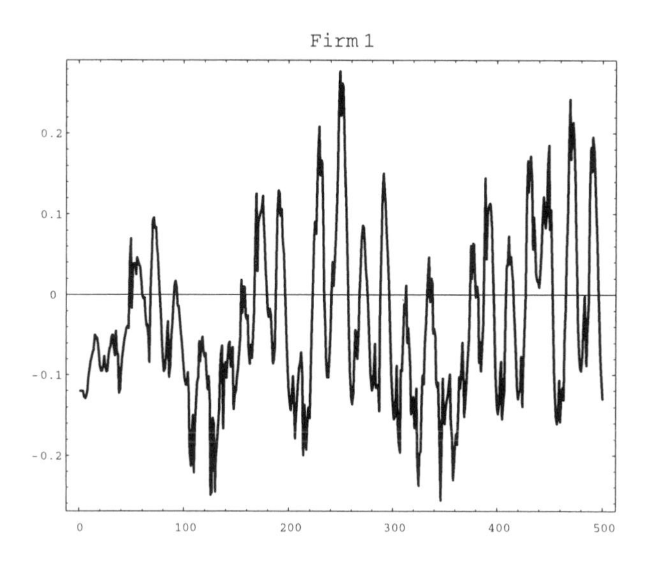

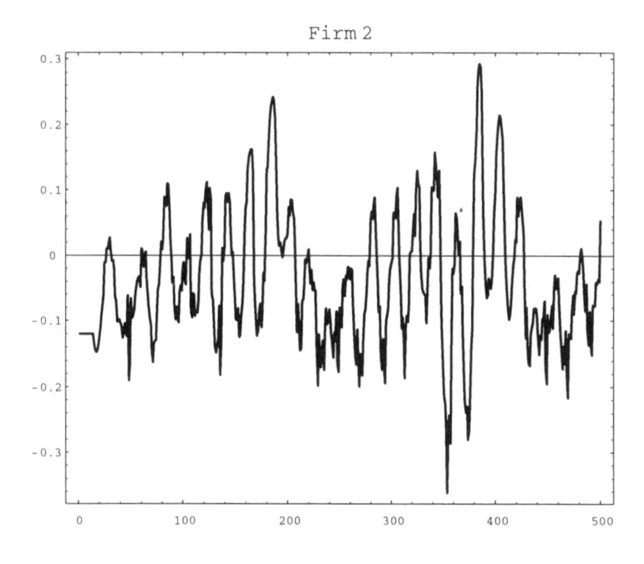

Simulation 3a (cont.): Unit Margin (Moving Average)

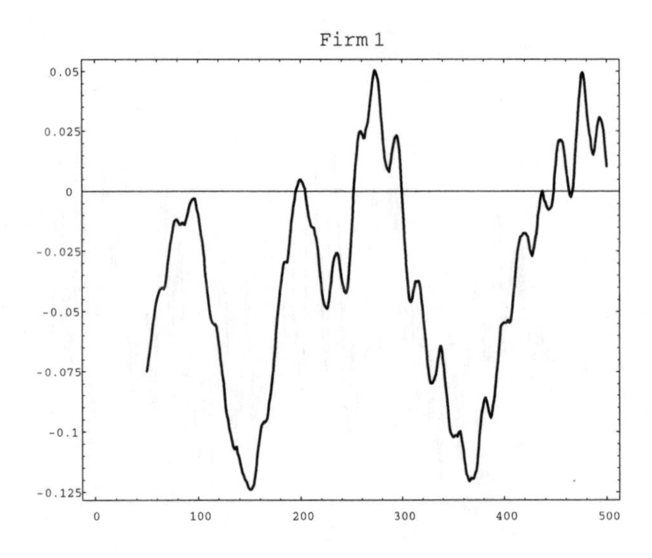

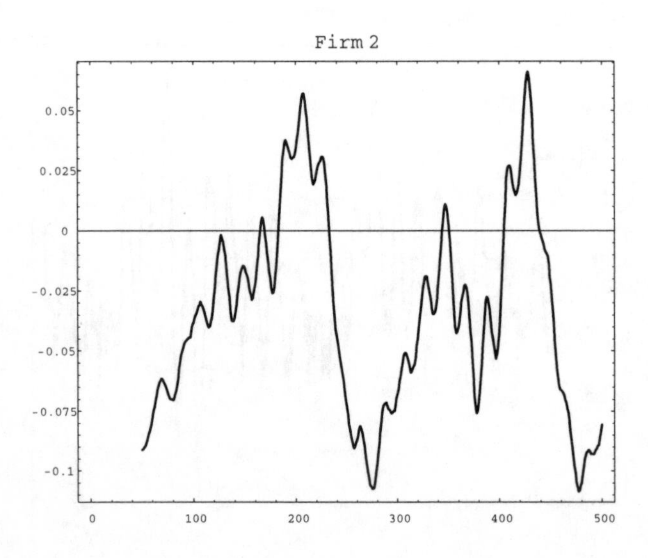

Simulation 3b: Price and Average Price

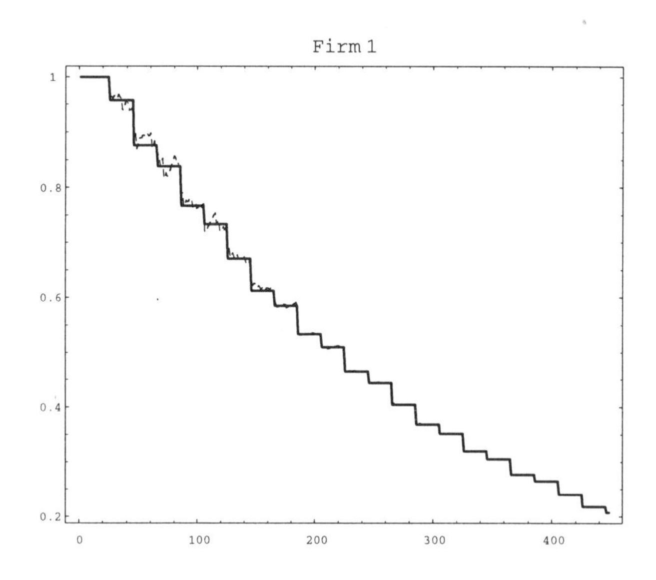

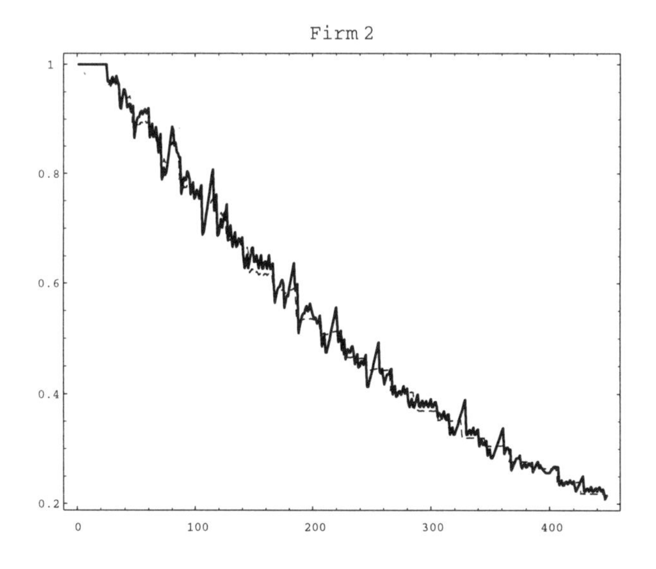

Simulation 3b (cont.): Market Shares

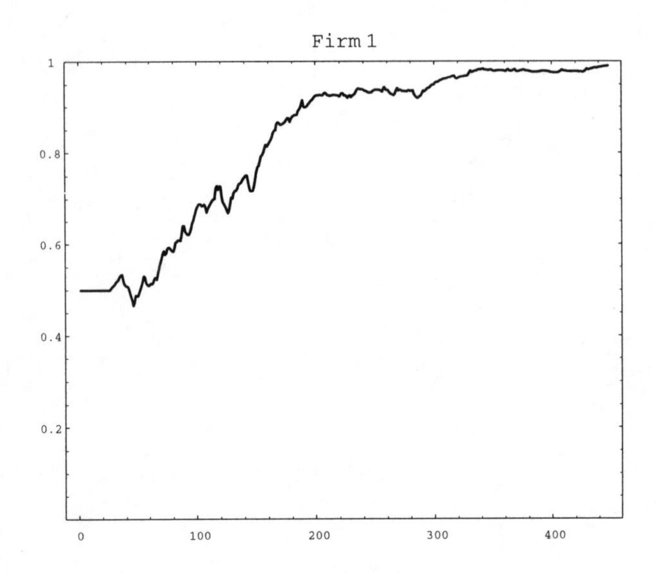

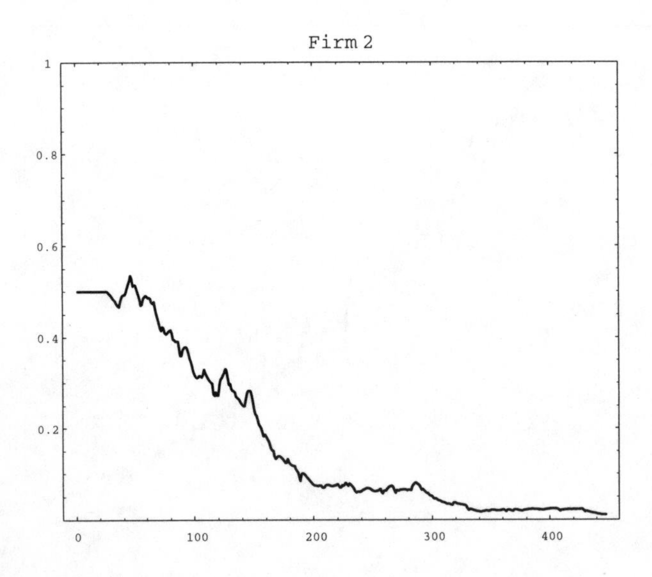

Simulation 3b (cont.): Rate of Capacity Utilization

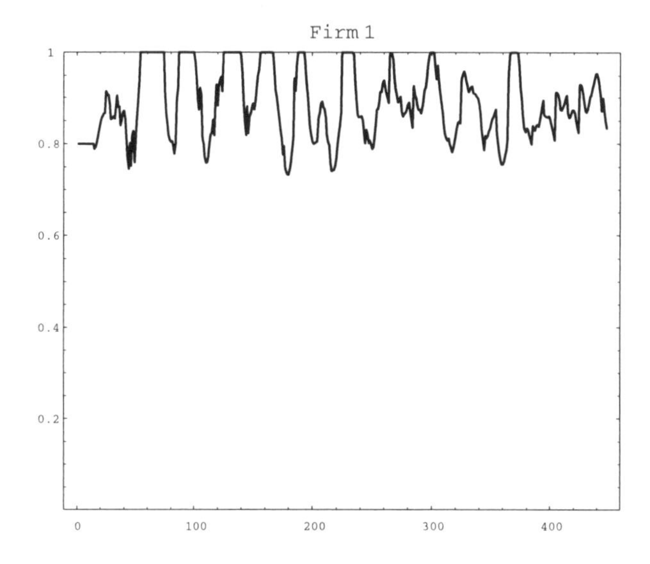

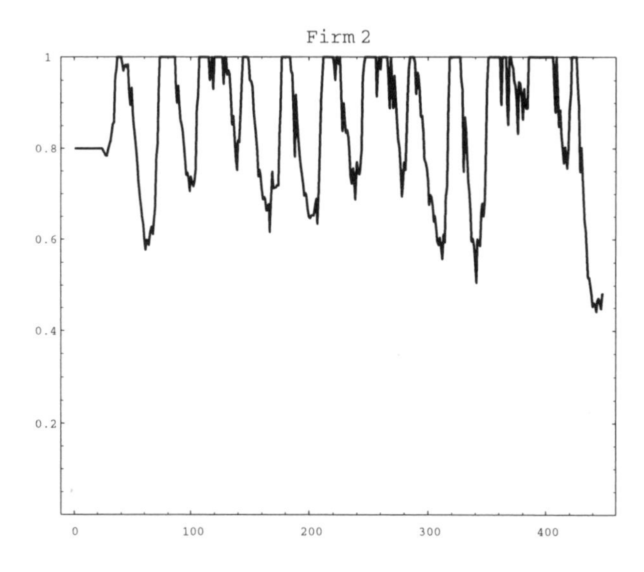

Simulation 3b (cont.): Unit Cost

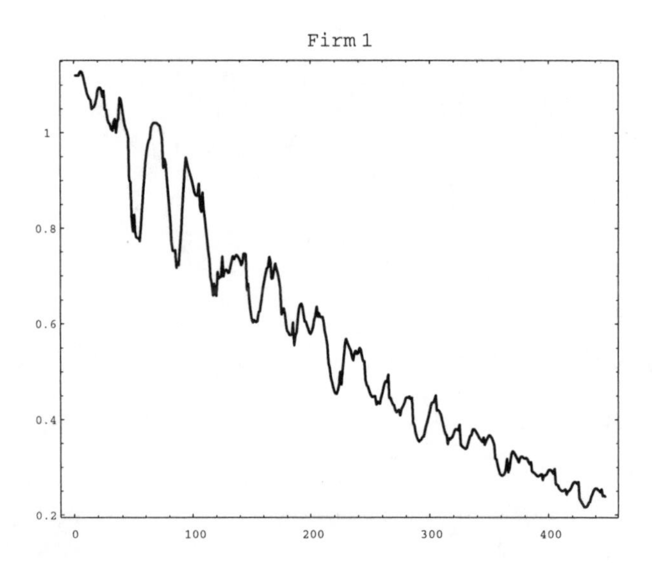

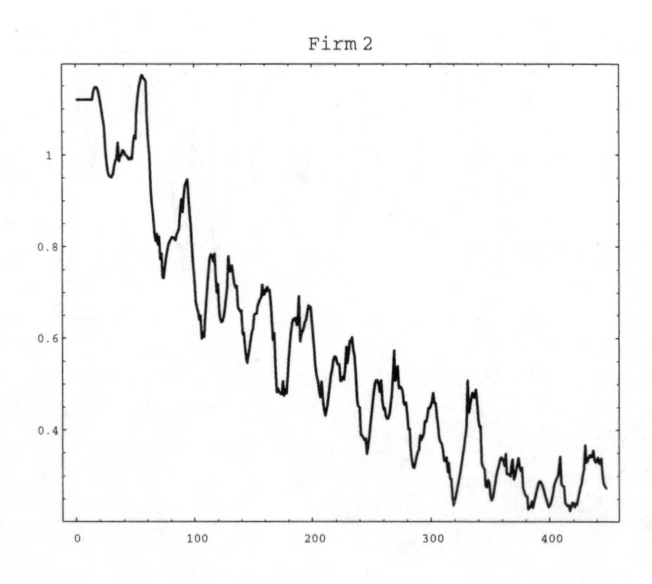

Simulation 3b (cont.): Unit Margin

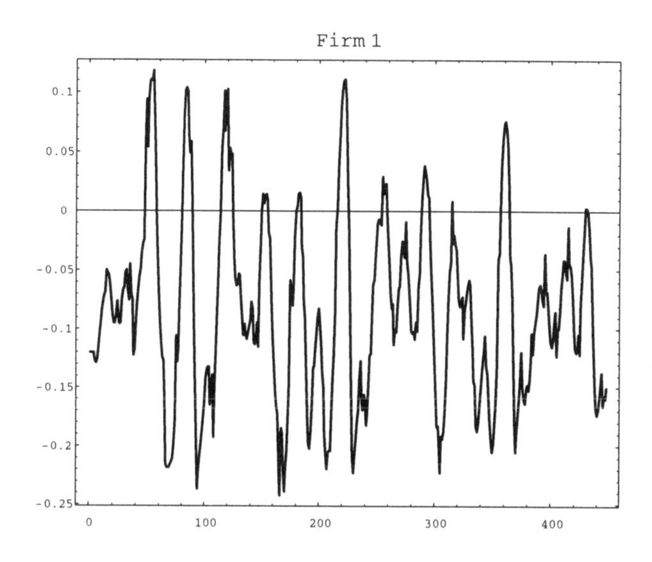

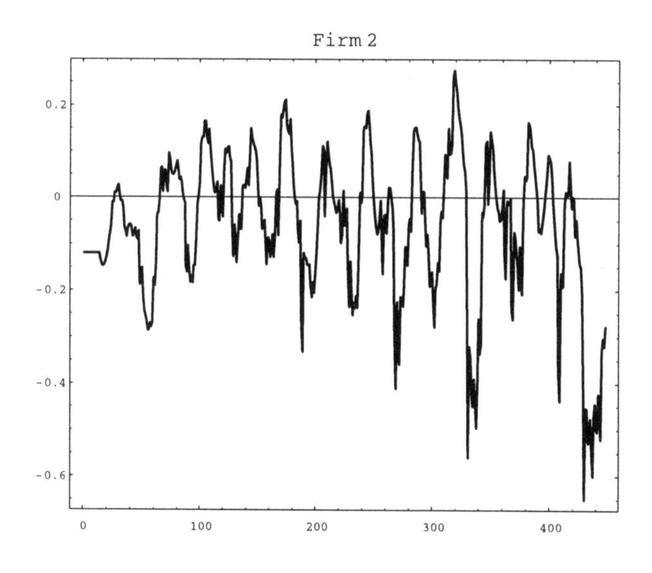

Simulation 3b (cont.): Unit Margin (Moving Average)

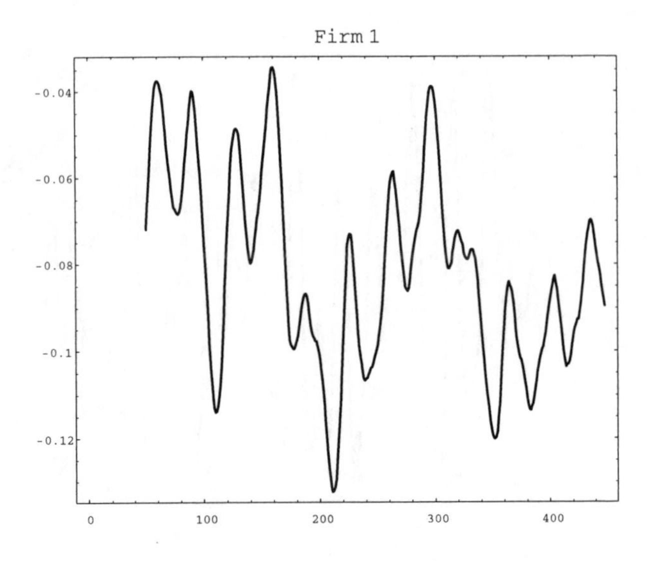

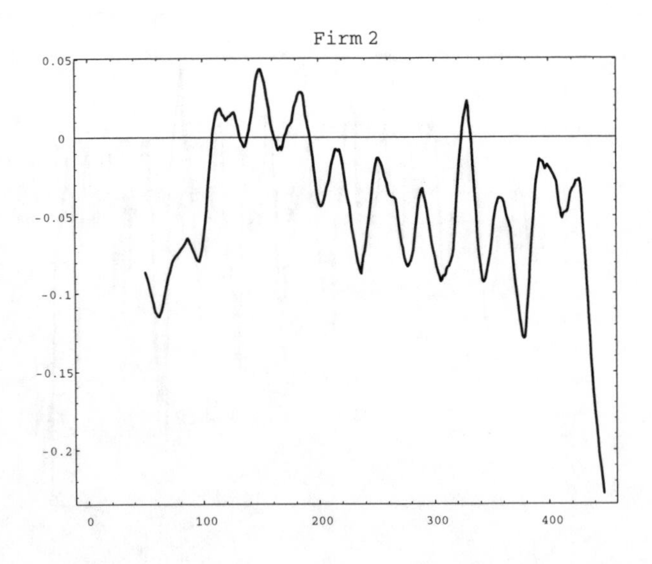

Simulation 3c: Price and Average Price

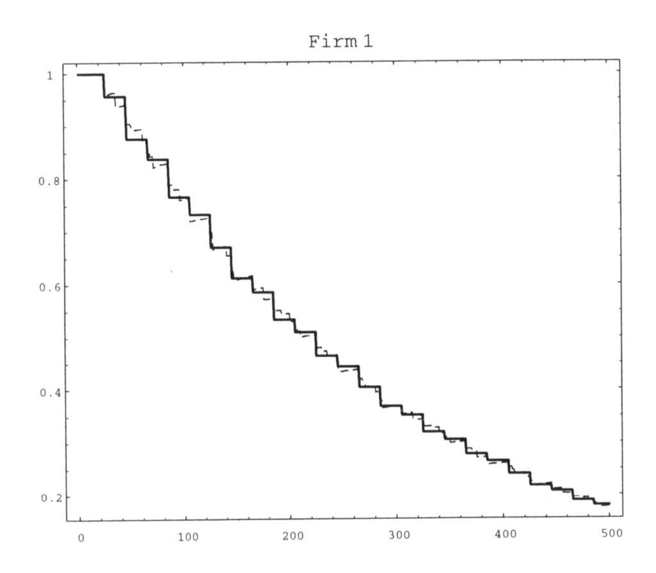

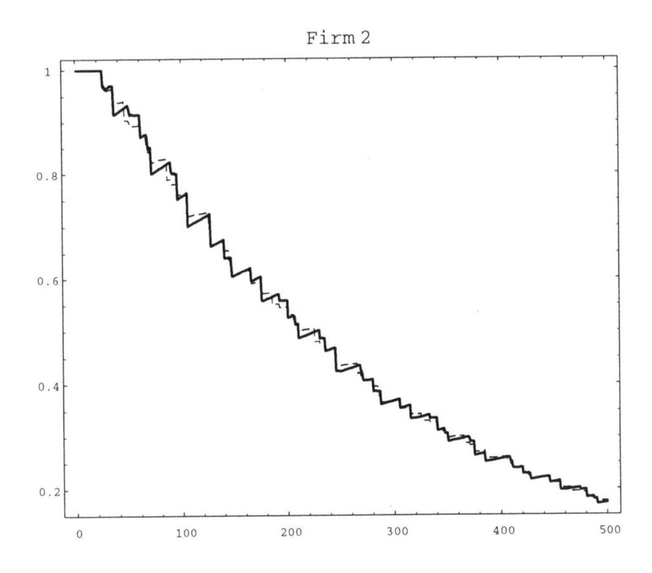

Simulation 3c (cont.): Market Shares

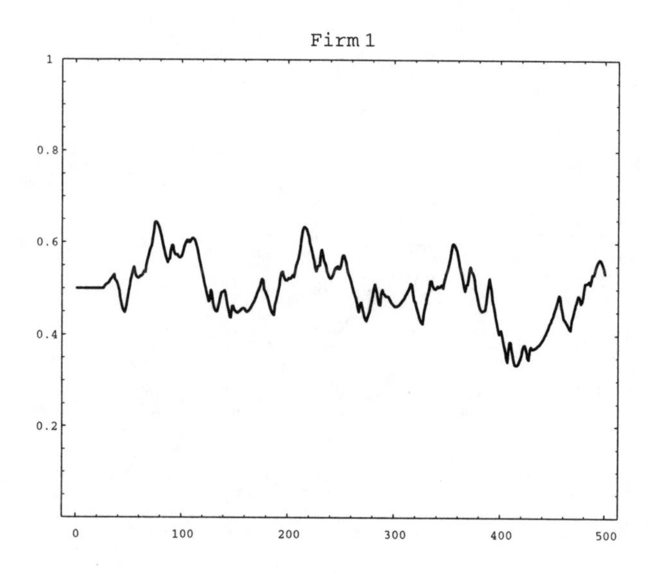

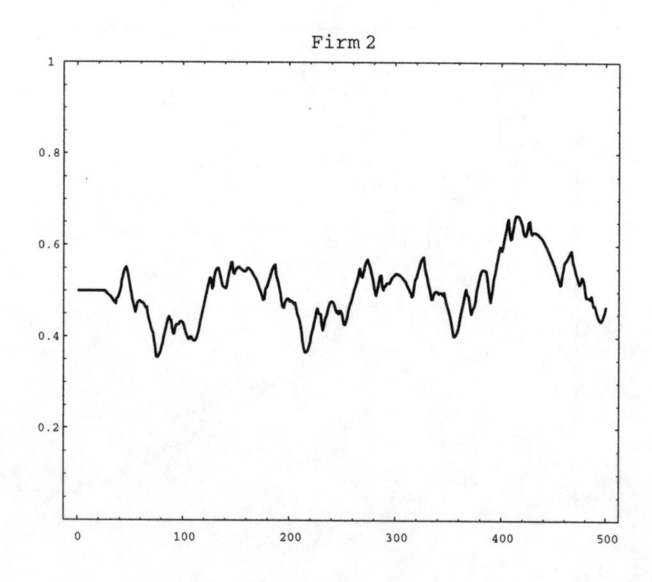

Simulation 3c (cont.): Rate of Capacity Utilization

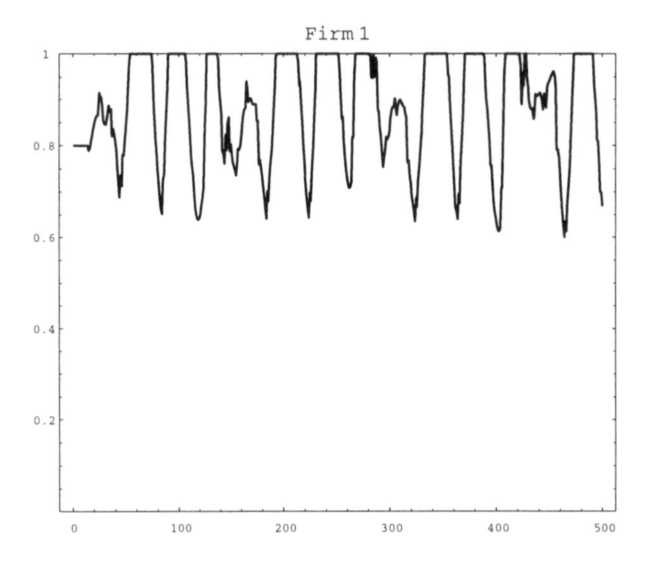

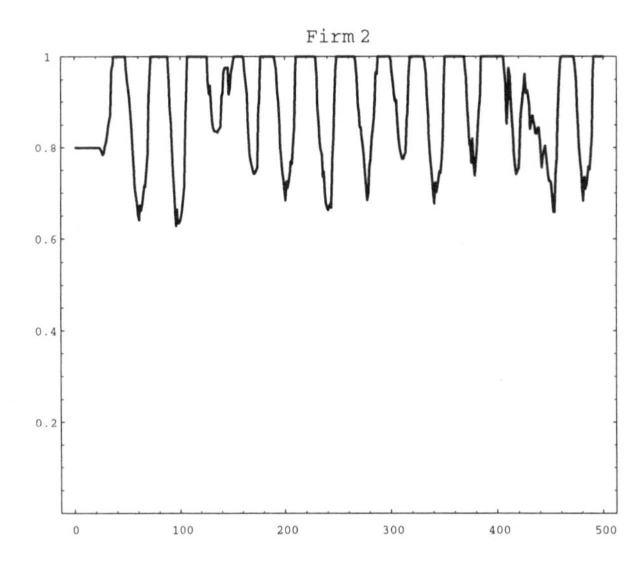

Simulation 3c (cont.): Unit Cost

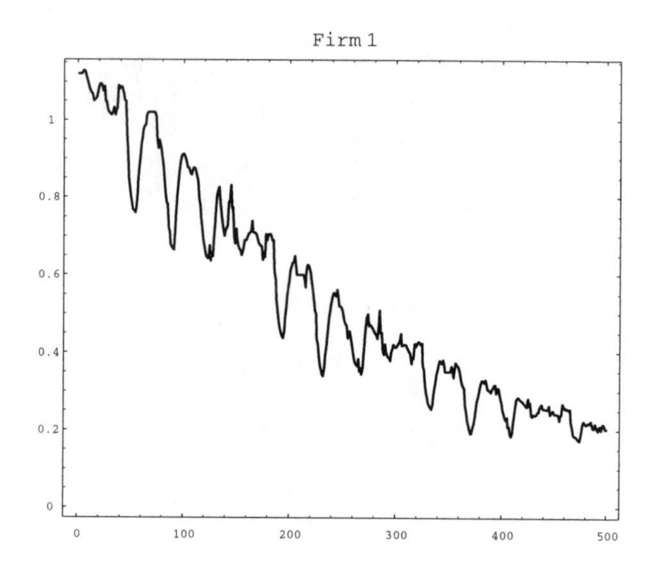

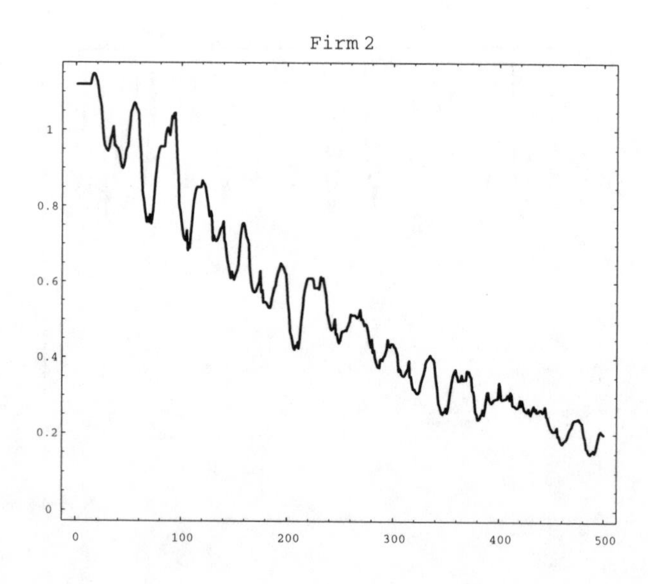

Simulation 3c (cont.): Unit Margin

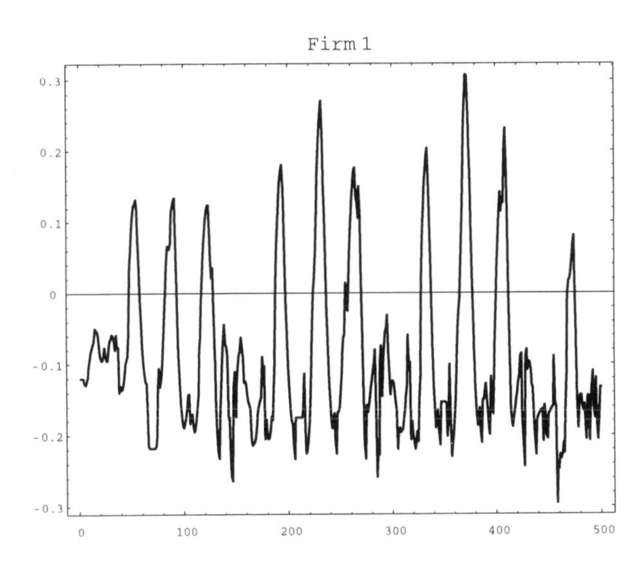

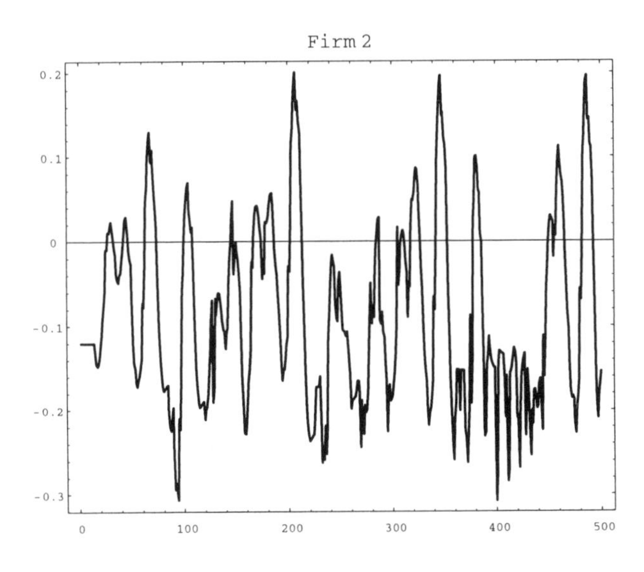

Simulation 3c (cont.): Unit Margin (Moving Average)

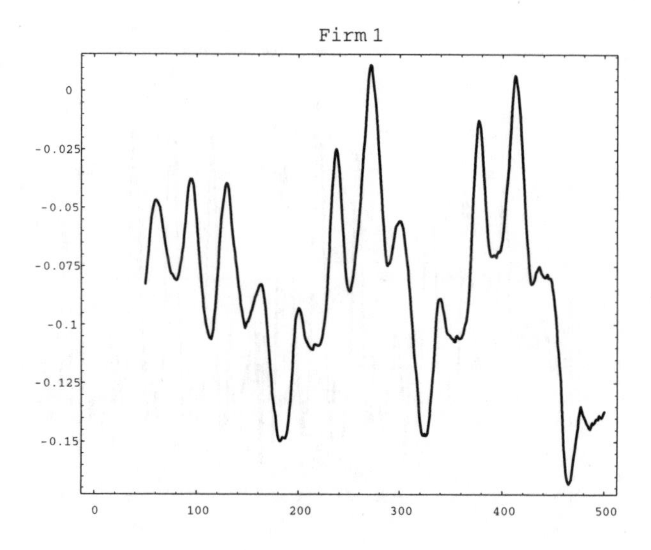

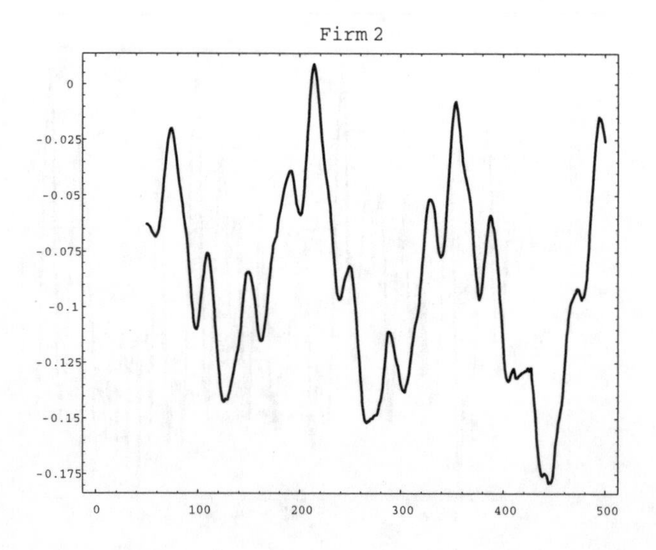

Simulation 4: Price and Average Price

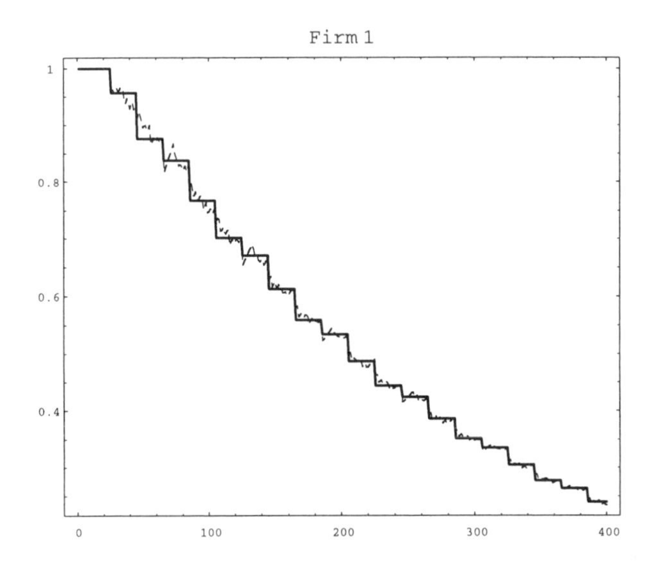

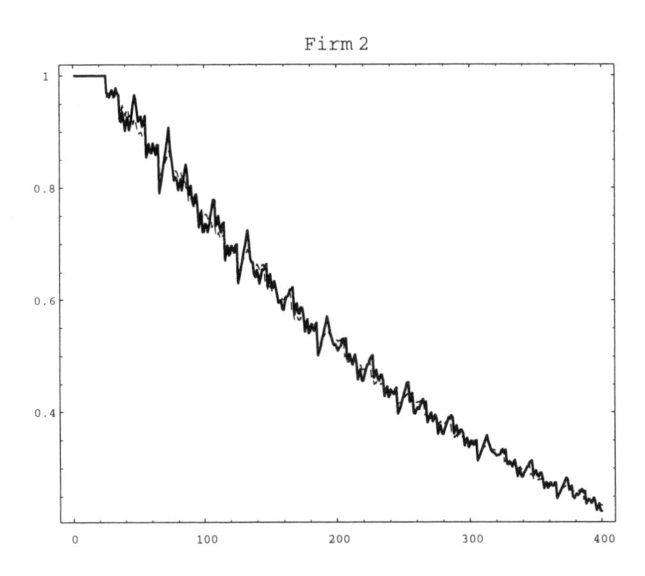

Simulation 4 (cont.): Market Shares

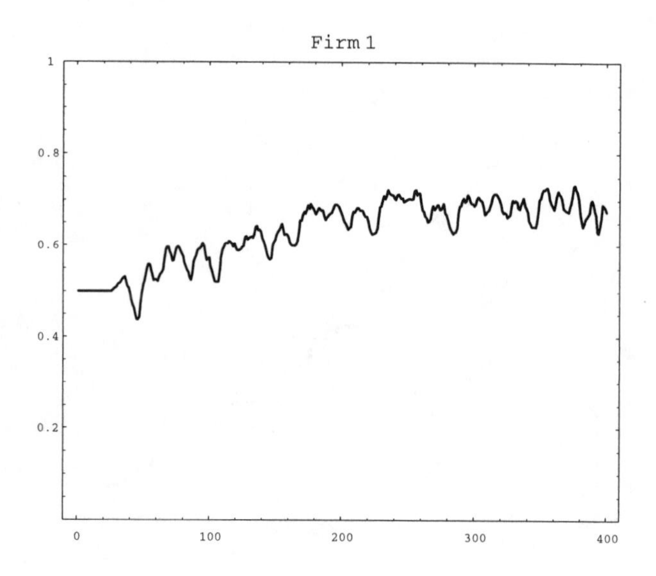

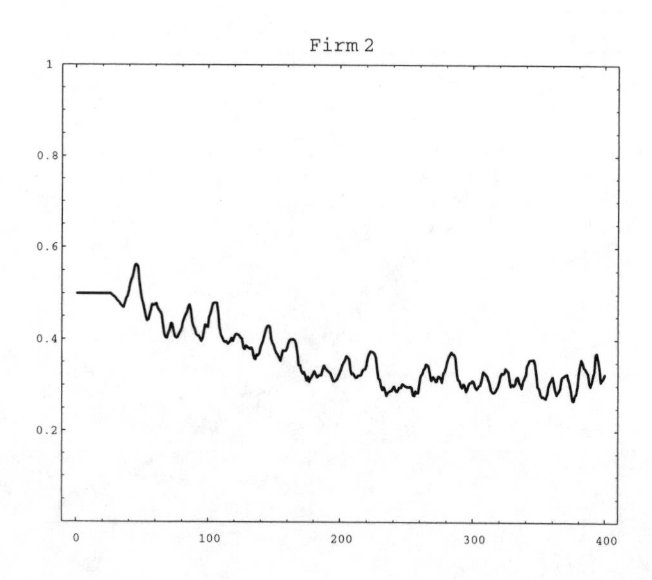

Simulation 4 (cont.): Rate of Capacity Utilization

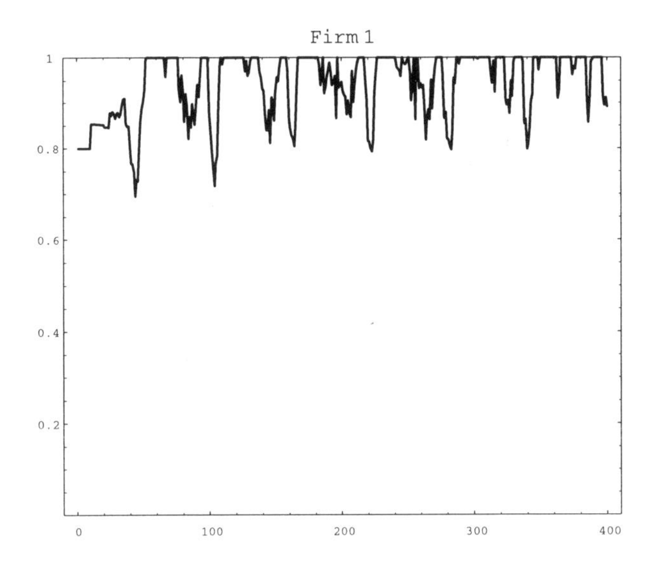

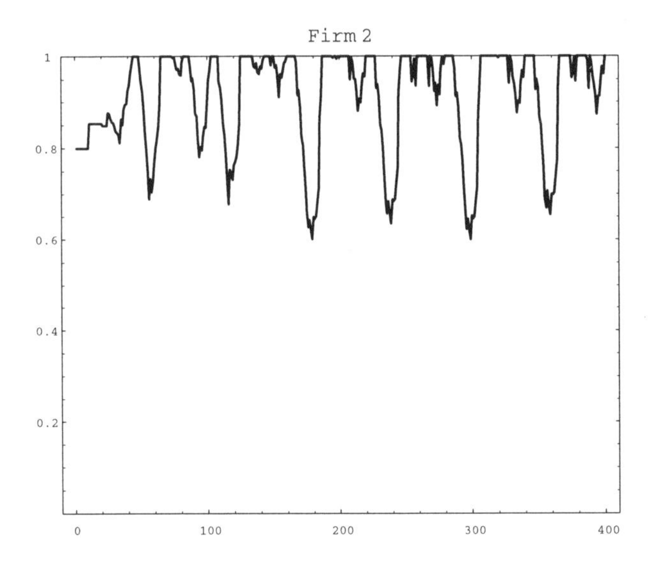

Simulation 4 (cont.): Unit Cost

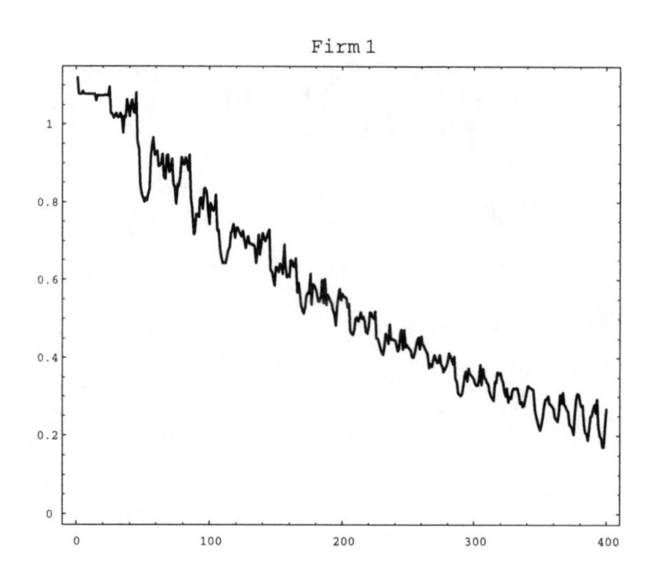

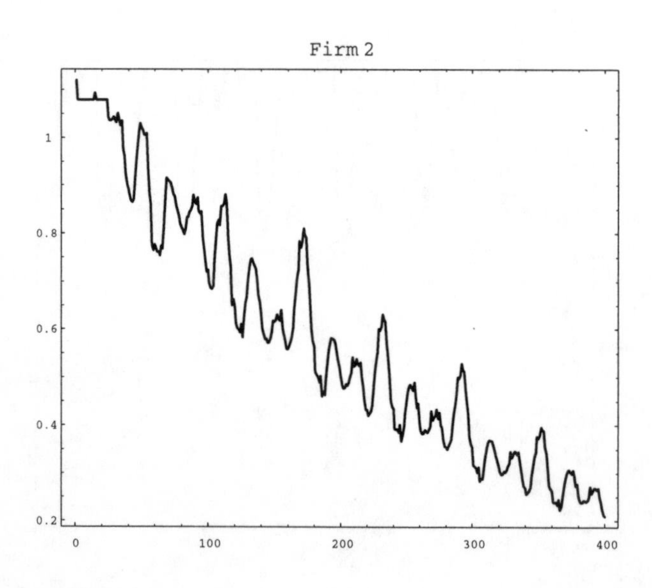

Simulation 4 (cont.): Unit Margin

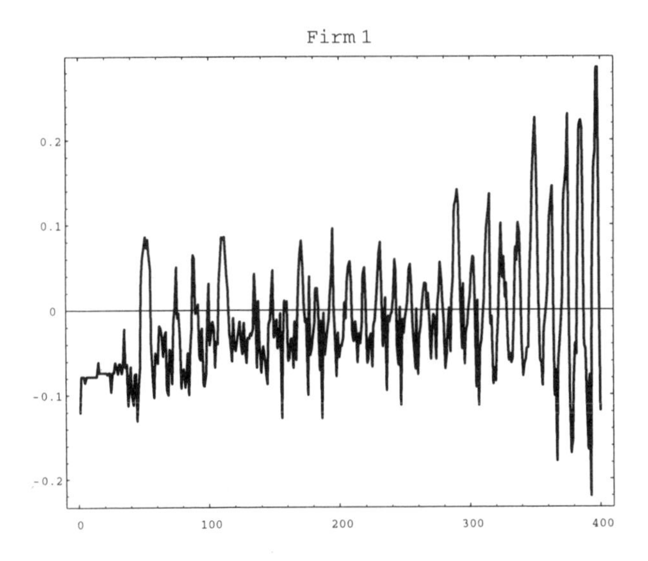

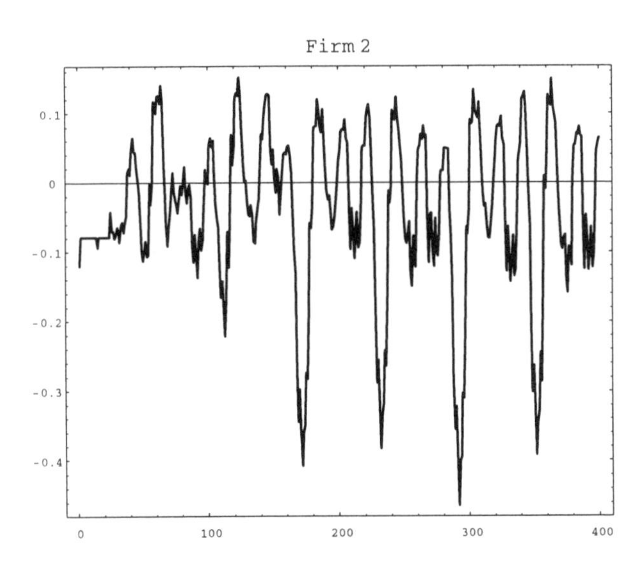

Simulation 4 (cont.): Unit Margin (Moving Average)

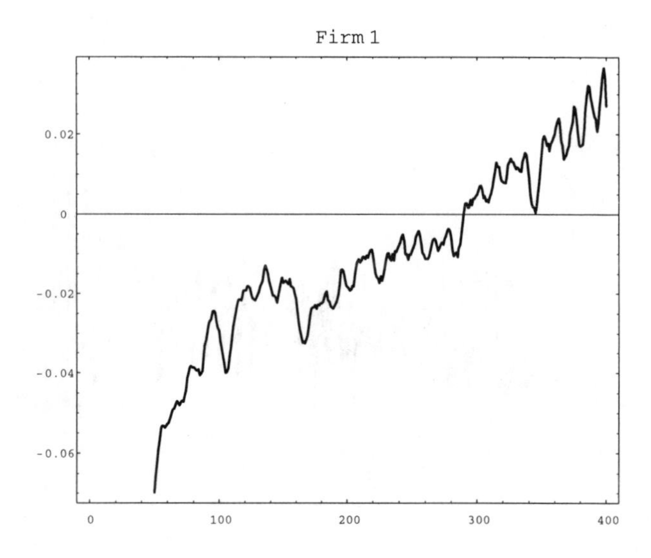

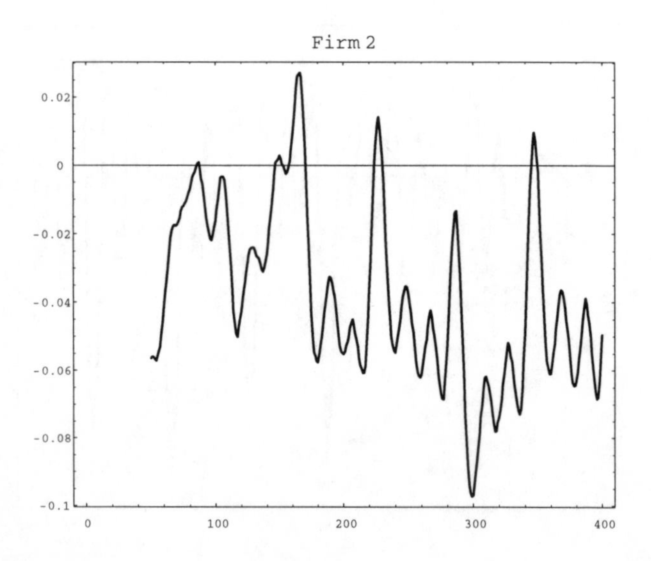

APPENDIX II

Tables 5.1 Value of key parameters in simulations

Simulation 1: v = 0

Parameters	Firm 1	Firm 2
First shock	5	15
Frequency	20	20
k	0.3	0.3
χ	0	0
$\Delta P_{upwards}$	0.5	0.5
$\Delta P_{downwards}$	0.5	0.5
$\Delta X_{1upwards}$	0.05	0.05
$\Delta X_{1downwards}$	0.05	0.05

Simulation 2: v = 0

Parameters	Firm 1	Firm 2
First shock	5	15
Frequency	20	21
k	0.3	0.3
χ	0	0
$\Delta P_{upwards}$	0.5	0.5
$\Delta P_{downwards}$	0.5	0.5
$\Delta X_{1upwards}$	0.05	0.05
$\Delta X_{1downwards}$	0.05	0.05

Simulation 3a: v = 0

Parameters	Firm 1	Firm 2
First shock	5	15
Frequency	20	22
k	0.3	0.3
χ	0	1.4
$\Delta P_{upwards}$	0.5	0.02
$\Delta P_{downwards}$	0.5	0.5
$\Delta X_{1upwards}$	0.05	0.05
$\Delta X_{1downwards}$	0.05	0.05

Simulation 3b: v = 0

Parameters	Firm 1	Firm 2
First shock	5	15
Frequency	20	35
k	0.3	0.3
χ	0	1.4
$\Delta P_{upwards}$	0.5	0.02
$\Delta P_{downwards}$	0.5	0.5
$\Delta X_{1upwards}$	0.05	0.05
$\Delta X_{1downwards}$	0.05	0.05

Simulation 3c: v = 0

Parameters	Firm 1	Firm 2
First shock	5	15
Frequency	20	35
k	0.3	0.3
χ	0	1.4
$\Delta P_{upwards}$	0.5	0.0016
$\Delta P_{downwards}$	0.5	0.5
$\Delta X_{1upwards}$	0.05	0.05
$\Delta X_{1downwards}$	0.05	0.05

Simulation 4: v = 0

Parameters	Firm 1	Firm 2
First shock	5	15
Frequency	20	30
k	0.1	0.1
χ	0	1.4
$\Delta P_{upwards}$	0.5	0.02
$\Delta P_{downwards}$	0.5	0.5
$\Delta X_{1upwards}$	0.05	0.05
$\Delta X_{1downwards}$	0.05	0.05

6. Strategy research and the market process perspective

Nicolai Foss and Volker Mahnke

1. INTRODUCTION[1]

As normally understood, strategy aims at the creation of sustained competitive advantage so that (it is hoped, long-lived) rent streams can be earned. Although this view is conventional, it is in no way uncontroversial or simple. What, for example, is meant by 'sustained' or 'long-lived' and how are these concepts dependent upon what we assume about the market process? Are (Ricardian, Paretian or monopoly) rents really the only relevant category of return – or may it also make sense to think of strategizing as aiming at reaping pure profit through intertemporal and interspatial processes of entrepreneurial discovery (à la Kirzner, 1973)?

This also relates to the way we conceive of the formulation and carrying out of strategies. A strategy is essentially a set of complex multivariate choices, including resources, activities and product market positioning. Thus consider Rumelt *et al.*'s (1994, p.9) discussion of firm strategy:

> Because of competition, firms have choices to make if they are to survive. Those that are *strategic* include: the selection of goals; the choice of products and services to offer; the design and configuration of policies determining how the firm positions itself to compete in product markets (e.g., competitive strategy); the choice of an appropriate level of scope and diversity; and the design of organization structure, administrative systems, and policies used to define and coordinate work . . . It is the integration (or reinforcing pattern) among these choices that makes a set a strategy.

A basic issue is how we conceive of those choices: are they essentially *given*, in what Kirzner (1973) calls a 'Robbinsian' manner, or are they best understood as being *constructed* through the entrepreneurial alertness of strategizers? This issue has been forcefully raised in the context of the theory of markets by Israel Kirzner in a string of publications (for example, 1973,

1992) and we shall draw on his work, as well as the work of other Austrian economists, in the ensuing pages.

More specifically, we shall concentrate on the implications for strategy research of what we assume about the markets in which firms wish to position themselves. In this connection, we argue that a number of important modern theories of firm strategy are characterized by what we call a 'market theory problem' (cf. Sautet, 1998). This is the problem of attempting to represent what are disequilibrium phenomena in terms of equilibrium. In our view, the phenomena that should be centre stage in a theory of firm strategy, such as change, entrepreneurship, knowledge accumulation and resource combination, are quintessentially disequilibrium phenomena. They are therefore likely to be seriously misrepresented by an equilibrium framework.

A theory of competition explains the nature and functioning of markets. If strategizing by firms influences market processes and market processes influence firm strategy, any explanation of how strategizing leads to competitive advantage merits theoretical attention to the interrelation between them. Existing explanations of the firm's competitive advantage (resource-based, structure conduct performance (SCP) or new industrial organization approaches) start from equilibrium assumptions of competition and portray the firm as a bundle of scarce resources (Barney, 1991; Peteraf, 1993) or, alternatively, as a unitary decision-making entity (Porter, 1980, 1985). Competitive advantage derives from market imperfection due to monopolistic restrictions on output (Porter, 1980) or from the distribution of access to valuable resources that yield rents to the extent that *ex post* or *ex ante* limits to competitions prevail (Barney, 1991; Peteraf, 1993). In either case, sustained competitive advantage is thought of as a property of equilibrium: an equilibrium exists in which firms earn a sustainable rent stream.

The literature on market processes, by contrast, describes competition as a process of continuous disequilibrium (Menger, 1871; Schumpeter, 1912; Mises, 1949; Hayek, 1948; Kirzner, 1973, 1992; Boettke and Prychitko, 1998), competition being driven by entrepreneurial discovery of given, but previously undiscovered, profit opportunities (Kirzner, 1973) and market creation based on new entrepreneurial resource combinations (Schumpeter, 1912). Markets and competition become a matter of learning and discovery in an essentially uncertain context (Kirzner, 1992). Competitive advantage fundamentally results from the subjective perception of profit opportunities, the exploitation of uncertainty and the coordination of learning and knowledge. Put differently: competitive advantage is based on subjective, individual cognition and its coordination for collective competitive action that a given company is able to undertake.

Like the market process literature, the recent literature on strategy processes deals with subjective cognition (for example, Hurst *et al.*, 1989; Aadne and Mahnke, 1998), the coordination of partly tacit knowledge (Hayek, 1945; Nonaka and Takeuchi, 1995), the discovery of profit opportunities (Kirzner, 1992; Ginsberg, 1994) and the entrepreneurial creation of profit opportunities through new resource combinations (Schumpeter, 1912) based on imagination (Shackle, 1958; Loasby, 1976; Prahalad and Hamel, 1994). These streams of literature, however, operate at different levels of analysis and have widely different disciplinary backgrounds. The market process literature focuses on market-level processes from a heterodox economics perspective, while the strategizing literature focuses on processes leading to firm strategy from a plethora of perspectives and disciplines, including sociology and psychology. However, we shall argue that insights from all this literature can usefully be integrated to address the dynamics of competitive advantage.

The remainder of the chapter is organized to address two major issues. First, what are the limitations of approaches to firm strategy that are rooted in equilibrium economics, where these approaches include the resource-based, the Porter industry analysis and the new industrial organization approaches? Second, what may a market process perspective add to the analysis of strategy and competitive advantage?

While this chapter is part of a more large-scale endeavour that aims at taking steps towards a more dynamic understanding of competitive advantage, its more limited ambition is to present the ground-clearing arguments as to why there is a need for a shift from an equilibrium foundation to a process foundation in strategy research.

2. EQUILIBRIUM EXPLANATIONS OF COMPETITIVE ADVANTAGE: THE MARKET THEORY PROBLEM

2.1. Three Equilibrium Approaches to Strategy

Three approaches are dominant among present-day economic approaches to strategy (content) research.[2] These are (a) the industry analysis approach associated with Michael Porter (1980), (b) approaches based on the new industrial organization and game-theoretic reasoning in general (Tirole, 1988; Shapiro, 1989), and (c) the resource-based view (Demsetz, 1973; Wernerfelt, 1984; Barney, 1986, 1991).

All three approaches are characterized by substantially relying on economic theory in order to put forward new arguments, clarify terminology, interpret existing insights, criticize other approaches, and so on. More specifically, the economics in question is largely mainstream, equilibrium economics, of either the basic UCLA–Chicago price-theory type (this is the case of the resource-based approach), old-fashioned industrial economics (the Porter industry analysis view) or the more fashionable new tools associated with game theory (new industrial organization).

In the following we briefly discuss these three approaches. Our purpose is to point out that they all suffer from what we here call a 'market theory problem'. While the theories in question are formulated as equilibrium theories, the phenomena that they scrutinize, namely the emergence and sustainability of competitive advantage, can only be fully understood by a market process approach that highlights the disequilibrium market process, and the role of differential entrepreneurial cognition and insight in that process. The latter are highlighted in market process theories, but neglected in mainstream economics. Thus theories of strategy that rests solidly on the foundation provided by equilibrium economics are likely to neglect these issues. This neglect is what we call 'the market theory problem'.

2.1.1. The industry analysis approach

In the mid-1970s, strategy scholars such as Richard Caves and Michael Porter realized that the Bain/Mason structuralist approach in industrial organization (IO) could be very usefully applied to the study of firm strategies and also for deriving practical recommendations. To Caves and Porter, basic IO concepts such as entry barriers and the collusion such barriers may foster offered an explanation of, for example, the observed persistence of above-normal profit. However, it was not entirely unproblematic to rely on IO in strategy research. For example, Bain (1959, pp.VII–VIII) explicitly excluded from the focus of IO any 'internal approach, more appropriate to the field of management science, such as could inquire how enterprises do and should behave in ordering their internal operations and would attempt to instruct them accordingly'. As this indicates, the would-be importer of IO to the strategy field confronted a basic translation problem, deriving from the explicit dissociation from any 'internal approach, more appropriate to the field of management science'.

Furthermore, IO was fundamentally static, did not seriously consider the diversified firm, saw the firm as a unitary decision maker, had an industry – rather than a firm – focus, operated with perfect competition as the ultimate yardstick for purposes of welfare comparisons and so on (Scherer, 1980; Porter, 1981). This was much in contrast to the mainstream of the strategy literature that from its emergence at the beginning of the 1960s saw strategy as involving entrepreneurial action in an uncertain and 'hard-to-predict' environment (Ansoff, 1965), did not neglect the large, diversified corporation (Chandler, 1962), was very much concerned with the internal workings of the firm (Bower, 1970) and so on.

Although Porter was well aware of the problems this raised for an application of IO to the strategy discipline (Porter, 1981), many of the unfortunate characteristics of IO did in fact carry over to his industry analysis approach (Porter, 1980). An example is the black-box conceptualization of the firm that is characteristic of older IO and which is clearly present in his best known book, *Competitive Strategy* (1980). Another one is the implicit equilibrium orientation: the focus is implicitly on non-cooperative equilibria where firms earn rents from their market power because of their ability to engage in tactics designed to build and maintain mobility and entry barriers.

With respect to the first problem, proponents of the resource-based perspective (such as Barney, 1991) have seen the neglect of the resource and capability side of firms as a major weakness of the Porter (1980) industry analysis approach. In contrast, they have not criticized the second problem, namely the underlying equilibrium orientation of the industry framework, because the resource-based approach is itself based on equilibrium economics, as we shall see later. For the moment, let us concentrate on the first problem.

Admittedly, it may be analytically permissible to 'black box' the firm for some purposes, such as, perhaps, understanding short-run business strategy in well-defined business environments. This may be so, because such issues do not necessarily involve significant changes in the firm's stock of resources. But this procedure may block understanding in other respects, such as explaining the direction of the firm's diversification activities (Montgomery and Wernerfelt, 1988), the inter-firm (imitation) barriers that block the equalization of rents among firms (Rumelt, 1984; Wernerfelt, 1984) and the growth strategies of firms (Penrose, 1959). Understanding such issues makes it necessary to treat the resource side of firms in some detail. However, this is arguably not fully recognized either in the next approach we consider, namely the new industrial organization.

2.1.2. The new industrial organization

The upsurge in work within the new IO took place at the beginning of the 1980s. Most research has been concerned with game-theoretic studies of behaviour and performance in imperfectly competitive markets (Tirole, 1988; Shapiro, 1989; Schmalensee and Willig, 1989; Saloner, 1994). More specifically, scholars specify a game among competing firms and solve that game using the concept of Nash equilibrium or one of its refinements (such as 'sub game perfection'). According to prominent new IO scholar, Carl Shapiro (1989), recent work in new IO can virtually be identified with 'the theory of business strategy'. Indeed, he goes as far as asserting that 'At this time, game theory provides the only coherent way of logically analyzing strategic behavior' (ibid., p.125). 'Strategic behavior', in this approach, means engaging in behaviour that by influencing rivals' expectations of one's future behaviour is able to significantly influence the behaviour of those rivals to the benefit of the strategizing firm.

Although the Porter industry analysis framework is not identical to the new IO, they have a common ancestor in older IO, and share many assumptions and concerns. In some ways, however, the new IO represents a distinct advance relative to the Porter framework. For example, firms in the new IO are not homogeneous. Thus they may differ not only in terms of their cost structures but also in terms of, for example, their reputations (Tirole, 1988, p.256). Moreover, the notions of factor/resource indivisibility and immobility become central, primarily because these notions play a key role in understanding entry deterrence and, more generally, the notions of credible threats and commitments.

In spite of these advances relative to the industry analysis approach, the new IO still suffers from weaknesses when perceived through the lens of market process theories. Most notably, there is no notion of an entrepreneurial discovery procedure (Kirzner, 1973), in the sense that firm managers are not supposed to discover and act on new opportunities in the market. Everything is essentially given from the beginning and specified by the analyst. Although the decision problem that strategizers confront in such models may be a good deal more complicated (because they have to consider extremely complicated game trees) than standard maximizing problems, everything is still presumed to be given to the decision maker/strategizer.

We can see this more specifically, if we ask, for example, why firms differ in the new IO. In general, the most important reasons for firms differing are that they (a) are placed in different environments, (b) come equipped with different initial endowments, (c) learn differently, and (d) are subject to different discretionary actions from management. Points (c) and (d) are the ones highlighted in market process theories, while point (a) is an explanation of firm heterogeneity in the industry analysis approach,[3] and point (b) represents the new IO approach to accounting for variety. Thus in new IO models of technological competition, firms make different *initial* R&D draws, face different constraints and incentives, and accordingly make different strategies (Tirole, 1988, chap.10). In contrast, points (c) and (d) are not featured in new IO as explanations of firm heterogeneity. Rather, the differences are already there, as it were, and do not change.

In this view, strategy becomes primarily a matter of deploying given resources to a product market, and utilizing them in sophisticated plays and counter-plays. Strategy becomes a matter of extracting maximum monopoly rents out of 'fixed factors over the planning horizon' (Caves, 1984, p.128). Thus firms in the new IO are clearly different, but the sources of heterogeneity are given and fixed; firms do not themselves create their own opportunity set. To some extent, this is because the agents that populate the new IO models are incredibly smart. Here a strategy involves anticipating any and all actions that other players might take in all future stages of the game, and calculating the optimal response. Since all players are able to do this, the equilibrium position is essentially given from the beginning. Players cannot be surprised by unexpected events, there is never any difference between the competence of players and the difficulty of decision problems, and although agents may formally learn in Bayesian games, their learning functions never change. This means that there cannot be any failed strategies and wrong conjectures, there is no need for restructuring organizations in the face of, for example, new competition from innovative entrants, no 'emergent' (unintended) strategies (Mintzberg, 1994), and no accumulation of resources (except as represented in a trivial way by learning by doing). But it also means that we cannot address endogenous firm heterogeneity in the context of the new IO. The problem, fundamentally, is that there is no notion of an entrepreneurial market process in the new IO; it too suffers from a market theory problem.

2.1.3. The resource-based perspective

In little more than a decade, the resource-based perspective (the RBP) has emerged as arguably the dominant modern approach to strategy (content) research – as perhaps the new orthodoxy in strategy research inspired by economics. The resource-based analysis of (sustained) competitive advantages may be seen as starting out from two basic empirical generalizations, namely that there are systematic differences across firms in the extent to which they control resources that are necessary for implementing strategies, and that these differences are relatively stable. The basic structure of the RBP emerges when these two generalizations are combined with fundamental assumptions that are to a large extent derived from economics. Among these assumptions are that differences in firms' resource endowments cause performance differences, and that firms seek to increase their economic performance.

The overall managerial implication is that firms may secure a strong performance by building or otherwise acquiring certain endowments of resources. More generally, the overall objective that informs the RBP is to account for the creation, maintenance and renewal of competitive advantage in terms of the resource side of firms. The fundamentals of the resource-based analysis of the conditions for sustained competitive advantage are basically simple (Peteraf, 1993): in order that resources yield a sustained competitive advantage, they should meet four basic criteria.

1. *Heterogeneity*: in lieu of efficiency differences across resources, there cannot be any differences in the rents which firms earn (in fact, there cannot be any rents at all). This indicates that resource heterogeneity, leading to

efficiency differences and therefore rents, is a basic necessary condition for competitive advantage.[4]

2. *Ex ante limits to competition*: resources have to be acquired at a price below their discounted net present value in order to yield rents. Otherwise, future rents will be fully absorbed in the price paid for the resource (Demsetz, 1973; Barney, 1986; Rumelt, 1987).
3. *Ex post limits to competition*: it should be difficult or impossible for competitors to imitate or substitute rent-yielding resources. As Dierickx and Cool (1989) clarify, there are a number of mechanisms at work that often make it hard for competitors to copy the sources of competitive advantage of a successful firm. For example, there may be 'causal ambiguity', which means that competitors confront difficulties ascertaining precisely how a bundle of resources contributes to success.
4. *Imperfect mobility*: the resource should be relatively specific to the firm. Otherwise, the superior bargaining position that is obtained from not being tied to a firm can be utilized by the resource (or the resource's owner) to appropriate the rent (or, at least a large portion of the rent) that the resource helps create. In other words, the key question to ask here is: who captures value from the resource, and how may the firm capture more value from this resource?

Several things are noteworthy about this basic analysis. First, it explicitly draws on economics, more precisely on basic, economic equilibrium price theory as set out in any standard textbook on the subject. Second, it actually tells us very little of direct value for understanding the more dynamic and managerial aspects of competitive advantage. For example, the analysis is painted with too broad a brush to be directly helpful in connection with issues relating to the renewal of competitive advantage. As this indicates, the RBP, too, suffers from a market theory problem, and again the reason has to do with the role of equilibrium assumptions.

It is easy to discern the role of equilibrium assumptions in the RBP. For example, Peteraf (1993) develops the concept of Ricardian rent using efficiency differences across firms under competitive equilibrium as a benchmark. And Barney (1986) utilizes the finance concepts of strong and weak efficiency to elucidate the reasoning behind the concepts of perfect factor markets and factor market imperfections. Indeed, the very concept of sustained competitive advantage is often defined in equilibrium terms: it is that advantage which lasts after all attempts at imitation have ceased. So (zero imitation) equilibrium is utilized as a yardstick to define and understand (sustained) competitive advantage.

But there is an apparent problem here. For using an equilibrium notion to define the concept of sustained competitive advantage implies that the concept loses direct contact with reality. For example, sustainability is not a matter of calendar time. It is a matter of the 'logical time' of equilibrium models, and cannot be directly translated into real time.[5] Furthermore, sustained competitive advantage exists only in (zero imitation) equilibrium (cf. Lippman and Rumelt, 1982); it simply makes no sense to speak of sustained competitive advantage outside of equilibrium, because equilibrium is defined as the absence of imitation. Given that one of the central aims of the resource-based perspective is to uncover the sources of sustained competitive advantage (Barney, 1991; Peteraf, 1993) in terms of concepts such as rareness, non-imitability, non-substitutability and so on, and of resources and capabilities, it appears that much of the important structure of the resource-based perspective is solidly founded on equilibrium methodology. This has the implication, unfortunately, that sustained competitive advantage has no meaning outside equilibrium, and that the concept is hard to operationalize. Thus the market theory problem again raises its ugly head – this time in the RBP.[6]

2.2. The Role of Equilibrium: Useful Benchmark or Hindrance for Theorizing?

It is necessary to understand that equilibrium theories may take different forms. It is one thing to say that all phenomena should be represented as if always in equilibrium – what we may call 'the equilibrium always world'. And it is quite another thing to admit equilibrium as a legitimate tool of analysis, for example, as a state that real-world markets are constantly tending towards (but perhaps not reaching) – a much softer notion of equilibrium, and one that many market process economists (and the present authors) would have no difficulties accepting.

Most strategy content research inspired by economics tends to adopt the hard version of equilibrium. Most notably, this is the case of both strategy research inspired by the new IO (for example, Ghemawat, 1997) and the RBP. Admittedly, both streams of literature suggest a *starting point* for the strategy process in the analysis of the industry or the company's resource endowment, respectively. However, neither of them provides any insight into the strategy process per se. More critically, perhaps, they implicitly suggest that the strategy process can somehow be separated from the content of a strategy, and that implementing strategy is trivial.

In contrast, we shall later argue that, if we begin from the market process premise that in *any* social system knowledge is subjective, partly tacit and dispersed, (a) it does not make sense to suppress process issues and concentrate on equilibrium only, (b) it is not legitimate to separate the strategy process from strategy content, and (c) it is not legitimate to neglect implementation issues. Even strategy content research is likely to be biased in a too narrow direction by the 'equilibrium always' assumption. This is because there are determinants of competitive advantage that only become visible in a process perspective, such as the ability in a big firm to make extensive use of dispersed, subjectively held and tacit knowledge in that firm.

The suppression of process is but one shortcoming in equilibrium-based strategy research. Another one is the tendency to see firms as unitary actors. If indeed the world is always in equilibrium, not only markets, but also the internal (principal-agent) relations between the agents who supply inputs (notably, work inputs) to the firm are in equilibrium. 'Equilibrium' in the latter sense means that incentives have been aligned through compensation schemes and so on. Given this, it makes sense to treat the firm as a unitary actor. However, the whole process of internal jockeying, aligning behaviours and the rest, which is a crucial aspect of strategy formation and implementation, is suppressed. Thus as in Porter's (1980, 1985) industry analysis approach, strategy is reduced to big decisions of firms-understood-as-unitary-actors, whether they concern product differentiation, cost leadership or focus (cf. Barney, 1994).

Although resource-based analysis explicitly starts from the assumption of firm heterogeneity, it is assumed in this approach that 'firms within an industry may possess different strategically relevant skills and capabilities . . . Skills and capabilities that enable the organization to conceive of, choose and implement strategies that exploit environmental opportunities' (Barney, 1994, p.67). Again, we have the implicit view of the firm as a unitary actor, which is also characteristic of other equilibrium approaches to strategy. And again we have the implicit supposition that all intra-firm agency-type problems, knowledge gaps and so on have been eliminated and all behaviours have been aligned.

By contrast, once we recognize that firms are multi-person coalitions populated by asymmetrically informed individuals who perceive the world subjectively, and that subjective knowledge and learning processes need to be somehow coordinated for successful strategy formation (Mintzberg, 1994), these separations begin to blur. For then the very activity of carrying through a strategic planning exercise may yield competitive advantage through the added knowledge it may bring top management of dispersed knowledge and learning processes in the firm.

Given the shortcomings of equilibrium-oriented strategy content research – that is, what we have called 'the market theory problem' – we seriously question the soundness of this research strategy. There are, in our view, no compelling logical or ontological reasons for such a commitment. In fact, we argue that the 'equilibrium always' strategy may be a serious hindrance to theorizing, precisely because of the market theory problem. For example, as already suggested, a tight connection between the understanding of competitive advantage and the 'equilibrium always' assumption surely hinders understanding a number of real-world phenomena. As a general matter, we are cut off from approaching the disequilibrium aspect of competitive advantage; for example, maintaining competitive advantage through engaging in learning and innovation activities. These activities involve, by definition, novelties in the sense of the acquisition or creation of novel knowledge – and such novelties are hard to force into an equilibrium straitjacket.

Equilibrium models may undeniably be useful in connection with tracing the effects of the creation of new knowledge – for example, the effects on factor prices of the creation and diffusion of new technical knowledge – but they tell us next to nothing about the process of creation and coordination of knowledge. Thus equilibrium concepts may also introduce a static bias and they may, if used in a too heavy-handed way, hinder understanding of process (disequilibrium) phenomena within the firm and within the market. Strategy is very much a matter of exploiting and perhaps initiating periods of disequilibrium and we wish to theorize this aspect of strategy, too. In our view, this necessitates that we turn to non-mainstream economics, more precisely to what we here call 'market process economics'.

3. AN ALTERNATIVE VIEW: MARKET PROCESS ECONOMICS

3.1. What is Market Process Economics?

Although Williamson (1986, p.94) observed that 'The proposition that process matters is widely resisted and has attracted little concerted research attention from economists', not everybody has resisted this 'proposition' and there has been some 'concerted' research effort,[7] taking place under the banner of 'market process economics' (Boettke and Prychitko, 1998). This line of thought includes the Austrian school of economics (for example, Mises, 1949; Hayek, 1948; Kirzner, 1973; Lachmann, 1986) and evolutionary (Nelson and Winter, 1982), Schumpeterian (Schumpeter, 1912) and post-Marshallian economics (Loasby, 1991), as well as some contributions with a more formal, neoclassical character (for example, Fisher, 1983). Fundamentally, these streams attempt to conceptualize and understand the mechanisms that drive disequilibrium processes of change, although these mechanisms are conceptualized somewhat differently among the streams.[8] In the following, we provide a detailed description of market process economics.

3.2. The Market Process

Our core concept is that of 'market process' understood in the sense of active rivalry (Kirzner, 1997). In contrast, there is a tendency in mainstream economics to conceptualize competition in terms of consistency of maximizing decisions taken by consumers and producers. Thus competition is understood in terms of equilibrium (competitive equilibrium). Moreover, since equilibrium basically means a state of rest (at least in older conceptualizations), this conceptualization gives a distinctly static character to the concept of competition (but see Vickers, 1995). However, as Friedrich Hayek noted more than 50 years ago, the economist's equilibrium understanding of competition differs significantly from lay understanding (Hayek, 1948, p.96):

> The peculiar nature of the assumptions from which the theory of competitive equilibrium starts stands out very clearly if we ask which of the activities that are commonly designated by the verb 'to compete' would still be possible if those conditions were all satisfied . . . I believe that the answer is exactly none. Advertising, undercutting, and improving ('differentiating') the goods and services are all excluded by definition – 'perfect' competition means indeed the absence of all competitive activities.

Furthermore, Hayek argued that, by portraying competition as a tranquil state rather than as a rivalrous process, what we want from competition, and how we get it, becomes basically obscured. If competition is indeed best understood in static terms (that is, as a state characterized by large numbers of sellers and buyers, perfect information, consistency between the maximizing decisions of consumers and producers, with the implied welfare properties) – then it is not necessarily unreasonable to think that this situation can best be achieved by public intervention (for example, market socialism), or, at least, that public policies can help society approximate the competitive equilibrium. But this basically misconstrues the nature of competition, what we can expect to get out of competition, and how competition is best promoted. Briefly, competition should not be understood as a static state of affairs, but as a rivalrous process. More specifically, competition is fundamentally a procedure for discovering (ibid., p.97) '*who* will serve us well: which grocer or travel agency, which department store or hotel, which doctor or solicitor, we can expect to provide the most satisfactory solution for whatever personal problem we may have to face'.

3.3. Knowledge and Entrepreneurship

Such knowledge is not in any meaningful sense *given* to a single mind who can somehow disseminate it across the economy and make sure that it is efficiently utilized; we rely on competition as the mechanism for mobilizing and disseminating such dispersed knowledge. It is important to appreciate that, when Austrians and other market process theorists talk about dispersed knowledge, what they have in mind is not 'imperfect' or 'asymmetric information' as these are understood in mainstream economics (for example, Nalebuff and Stiglitz, 1983). Although these are important analytical categories, there is a further category that is not treated in mainstream economics, namely sheer (or unknown) ignorance. Becoming aware of something (for example, a profit opportunity) that one had previously overlooked (and not *searched* for) is what is meant by discovery. Kirzner's argument (which is discussed more fully below) is then that the competitive market is a superior setting for generating entrepreneurial discoveries through the exercise of alertness. For, although the entrepreneur may not search for any profit opportunity in particular, the lure of pure profit may nevertheless lead him to continually scan the horizon, as it were (Kirzner, 1997, p.72).

We rely, in short, on competition because it is an effective procedure for discovering knowledge that we do not yet know is available or, indeed, needed at all (Hayek, 1968). To the extent that this is the social function of competition, it is to misconstrue competition to portray it as a state in which each market participant has either deterministically perfect or stochastically perfect knowledge. More broadly, it is to misunderstand the character of the economic problem facing society (Hayek, 1945, p.78):

> The peculiar character of the problem of a rational economic order is determined precisely by the fact that the knowledge of the circumstances of which we must make use never exists in concentrated or integrated form but solely as the dispersed bits of incomplete and frequently contradictory knowledge which all the separate individuals possess. The economic problem of society is thus not merely a problem of how to allocate 'given' resources – if 'given' is taken to mean given to a single mind which deliberately solves the problem set by these 'data'. It is rather a problem of how to secure the best use of resources known to any of the members of society, for ends whose relative importance only these individuals know. Or, to put it briefly, it is a problem of the utilization of knowledge which is not given to anyone in its totality.

What seems to have prompted the emergence of these insights is Hayek's involvement during the 1930s in a debate on the economic feasibility of socialism, now called 'the socialist calculation debate' (Lavoie, 1985). Hayek's socialist opponents here either maintained that all relevant knowledge could in fact be centralized, or, if it could not, the problem could be solved by telling socialist managers to obey simple price-setting rules that would lead to an optimal allocation of resources.

Against this, Hayek argued that the market socialists basically overlooked (a) problems of incentive compatibility, (b) tacit local knowledge (which could not be centralized) and (c) the need for rapid adaptation to unexpected contingencies/novelties (which made centralization inefficient). With respect to the last point, (Hayek, 1945, pp.83–4) observed that:

> If we can agree that the economic problem of society is mainly one of rapid adaptation to changes in the particular circumstances of time and place, it would seem to follow that the ultimate decisions must be left to the people who are familiar with these circumstances, who know directly of the relevant changes and of the resources immediately available to meet them. We cannot expect that this problem will be solved by first communicating all this knowledge to a central board which, after integrating all knowledge, issues its orders.

Hayek's point, of course, is that a 'central board' is not at all necessary: a market system, meaning a system with alienable property rights, promotes a tendency towards allocating property rights to those who can make best use of them and competition ensures that best use is indeed made of these rights.

3.4. Action and Entrepreneurship

However, it has been left to Israel Kirzner (1973, 1992) in particular to elaborate the details of the Austrian view of the market process. In doing this, he has put primary emphasis on the entrepreneur. As Kirzner (1973, p.14) argues 'our confidence in the market's ability to learn and to harness the continuous flow of information to generate the market process depends crucially on our belief in the benign presence of the entrepreneurial element'. The foundation of this claim lies in Kirzner's distinction between 'Robbinsian maximizing' and 'entrepreneurial alertness'. The first behavioural category conforms to the standard picture of economic man as basically applying given means to best satisfy given but conflicting ends in a fundamentally mechanical way (Robbins, 1932). Since everything is given, action becomes purely a matter of calculation. Kirzner points out that, within this conceptualization of behaviour, the discovery of new means, of new ends, and the setting up of new means-ends structures simply cannot be rationalized.

As a result, the dynamic market process cannot be understood in terms of the passive mode of behaviour of Robbinsian maximizing; we need another behavioural quality, the quality of entrepreneurial alertness to hitherto unexploited profit opportunities. This alertness factor ranges from the discovery of a ten dollar bill on the street to the discovery of a need for a new, potentially extremely profitable, drug. Thus entrepreneurs are discoverers; they discover new resource uses, new products, new markets, new possibilities for arbitrage: in short, new possibilities for profitable trade.

Combining his notion of entrepreneurial behaviour with Hayek's notion of the market as a dynamic process, Kirzner paints a broad picture of the market process as a continual process of entrepreneurial discovery of hitherto unnoticed opportunities for pure profit. The profits earned in this process are discovered profits – profits that are earned because of the discovery, creation and exploitation of profit opportunities that would not be grasped in the absence of entrepreneurial activity. Thus the entrepreneurial function is beneficial because it alleviates the problem introduced by the division of knowledge. It is not only that entrepreneurial activity reduces our lack of knowledge about which products, processes, new organizational forms and so on are needed; it is more fundamentally that entrepreneurial activity alleviates our ignorance about what we do not know.

3.5. Summing Up

So far we have argued that the dominant approaches to firm strategy build on equilibrium economics and an understanding of competition that is derived from it. We have suggested that this perspective on firm strategy has several shortcomings when it comes to conceptualizing what strategy is about and how successful strategies emerge. Thus an 'equilibrium always' perspective runs into what we have called 'the market theory problem', which in the present context refers to the inability to make sense out of the disequilibrium aspects of competitive advantage, and also, we wish to add, the inability to conceptualize the strategy process.

The purpose of the present section has been to present an alternative view of competition: that contained in market process economics. In this view competition is driven by the combined forces of (a) entrepreneurial discovery of given, but previously undiscovered, profit opportunities (Kirzner, 1973), (b) market creation based on new entrepreneurial resource combinations (Schumpeter, 1912) and (c) market making (Casson, 1982). Markets and competition become a matter of learning and discovery in an essentially uncertain context (Kirzner, 1992). This view suggests a different understanding of competitive advantage. Competitive advantage fundamentally results from the subjective perception of profit opportunities, the creation and exploitation of uncertainty, and the coordination of learning and knowledge. Table 6.1 summarizes a number of the crucial differences between a market process view and an equilibrium view.

Table 6.1 Differences between a market process view and an equilibrium view

	Equilibrium economics	Market process economics
Role of equilibrium	All economic phenomena must be portrayed as if in equilibria: 'Equilibrium always'	At most a state towards which some tendencies in the market reach
The entrepreneur	Not considered	Crucial; the driving force of the market process
Knowledge	Information: asymmetric and imperfect, but at least stochastically given; given learning functions	Subjective, dispersed and tacit; surprises take place; genuine uncertainty
Cognition	Uniform	Differential (subjectivism)
Innovation	Excluded, or exogenous; not of substantial importance	Included, endogenous; of crucial importance, new resource combination
Institutions	Embody incentives	Embody incentives and reduce uncertainty
The market	A costless price mechanism working through auctioneer, common knowledge, etc	A costly discovery, coordination and learning process
Adaptation	Simultaneous	Sequential
Competition	Action within known contexts, such as price taking	Creation of new markets, innovation, discovery
Competitive advantage	Based on equilibrium	Based on mobilization of locally dispersed intelligence, creation and utilization of disequilibrium

In the following section, we argue that it makes a difference to the way we conceive of the task of building theories in strategic management whether we take our starting point in equilibrium economics or in market process theories. In particular, we (a) discuss the affinity between cognitive theories of strategizing and market process theory, (b) consider the implications for linking strategy content to process, (c) illustrate some implications for advances in strategy research, (d) advocate a new understanding of competitive advantage based on a market process perspective.

4. STRATEGIZING, THE MARKET PROCESS AND COMPETITIVE ADVANTAGE

The key issue to be addressed here is: how does it make a difference that we rely on market process economics rather than on equilibrium economics when theorizing about strategy? Our argument proceeds along the following lines. First, although several authors have called for a theory of strategy that integrates strategy content (to what end should strategy processes work?) and process research (how does the strategy process proceed?), this integration is still missing to a large extent. Secondly, we argue that an integration of strategy content and process research may best proceed on a set of shared assumptions. Building on market process assumptions regarding individual cognition, the dispersion of knowledge, and entrepreneurial imagination and discovery is crucial for a dynamic theory of competitive advantage and a coherent theory of strategy. This view is supported by a number of management scholars who have called for a more process-oriented and cognitive-oriented strategic management research. Thirdly, joining the insights of market process economics and cognitive strategy process research, we can envision a coherent theory of strategy to advance. To this end we tentatively suggest that strategy content consists of (a) the utilization of opportunities for spatial and intertemporal arbitrage, (b) the discovery and imagination of new resource combinations, based on which (c) new markets are created. We also discuss intra-firm processes that may support such outcomes.

4.1. Linking Strategy Process to Strategy Content Research

Recently, a number of influential management scholars (for example, Pettigrew, 1992) have forcefully argued that strategy research should treat the two dimensions of strategy (content and process) in a more integrated manner. For example, with Dan Schendel (1992, p.2) we may ask, when the 'challenge is to use administrative process to shape or develop good strategy, and then go on to develop those processes necessary to use the strategy to operate the firm . . . does it make sense to construct dichotomies of content and process?' Using stronger words, Andrew Pettigrew (1992, p.6) urges us to 'to abandon the intellectual trap . . . in classifying strategy research into content and process domains', and argues that this is necessary for the strategy field to proceed. Moreover, when content research is increasingly concerned with more dynamic questions (Porter, 1994; Rumelt *et al.*, 1994; Nelson, 1994; Prahalad and Hamel, 1994), questions about the interrelation between strategy content and process become much more pressing.

While we agree with the call of the above authors to join research in strategy content and process, cognitively oriented strategy process researchers have so far hardly linked their process theories to traditional strategy content research. That the two streams of strategy research have developed rather independently from each other is the less surprising the more we understand that both rest on fundamentally incompatible assumptions which makes fruitful integration difficult. Traditionally, strategy content research rests on equilibrium assumptions, whereas cognitively oriented strategy process research – like market process theory – tries to account for the dynamic coordination of subjective knowledge and learning. An integration of strategy process and strategy content research will be impeded as long as strategy content research remains committed to equilibrium reasoning. This is because existing strategy process research already emphasizes dispersed knowledge, subjectivity and disequilibrium, while traditional strategy content research precisely eliminates such process phenomena by importing equilibrium assumptions. In our view, this suggests that market process economics may be an attractive substitute on the basis of which to advance integrated process and content research in the realm of strategy.

4.2. Shared Assumptions and Point of Views

In contrast to equilibrium-based strategy content research, much cognitive strategy process research is already based on assumptions that are similar to or compatible with those of market process economics. Although theories of the strategy process (for example, Burgelman, 1994; Hurst *et al.*, 1989; Mintzberg, 1994; Nonaka, 1994; Huff *et al.*, 1992; Hamel, 1996; Aadne and Mahnke, 1998) focus on different issues, such as participation (top management versus wider participation), directionality (top-down versus bottom-up) and speed (incremental adjustment versus revolution, punctuated change), taken together they argue in favour of the positions that (a) knowledge in firms is dispersed, partly tacit and subjectively held; (b) managerial attention spans are limited; (c) the strategy process is to a large extent a process of coordinating dispersed knowledge and learning; (d) cognitive processes of imagining and developing the company's own future road map are important, and (e) strategic realities in organizations are developed through the complex interaction between subjective cognitive processes and tangible or objective elements in the environment. Table 6.2 illustrates the affinity of assumption between market process theory and recent findings in modern strategy process research.

Table 6.2 Affinities between market process economics and strategy process research

	Market process economics	Strategy process research
The entrepreneur	Crucial; the driving force of the market process	Intrapreneurship unleashes existing and untapped ideas and potentials through autonomous and unplanned initiative (Hamel, 1996; Burgelman, 1994)
Knowledge and cognition	Subjective, dispersed and tacit; surprises take place; genuine uncertainty	A strategy process that avoids cognitive rigidities and inertia involves managers and employees who are able to perceive strategic issues through different lenses (Hurst *et al.*, 1989; Huff *et al.*, 1992)
Innovation	Included, endogenous; of crucial importance, new resource combination	Innovation can be understood as a process in which firms create new problems and then actively develop knowledge to solve them (Nonaka, 1994, p.14)
The market process	A costly discovery, coordination and learning process	The strategy process mobilizes dispersed knowledge, and involves coadaptive learning (Aadne and Mahnke, 1998)
Adaptation	Sequentially emergent patterns	The strategy process involves not first grand design and later implementation; it is a process where patterns of action emerge (Mintzberg, 1994)
Competition	Creation of new markets, innovation, discovery	The strategy process leads to imagination and market foresight (Prahalad and Hamel, 1990, 1994)

4.3. Integrating the Dimensions of Strategy Research

An advanced theory of strategy integrates strategy content and process based on a set a realistic assumptions. Since strategy content derives from a theory of competition, and market process theory offers such a theory which is already based on assumptions similar to modern strategy process research, we argue that a more integrated theory of strategy may usefully subscribe to this underlying view of competition. In such a perspective, strategy processes in the company would support strategy content, exemplified by (a) the utilization of opportunities for spatial and intertemporal arbitrage, (b) the discovery and imagination of new resource combinations, based on which (c) new markets are created. Figure 6.1 illustrates how an integrated strategy research agenda might proceed.

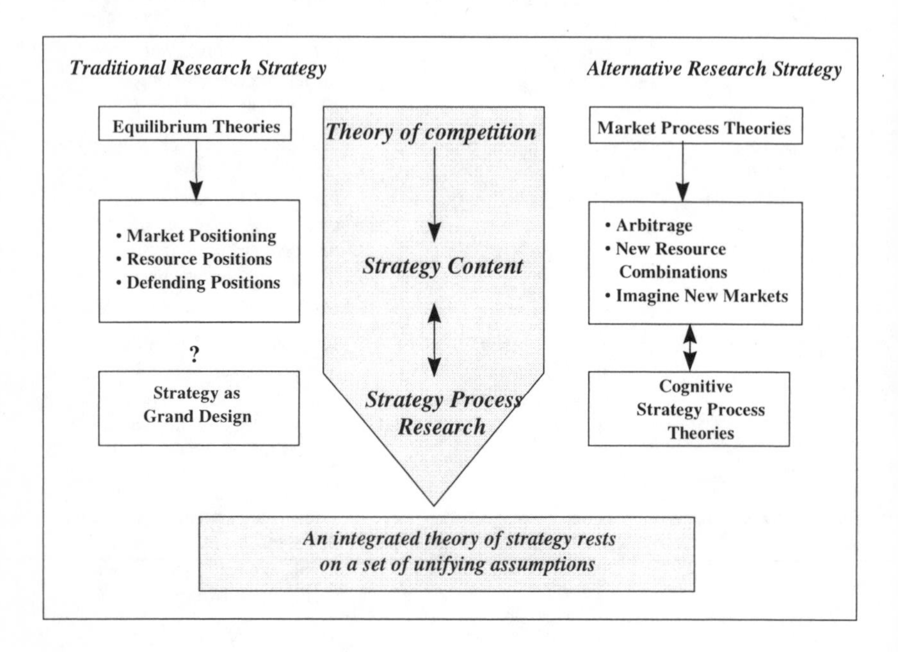

Figure 6.1 Alternative research strategies

As we have repeatedly argued, much strategy research clearly suffers from a market theory problem. Here we suggest that this also causes a problem with conceptualizing and understanding the strategy process. Although the theories of strategic content that we have discussed offer insights into where strategy analysis might start (for example, a given industry, the firm's resource endowment), they have next to nothing to say about how strategy formation proceeds. In that type of strategy research that relies on equilibrium economics, the strategy process becomes reduced to an initial grand design. The formulation of strategy, in this view, starts from analysing a well-defined problem set on the basis of which strategy is first formulated and then executed in a straightforward manner. In this view there is also a basic optimism that the knowledge that it is necessary to control in order to formulate and implement such a grand strategy design can in fact be centralized, accumulated and prepared for top management decisions in central planning departments. This picture of strategy leaves out several important questions, for example how local knowledge is mobilized for strategic outcomes, whether it can be aggregated for decision making at all, how intrapreneurship brings about emergent opportunities, and whether strategy is adequately seen as choice in well-defined decision arenas.

Some of these points are clearly reminiscent of the Austrian critique in the socialist calculation debate and it is not surprising to find strategy theorist Henry Mintzberg (1994) arguing against the rationalistic pretences of the so-called 'design school' (of Ansoff and others) in terms that are plainly Hayekian. Large-scale strategic planning exercises of the sort that were in vogue at the end of the 1960s have now fallen out of fashion. This is because they did not deliver what they promised and because they received sustained criticism from the likes of Mintzberg and Quinn, who employed arguments against 'grand design' type strategic planning in firms that were closely akin to those employed by Hayek in his critique of large-scale socialist planning. However, many firms continue to do strategic planning, albeit of a more limited scope, which suggests that there must be something valuable in the activity. Clearly, this has something to do with the sense of direction and motivation that the process of articulating a strategy may provide. But, more importantly, there are other reasons that have to do with the question from which assumptions strategy works.

Leaving aside the traditional perspective on strategy which rests on equilibrium assumptions, the alternative view on strategy works from the shared assumptions of cognitive theories of strategy process and market process theory, as outlined above. Seen from this alternative perspective, strategic planning takes on new meaning. Here strategic planning exercises are initiated to reveal dispersed knowledge and learning processes that top management were not aware of at all. While top management may not have direct access to this knowledge and learning, they may nevertheless, through direction, make use of it, for example by transferring it to other uses in the organization. Therefore, from a process perspective, a distinct advantage of the strategy process is not so much that it helps to give the firm direction, but that it stimulates the discovery of dispersed knowledge and learning in the firm.

Of course, from a market process perspective, the ability of top management to directly discover and make use of dispersed knowledge is narrowly circumscribed. Firms of even a moderate size confront a Hayekian knowledge problem, which is bound to produce outcomes that are, at least to some extent, unanticipated and unintended by top management. If management is unable to centralize all dispersed and tacit knowledge possessed by the employees, an implication will be that the latter will in general have a more fine-grained understanding of their environments than managers. In addition, they are likely to also know more about the realizations of their action sets. As Sautet (1998) points out, management confronts a 'double Hayekian knowledge problem': it is not just that it does not know what it does not know in the market; it is also the case that it does not know what it does not know about the firm's employees. The ability to solve the double Hayekian knowledge problem may be a critical source of competitive advantage.

The ability to do this, in turn, hinges on top management's luck and ability to stimulate a discovery process that is internal to the firm. In such a perspective, incentives have a different role relative to the role they play in the more standard economics of organization (for example, of the principal-agent variety): it is not so much a matter of bringing effort closer to a pre-specified level or of selecting an action out of an already known action set; rather, it is a matter of stimulating entrepreneurial alertness among the firm's employees, that is, of fostering a social learning process inside the firm.

A market process and subjectivist perspective also suggests that such organizational learning may be promoted by interaction among agents that hold different subjective conceptions. This implies that organizational learning may be an emergent property of the interaction of individual learning processes. Thus organizational learning is at least partly a spontaneous order. To the extent that stimulating and influencing organizational learning is an important strategic task and that the outcomes of organizational learning may have strategic value, this suggests why traditional thinking of strategy as grand design needs to be rethought to the extent that the assumptions made in market process theory and cognitive strategy process theory turn out to be valid.

5. CONCLUDING COMMENTS: TOWARDS A PROCESS THEORY OF COMPETITIVE ADVANTAGE

We began by noting that, conventionally, strategizing is seen as an activity aiming at the creation of sustained competitive advantage so that rent streams can be earned. The economics-inspired literature on firm strategy focuses on earning either monopoly rents or Ricardian rents, where both of these returns are evaluated relative to a perfect competition equilibrium. We have called this 'the equilibrium always view'. Moreover, the economics of strategy has so far had very little to say about the attainment of competitive advantage; what has captured the theorist's mind is the sustainability of rents in equilibrium.

The obvious (we think) problem with this is that the 'equilibrium always view' hinders understanding a number of issues that are crucial to understanding the emergence and sustainability of competitive advantage. This is what we called 'the market theory problem'. In contrast, we have argued that a market process view is likely to substantially change the way we think about competitive advantage. Most notably, we can find room for entrepreneurship, endogenous change and returns that stem from exploiting disequilibrium conditions. More methodologically, there are numerous appealing overlaps between market process theory and recent strategy process research that may constitute a platform for aligning process and content research in strategy with market process theory. Together, these may help to rethink competitive advantage based on an integrated theory of strategy.

NOTES

1. We are grateful to our colleagues in LINK for inspiration and discussion.
2. It is customary in the strategy literature to make a rather sharp distinction between 'strategy content research' (that is, what is or should be the product of strategizing processes) and 'strategy process research' (that is, the process through which a strategy is actually arrived at). We shall later argue that this separation is less watertight than it may look.
3. And, we may add, in conventional economics as well.
4. An alternative formulation – put forward by Barney (1991) – is that, with homogeneous resources, all firms can implement the same strategies; hence, no firm can differentiate itself from other firms, and nobody will have a competitive advantage.
5. Barney (1991, p.102) explicitly makes this point. For discussions of the complex issue of time in economic models, see Shackle (1972) and O'Driscoll and Rizzo (1985).
6. In fairness, it should be noted that many researchers have seen it as a distinct advantage of the RBP that it helped aligning strategy and economic equilibrium. As Spender (1993, p.42) noted in a related context 'The notion of rents is simply a way of bringing the homogeneity of economic thought together with the heterogeneity of the real world'. For example, if information costs are positive, we can have an equilibrium with firms of different efficiencies and rents (and therefore different competitive advantages) and we can perform the usual comparative static exercises in this setting (Demsetz, 1973, Lippman and Rumelt, 1982). Moreover, equilibrium, in the eyes of writers such as Barney, is a useful benchmark, one that can be used for analysing factor market imperfections and sustained competitive advantage.
7. Historically, the suppression of process in economics is largely a post-Second World War phenomenon (Foss, 1994, 1996, 1997, 1997b; Machovec, 1995).
8. For example, evolutionary economics gives more attention to forces of inertia than Austrian economics does.

REFERENCES

Aadne, J. and V. Mahnke (1998), 'The Role of Speed and Breakdown in the Process of Strategic Renewal', *Academy of Best Papers Proceedings*, St. Diego.

Ansoff, I. (1965), *Corporate Strategy: An Analytical Approach to Business Policy for Growth and Expansion,* New York: McGraw-Hill.

Bain, J. (1959), *Industrial Organization*, New York: Wiley.

Barney, J. (1986), 'Strategic Factor Markets', *Management Science,* **32**, 1231–41.

Barney, J. (1991), 'Firm Resources and Sustained Competitive Advantage', *Journal of Management,* **17**, 99–120.

Barney, J. (1994), 'Beyond Individual Metaphors in Understanding How Firms Behave: A Comment on Game Theory and Prospect Theory Models of Firm Behaviour', in R. Rumelt, D. Schendel and D. Teece (eds), *Fundamental Issues in Strategy*, Boston: Harvard Business School Press.

Boettke, P. and D. Prychitko (eds) (1998), *Market Process Theories,* 2 vols, Cheltenham, UK and Lyme, US: Edward Elgar.

Bower, J. (1970), *Managing the Resource Allocation Process*, Boston: Harvard University Press.

Burgelman, R. (1994), 'Fading Memories: a Process Theory of Strategic Business Exit in Dynamic Environments', *Administrative Science Quarterly*, **39** (1), 24–56.

Casson, M. (1982), *The Entrepreneur*, Oxford: Basil Blackwell.

Caves, R. (1984), 'Economic Analysis and the Quest for Competitive Advantage', *American Economic Review, Papers and Proceedings,* **74**, 127–32.

Chandler, A. (1962), *Strategy and Structure*, Cambridge, Mass.: MIT Press.

Demsetz, H. (1973), 'Industrial Structure, Market Rivalry and Public Policy', *Journal of Law and Economics*, **16**, 1–10.

Dierickx, I. and K. Cool (1989), 'Asset Stock Accumulation and Sustainability of Competitive Advantage', *Management Science*, **35**, 1504–11.

Fisher, F. (1983), *Disequilibrium Foundations for Equilibrium Economics*, Cambridge, Mass.: Cambridge University Press.

Foss, N. (1994) 'The Biological Analogy and the Theory of the Firm', *Journal of Economic Issues*, **18**, 1115–36; reprinted in G. Hodgson (ed.) (1998), *The Foundations of Evolutionary Economics*, Cheltenham, UK and Lyme, US: Edward Elgar.

Foss, N. (1996), 'Research in Strategy, Economics and Michael Porter', *Journal of Management Studies*, **33**, 1–24.

Foss, N. (1997), 'Austrian Insights and the Theory of the Firm', *Advances in Market Process Economics,* **4**, 175–98.

Foss, N. (1997b), *Resources and Strategy: A Reader*, Oxford: Oxford University Press.

Ghemawat, P. (1997), *Games Business Plays*, Cambridge, Mass.: MIT Press.

Ginsberg, A. (1994), 'Minding the Competition: From Mapping to Mastery', *Strategic Management Journal*, **15**, 153–74.

Hamel, G. (1996), 'Strategy as Revolution', *Harvard Business Review,* **2**, 56–73.

Hayek, F. (1945), 'The Use of Knowledge in Society', reprinted in *Individualism and Economic Order* (1948), Chicago: University of Chicago Press.

Hayek, F. (1948), *Individualism and Economic Order*, Chicago: University of Chicago Press.

Hayek, F. (1968), 'Competition as a Discovery Procedure', reprinted in *New Studies in Philosophy, Economics, Politics, and the History of Ideas* (1978), London: Routledge and Kegan Paul.

Huff, J., A. Huff and H. Thomas (1992), 'Strategic Renewal and the Interaction of Cumulative Stress and Inertia', *Strategic Management Journal*, **13**, 55–75.

Hurst, D., J. Rush and R. White (1989), 'Top Management Teams and Organizational Renewal', *Strategic Management Journal*, **10**, 87–105.

Kirzner, I. (1973), *Entrepreneurship and Competition,* Chicago: University of Chicago Press.

Kirzner, I. (1992), *The Meaning of the Market Process*, London: Routledge.

Kirzner, I. (1997), 'Entrepreneurial Discovery and the Competitive Market Process: An Austrian Approach', *Journal of Economic Literature,* **35**, 60–85.
Lachmann, L. (1986), *The Market as an Economic Process*, Oxford: Basil Blackwell.
Lavoie, D. (1985), *Rivalry and Central Planning*, Cambridge, Mass.: Cambridge University Press.
Lippman, S. and R. Rumelt (1982), 'Uncertain Imitability: An Analysis of Interfirm Differences Under Competition', *Bell Journal of Economics,* **13**, 418–38.
Loasby, B. (1976), *Choice, Complexity and Ignorance*, Cambridge, Mass.: Cambridge University Press.
Loasby, B. (1991), *Equilibrium and Evolution*, Manchester: Manchester University Press.
Machovec, F. (1995), *Perfect Competition and the Transformation of Economics*, London: Routledge.
Menger, C. (1871), *Principles of Economics*, New York: New York University Press.
Mintzberg, H. (1994), *The Rise and Fall of Strategic Planning*, New York: Prentice-Hall.
Mises, L. (1949), *Human Action: A Treatise on Economics*, New Haven: Yale University Press
Montgomery, C. and B. Wernerfelt (1988), 'Diversification, Ricardian Rents and Tobin's q', *Rand Journal of Economics,* **19**, 622–33.
Nalebuff, B. and J. Stiglitz (1983), 'Prizes and Incentives: Towards a General Theory of Compensation and Competition', *Bell Journal of Economics,* **14**, 21–43.
Nelson, R. (1994), 'Why do Firms Differ and How Does it Matter?', in R. Rumelt, D. Schendel and D. Teece (eds), *Fundamental Issues in Strategy*, Boston: Harvard Business School Press.
Nelson, R. and S. Winter (1982), *An Evolutionary Theory of Economic Change*, Cambridge, Mass.: The Belknap Press.
Nonaka, I. (1994), 'A Dynamic Theory of Organizational Knowledge Creation', *Organization Science*, **5**, 14–37.
Nonaka, I. and H. Takeuchi (1995), *The Knowledge-Creating Company*, Oxford: Oxford University Press.
O'Driscoll, G. and M. Rizzo (1985), *The Economics of Time and Ignorance*, Oxford: Basil Blackwell.
Penrose, E. (1959), *The Theory of the Growth of the Firm*, Oxford: Oxford University Press.
Peteraf, M. (1993), 'The Cornerstones of Competitive Advantage: A Resource-Based View', *Strategic Management Journal,* **14**, 179–91.
Pettigrew, A. (1992), 'The Character and Significance of Strategy Process Research', *Strategic Management Journal,* **13**, 5–16.
Porter, M. (1980), *Competitive Strategy*, New York: Free Press.
Porter, M. (1981), 'The Contributions of Industrial Organization to Strategic Management', *Academy of Management Review,* **6**, 609–20.
Porter, M. (1985), *Competitive Advantage*, New York: Free Press.
Porter, M. (1994), 'Towards a Dynamic Theory of Strategy', in R. Rumelt, D. Schendel and D. Teece (eds), *Fundamental Issues in Strategy*, Boston: Harvard Business School Press.
Prahalad, C. and G. Hamel (1990), 'The Core Competence of the Corporation', *Harvard Business Review,* **66**, 79–91.
Prahalad, C. and G. Hamel (1994), *Competing for the Future*, Boston: Harvard Business School Press.

Robbins, L. (1932), *An Essay on the Nature and Significance of Economic Science*, London: Macmillan.
Rumelt, R. (1984), 'Towards a Strategic Theory of the Firm', in R. Lamb (ed.), *Competitive Strategic Management*, Englewood Cliffs, NJ: Prentice-Hall.
Rumelt, R. (1987), 'Theory, Strategy and Entrepreneurship', in D. Teece (ed.), *The Competitive Challenge*, Cambridge, Mass.: Ballinger.
Rumelt, R., D. Schendel and D. Teece (eds) (1994), *Fundamental Issues in Strategy: A Research Agenda*, Boston: Harvard Business School Press.
Saloner, G. (1994), 'Game Theory and Strategic Management: Contributions, Applications and Limitations', in R. Rumelt, D. Schendel and D. Teece (eds), *Fundamental Issues in Strategy Research*, Boston: Harvard Business School Press.
Sautet, F. (1998), 'Une Théorie Entrepreneuriale de la Firme' ('An Entrepreneurial Theory of the Firm'), PhD dissertation, Université Paris IX, Dauphine.
Schendel, D. (1992), 'Introduction to Special Issue on Strategy Process', *Strategic Management Journal*, **13**, 1–5.
Scherer, F. (1980), *Industrial Market Structure and Economic Performance*, Boston: Houghton-Mifflin.
Schmalensee, R. and T. Willig (1989), *Handbook of Industrial Organization*, Amsterdam: North-Holland.
Schumpeter, J. (1912), *The Theory of Economic Development*, Cambridge, Mass: Harvard University Press.
Shackle, G. (1958), *Time in Economics*, Cambridge, Mass.: Cambridge University Press.
Shackle, G. (1972), *Economics and Epistemics*, Cambridge, Mass.: Cambridge University Press.
Shapiro, C. (1989), 'The Theory of Strategy', *Rand Journal of Economics*, **20**, 125–37.
Spender, J. (1993), 'Some Frontier Activities around Strategy Theorizing', *Journal of Management Studies*, **30** (1), 11–30.
Tirole, J. (1988), *The Theory of Industrial Organization,* Cambridge, Mass.: MIT Press.
Vickers, J. (1995), 'Concepts of Competition', *Oxford Economic Papers*, **47**, 1–23.
Wernerfelt, B. (1984), 'A Resource-Based View of the Firm', *Strategic Management Journal*, **5**, 171–80.
Williamson, O. (1986), 'The Economics of Governance: Framework and Applications', in R. Langlois (ed.) (1986), *Economics as a Process: Essays in the New Institutional Economics*, Cambridge, Mass.: Cambridge University Press.

7. Competition and industrial coordination

Jackie Krafft and Jacques-Laurent Ravix

1. INTRODUCTION

This chapter aims at studying the adjustment process implemented by competing firms. The process of competition between firms may lead to different positions. Competition may arrive at perfect coordination and the adjustment process exhibits a convergence to an equilibrium. Competition may also imply a more problematic position of imperfect coordination and the emergence of durable and cumulative disequilibria. In both situations, specific institutional arrangements such as mergers and acquisitions, cooperation and alliances have to be elaborated by firms to prevent the occurrence of these disequilibria and, to some extent, to organise the process of competition. In fact, the role of business institutions is different with respect to each type of coordination. Being considered as a simple response to market failures when coordination is perfect, they must be endowed with a more endogenous status when coordination is imperfect.

To analyse these issues, we will assume that, within the competitive process, interacting firms are facing two problems at the same time. Firms have to acquire a productive knowledge (how can the productive capacity be developed?) and a market knowledge (how do other firms behave?). We will argue on the one hand that, if productive knowledge is perfect, the concern is only in the treatment of market coordination. On the other hand, if both market and productive knowledge are imperfect, the concern is in what we may label the 'coordination of industry'.

In the analysis of market coordination, general equilibrium economics had for a long time led economists to be used to represent a system of decentralized market interactions by the abstract device of centralized coordination. In fact, general competitive equilibrium theory is essentially 'top-down' for, in the absence of externalities, it reduces to the optimal solution of a social planner's problem. Using a computer analogy,

Leijonhufvud has advocated a 'bottom-up' view of the system where 'the economy is best conceived of as a network of interacting processors' (Leijonhufvud, 1993). While centralized top-down coordination can work with static and perfect information hypotheses, decentralized bottom-up coordination is naturally characterized as a dynamic step-by-step problem solving process. In this case institutions and behavioural conventions emerge to cope with partial ignorance and strong uncertainties affecting the individual agent. We shall see in the next section that there have been two ways of treating the link between market coordination and institutions from a bottom-up point of view. Hayek argued that coordination of dispersed knowledge is mainly dedicated to the acquisition of market knowledge, while Marshall developed a notion of organization which opens the way to analysing industry.

In the analysis of industrial coordination, the releasing of the perfect productive knowledge assumption, along with the assumption of perfect market information, shows a limited ability of agents to process information and to coordinate their activities in a complex and unstable environment. Thus the main requisite of bottom-up coordination is 'computational feasibility' (ibid.). That is, decision rules and learning procedures, including expectations formation, should be capable of algorithmic representations. In this case, we shall use in the third section the work of Richardson to propose an algorithm where decision making in production processes serves as a computational device for the market process. Referring to this framework, we will show that competition is a dynamic process based on recurrent coordination failures. Within this process firms have to implement institutional arrangements (integration, cooperation or market relation) to avoid dramatic disequilibria.

2. MARKET COORDINATION AND INSTITUTIONS

The assumption of imperfect market information in the theory of prices makes it necessary to consider the market as an institution. This comes from the idea that institutions may in some way compensate for the unavailability or dispersion of market knowledge. We will show that, in Hayek's analysis of competition, the prevalence of a market order suggests the existence of perfect coordination where institutions are essentially exogenous to the adjustment process. In Marshall's work, on the contrary, there is an essential recognition that the adjustment process can fail and may lead to imperfect coordination. The focus on internal business organization and external trade connections, together with the linking of knowledge and organization, tends to make institutions endogenous in the description of competition.

2.1. Division of Knowledge and the Adjustment Process

The coordination problem has been stated in terms of knowledge and information by Hayek in 'Economics and Knowledge' (Hayek, 1937). In this article, the author dismisses the static allocative efficiency criterion of the 'Pure Logic of Choice' to the benefit of a coordination process perspective. According to Kirzner, this is a step logically prior to the operation consisting in allocating given resources to pre-established ends (Kirzner, 1982, 1984). To study the coordination process is to analyse the tendency towards equilibrium, which means that the knowledge of the different members of society comes more and more into agreement and that the expectations of individuals, particularly of the entrepreneurs, become more and more correct. This implies taking into account the problem of 'the *division of knowledge* which is quite analogous to, and at least as important as, the problem of the division of labor' (Hayek, 1937, original emphasis). The former has been neglected, although it seems 'to be the really central problem of economics as a social science'. That is (ibid., pp.50–51):

> how the spontaneous interaction of a number of people, each possessing only bits of knowledge, brings about a state of affairs in which prices correspond to costs, etc., and which could be brought about by deliberate direction only by somebody who possessed the combined knowledge of all those individuals.

The only relevant knowledge different people must possess in order that equilibrium may prevail is the one they acquire in carrying out their original plans. They do not dispose of all the information, especially the information which, 'if acquired by accident', would lead them to change their plans. Therefore this equilibrium is not an optimum position. Further conditions should be met in order that 'the results of the combination of individuals bits of knowledge should be comparable to the results of direction by an omniscient dictator' (ibid., p.53).

These references to deliberate direction, omniscient planner or 'directing mind' (ibid., p.54), even if alluded to in the negative, reveal the difficulties met in attempting to treat theoretically the division of knowledge (cf. Böhm, 1995, pp.162–3). Even if market knowledge can be considered as a social device which cannot be acquired individually, 'Hayek conveys the impression . . . that the outcomes of competitive market transactions are independent of the processes generating them' (ibid., p.162). This inability to solve analytically the problem of convergence to equilibrium in 'Economics and Knowledge' led to 'Hayek's transformation', identified by Caldwell (1995), involving a turning away from a theory of learning and expectation formation to the more pragmatic task of investigating the use of dispersed or fragmented knowledge according to different institutional arrangements. The historical emergence and extension of the competitive market became the main topics of the author's work (Ege, 1992). Spread out all over this work, they constitute the subject matter of a number of articles proposing a critical reading of price and exchange theory.

'The Use of Knowledge in Society' (Hayek, 1945) deals more precisely with the problem confronted by society to make a rational economic order emerge in a situation where the separate individuals only possess 'dispersed bits of incomplete and frequently contradictory knowledge' (ibid., p.519). The economic problem of society is not merely one of allocating given resources, but mainly one of 'rapid adaptation to changes in the particular circumstances of time and place' (ibid., p.524). The real function of competitive market is to coordinate the separate actions of different people with the price system which is 'a mechanism for communicating information' (ibid., p.526). The level of knowledge necessary to individual participants in this system is very low, being compensated by 'constant use of formulas, symbols and rules whose meaning we do not understand' and by the development of 'practices and institutions'. The price system is one of those formations 'which man has learned to use . . . after he had stumbled upon it without understanding it' (ibid., p.528). Starting from this notion of dispersed knowledge, the basic idea is to define the market as the locus of a 'process of competition' as opposed to competition as a 'state of affairs' used in price theory where the essential characteristics of a dynamic process has been assumed away (Hayek, 1946). Competition itself is defined as a 'discovery procedure' (Hayek, 1978) the operation of which leads to an 'order'. This order, 'being approached to various degrees' and 'preserved throughout a process of change', is different from the notion of an economic equilibrium which 'never really exists' (ibid., p.184).

In spite of the open-endedness and creative aspects of the market process as described by Hayek, the critical function of his analysis is reduced by the teleological aspect of his notion of an economic order constitutive of these processes. The analogy between market adjustments and the results obtained by an 'omniscient dictator' already noticed in our comment on Hayek (1937) must be compared to the statement that, although the specific outcomes of a discovery procedure are in their nature unpredictable, 'the market order produces in some sense a maximum or an optimum' (Hayek, 1978, p.183).[1] What one may conclude from these remarks is that the procedure of decentralized coordination as expressed by Hayek always tends towards an order which is defined outside the economic sphere. In the words of Foss (1995, p.29), 'Hayek (1937) was content with stating the co-ordination problem, and then later on seeking a solution to it outside economics, namely in classical liberalism's traditional emphasis on evolved institutions and how such institutions stimulated spontaneous orders'.

Thus the role of institutions is reduced to the confirmation of 'the empirical observation that *prices do tend to correspond to costs*' (Hayek, 1937, p.51, emphasis added). It only shows that the coordination procedure cannot fail, so that there is no need for the agents to compute this 'spontaneous order'. In Hayek's analysis, the adjustment process is definitely a spontaneous process leaving no role to computation. Thus, to construct an analysis of the adjustment process, it becomes necessary to consider endogenous institutions that make this computation possible.

Investigating the problems of information related to the perfect competition model, Leijonhufvud (1968, p.70) quotes Hayek's (1945) remark about how little the individual participants in the price system need to know in order to take the right action, and argues that what the individual transactor needs to know is precisely the equilibrium prices. When one tries to interpret the abstract competitive model as an actual process, there emerge two features (Leijonhufvud, 1968, p.70):[2] '(a) the information required by individual transactors is "produced" apart from the actual process of exchange (and production) and (b) it is "distributed" at no cost to transactors'.

Thus there appears the necessity of investigating how some kind of institutional arrangement emerges to do the coordinating job. In fact, computable economics has to be set into some institutional context, so as to ensure 'computational feasibility'.

Even a centralized top-down general equilibrium system needs some organization, as soon as it is considered as a concrete issue. Taking as a point of departure a model with a central coordinator, as in the case of established general competitive analysis, Clower and Leijonhufvud (1975) modify it so that it can be used to deal with real and not only virtual disequilibria. This implies getting rid of the two hypotheses pointed out above, so that: (a) trades can take place at prices that do not ensure the collective consistency of individual plans, and (b) transactions are costly. From this follows the model of the 'central supermarket' where individual agents can in pairwise fashion trade at will any one good for any other, under the control of a 'central trade coordinator'. This coordinator is holding such quantities of tradable commodities as to meet the requirement that individuals may be able to trade at dates and in amounts they choose, and determines exchange rates so as to meet operating expenses and adjust aggregate inventories through time. Under some appropriate requirements ensuring that this economy behaves not too irrationally (or reasonably enough), the existence and stability conditions of equilibria can be derived. However, the existence conditions appear to be rather artificial. The organized barter economy portrayed by the supermarket model necessitates that the coordinator deal in every kind of commodities, including employment contracts, future contracts and so on, in the same way as spot trading of physical objects. The protection against opportunism, fraud or overcommitments would need such costly monitoring and enforcement devices that this kind of uneasy and long-term contracts should be 'severely limited' (ibid., p.185). The same applies to stability which is less conditioned by mechanical reactions of the model than by the necessity of invoking some 'reasoned and intelligent decisions of the trade coordinator' (ibid., p.186).

Such clauses are designed to set limited magnitude and bounded duration to departures from equilibrium in a barter economy, showing through the institutional requirements for informational structures and incentives schemes used in modern microeconomics theory. Nevertheless, all these pseudo-institutional forms cannot protect the system from being threatened by the occurrence of coordination failures, as soon as a substantial proportion of traded commodities are highly durable goods or, worse, if monetary or credit complications are introduced into the model. These coordination failures then become violent and cumulative.

2.2. Knowledge and Organization: Internalizing Institutions

When institutions are maintained outside the analysis of equilibrating processes, they are only used as an explanation of the existence of an economic order towards which the system will tend spontaneously. Conversely, when institutions are part of the process, they can be considered as playing a more effective role in compensating coordination failures. Internalizing institutions thus gives to the analysis a more realistic content, in the sense that one may consider now that the coordination process can fail. The problem is essentially to answer the question why aggregate outcomes of rational agents' interaction could be less rational than the Austrian 'market order' defined as the unintended result of purposeful individual actions.

The emergence of effective intermediate institutions (middlemen, specialized merchant traders or organized markets) becomes an analytical necessity in dealing with such a coordination problem where there is no medium course between ultrarational stability and chaotic unstability. As far as a real organization of trade is concerned, the work of Marshall naturally comes into play. In fact, '[M]arshall's economics . . . *is not based on choice theory* [but rather on] simple feedback-based *decision rules* in less than completely known environments' (Leijonhufvud, 1993, p.9, original emphasis).

Knowing the marginal utility of money and having a subjective marginal utility function for each separate good, the boundedly rational consumer follows a sequential process of consecutive buying decisions ending up with the exhaustion of his or her budget constraint. This process is open to error in that prices are discovered one after the other, so that it can be corrected before spending next month's wages.

The notion of Marshallian competition as a real discovery procedure is more specifically studied by Loasby (1989, chap.4 ; 1990). It is argued that Marshall's theory of economic progress, as well as his theory of coordination, were based on the relationship between knowledge and organization, the 'twin themes' of Book IV of Marshall's *Principles* being 'the effects of the growth of knowledge on organisation and costs of production, and the effects of the organisation of production on the growth of knowledge' (ibid., p.54). In Marshall's own words (Marshall, 1920, p.115):

> Capital consists in a great part of knowledge and organisation . . . Knowledge is our most powerful engine of production . . . Organisation aids knowledge; it has many forms, *e.g.* that of a single business, that of various businesses in the same trade, that of various trades relatively to one another, and that of the State providing security for all and help for many.

Indeed, this description draws a more complete picture of the organization of industry than the usual industrial organization literature. Beginning his chapter on 'Industrial Organisation' (Marshall, 1920, book IV, chap. VIII), the author combines the Smithian division of labour with Darwinian theory, pointing out 'the many profound analogies which have been discovered between social and especially industrial organisation on the one side and the physical organisation of the higher animals on the other' (ibid., p.200). In fact, there is:

> a fundamental unity of action between the laws of nature in the physical and in the moral world. This central unity is set forth in the general rule, to which there are not very many exceptions, that the development of the organism, whether social or physical, involves an increasing subdivision of functions between its separate parts on the one hand, and on the other a more intimate connection between them. (Ibid., p.200–201)

The ways in which the various forms of organization aid knowledge and knowledge improves organization, thus making coordination possible, are not really presented in a well structured fashion by Marshall. Nonetheless, Loasby has spent a good deal of energy and ingenuity in regrouping the elements scattered through the *Principles* and *Industry and Trade*, and constructing a convincing picture of the coordination problem treated by Marshall as a consequence of both the division of labour and the division of knowledge (see Loasby, 1989, 1990, 1994). The most significant result of this reconstruction is certainly the one which relates internal business organization and external trade connections to the processes leading to internal and external economies, these processes being much more a matter of improvements in knowledge and organization than a matter of standard definition in terms of scale economies. See, for instance, Marshall's wording of the 'law of increasing returns': 'An increase of labour and capital leads generally to improved organisation, which increases the efficiency of the work of labour and capital' (Marshall, 1920, p.265). As pointed out by Loasby (1989, p.57), Marshall draws attention to 'the length of time that is necessarily occupied by each individual business in extending its internal, and still more its external organisation' (Marshall, 1920, p.414). The term 'external organisation' suggests 'the network of social, technical and commercial arrangements which link a business with its customers, suppliers (who are usually of many kinds), and also its rivals, whose own experiments provide it with both incentive and information' (Loasby, 1989, p.57). Moreover, for all information dispensed by these trade connections, prices cannot be 'sufficient statistics' (Loasby, 1994, p.259). Therefore, contrary to Hayek's treatment of the same subject, Marshall's analysis of price is based on an institutional foundation which internally provides the means of coordination.

The consequences for an adjustment theory are the following. The coordination of the economic system should be described through trade connections linking firms one another in a process implying both market and productive information, as well as market and productive organizations. This leads naturally to Richardson who, as an 'Austrian Marshallian' (Foss, 1995), developed the Hayekian theme of the division of knowledge and the Marshallian theme of the link between knowledge and organization. These themes turn directly on issues of industrial coordination and the role of business institutions in this adjustment process. Indeed, Richardson 'sought a solution to the co-ordination problem that was internal to economic theory' (ibid., p.29).

3. INDUSTRIAL COORDINATION AND BUSINESS INSTITUTIONS

A situation in which both imperfect market and productive knowledge are simultaneously experienced leads to the threat of coordination failures that could result in the occurrence of durable and cumulative disequilibria between supply and demand. However, integrating the productive dimension in the way Richardson does will allow us to work out a 'computational algorithm' for both decision rules and learning procedures, whereas economists generally give up searching for an explanation of coordination in such a complex situation. More than simply coping with an intricate situation, the algorithm we propose highlights the function that business institutions have to perform with regard to the coordination problem.[3] Within the process of competition the role of these institutions is to ensure industrial coordination and not only informational coordination.

3.1. Market and Productive Knowledge

3.1.1. Defining an algorithm of decision in a complex environment

In a 1959 paper, Richardson introduces two types of information, namely 'primary information' and 'secondary information'. Primary information when imperfect implies that the technique of production may evolve through time in a way which is not always known or even predictable by the firm itself. Capabilities have to be developed step by step by the firm, if need be through the joint effort of other firms. Secondary information when imperfect implies that the market behaviours of other firms are not known by the firm. Within this framework, an acquisition of productive knowledge problem is added to the existing problem of access to market knowledge we referred to in the preceding section.[4] Market knowledge relates to the strategic activities which are engaged in by the competitors of a given firm, but also by its customers, suppliers or partners. Productive knowledge characterizes the specific investments which are implemented by this firm, either by itself or in cooperation with other firms. These two problems are also defined in terms of 'delays' or 'time periods' (cf. Richardson, 1960) because the acquisition of these two types of knowledge is delayed through time: market knowledge and productive knowledge will be acquired by the firm only after a lapse of time, the length of which is unknown by the firm.

The profitability of the investment of a given firm 'F' is then submitted to a couple of different delays: (a) the 'information transmission period', meaning that information concerning the strategic decisions of other firms (different from F) will appear only after a certain lapse of time, and (b) the 'investment gestation period', which means that receipts of the investment of the firm F will be available at the end of an irreducible and uncertain period.

Furthermore, in order to control the profitability of its investment, firm F has to face two kinds of investments constraints: (a) 'competitive investments' which, if they are engaged in by other firms and, especially by rivals, will decrease the profitability of the investment of firm F, and (b) 'complementary investments' which, if they are effectively implemented by firm F or by a group of cooperating firms, will increase the profitability of the investment of firm F.

If the respective lengths of the two defined periods were known, the problem of the firm would be easily solvable, using an optimization programme. In our case, however, these lengths are simply unknown by firm F, so that an equilibrium cannot be found. Economists are often discouraged from asking such a complex question, mainly because it cannot be solved in equilibrium and rational behaviour terms. This question can be answered if we move to a computable economics analysis. As Leijonhufvud (1993, p.5) puts it: 'The rule for Computable Economics modelling will be that you may assume as much ''rationality'' on the part of decision-makers as you want as long as you can also specify a corresponding implementable algorithm by which they could make decisions'.

Our basic point is to describe a situation in which firms are only endowed with local, private and tacit knowledge. These firms implement competencies in developing specific production plans, and they take decisions from a limited information set. Because the industrial system is based on interactions between firms of this kind, it may experience coordination failures implying that erroneous choices are necessarily made, and disequilibria between supply and demand are observed (Richardson, 1960, chaps III and IV). The crucial issue is then to avoid the persistence of such disequilibria through time and to limit their cumulative effects. To achieve this result, firms have to maintain the industrial system between some threshold limits, that is within what could be called a viability corridor.

Taking into account the assumptions about information transmission and investment gestation delays made above, the algorithm takes the following form for firm F:

Develop some 'elements of control' in order to:

- *maintain competitive investments under a maximum threshold level.* The volume of competitive investments can be determined by available demand. In order to ensure profitability, firm F has to restrict the actions of its rivals. In this case, the elements of control come in the form of constraints and inertia so as to maintain market shares of firm F;
- *maintain complementary investments over a minimum threshold level.* In order to ensure profitability, firm F has to implement mutual actions with other firms. In this case, the elements of control are implemented so as to maintain the continuity of the production process. Firm F has to ensure the sequential development of complementary investments which are engaged by firm F itself or in collaboration with other firms.

The viability of the industrial system is ensured only if the two conditions are proved simultaneously. As time passes, firm F must create a coordination of both competitive and complementary investments. This point highlights the fact that, in such an algorithm, market coordination cannot be conceived apart from productive coordination. Business institutions are implemented because they provide a basis for 'reliable interactions' (Leijonhufvud, 1993, p.4) or 'reliable beliefs' (Richardson, 1960). In fact, these agreements help to decode this complex environment where firm F evolves by ensuring occurrence or non-occurrence of some event or the action or inaction of another firm, this latter firm being supplier, customer, partner or competitor of firm F.

3.1.2. Controlling industrial coordination through business institutions

Different elements of control may be implementable by firm F through different types of business institutions. There may be informal agreements or more formal agreements concerning price, quality, reputation, distribution and innovation strategies. The literature has focused intensively on the latter case because of the strong uncertainty involved in an innovative setting which requires a wide range of potential elements of control and business institutions to be developed. For instance, some firms may implement a strategy of 'premature announcement' for their new products (cf. IBM's case, Fisher, 1989). This strategy is intended to give time to customers (especially downstream firms) to adapt their productive or distributive structure to the upstream requirements. Other firms engage with their subsidiaries in some licensing strategies the purpose of which is to realize direct technological information transfers which in turn ensure a greater number of users. In the medium or long term, these practices may be turned into pure integration strategies. A group of firms may also organize themselves within 'technological consortia' (cf. Baumol, 1993) in order to acquire both market and productive knowledge. These different contributions are related to the debate over the institutional forms most conducive to innovation and more generally to economic growth (Langlois and Robertson, 1995a). Different points of views are expressed here. On the one hand, the evidence collected by Chandler (1977, 1990) on the emergence of giant firms at the beginning of the twentieth century, together with the economic analysis of this phenomenon by Lazonick (1991), tends to show that largely integrated firms are in the best position to develop and exploit major innovations. On the other hand, Piore and Sabel (1984) claim that small specialized firms are more flexible and better adapted to generating and adopting innovations.

This debate carries critical and unresolved issues that have led in recent years to an in-depth investigation of the link between the nature of innovation and the relevant business institutions (Teece, 1986, 1996; Langlois and Robertson, 1995b). The key dimensions are the characteristics of innovation and the availability of capabilities. In the words of Teece (1986), innovation can be either 'autonomous' or 'systemic'. When innovation is systemic this means that a simultaneous change in several stages of production has to be implemented. In this case the existing assets are obsolete and the production of the required assets implies the development of new capabilities. When innovation is autonomous the connections between the different stages of production are well defined because of the relative standardization of the different components. The change involved by autonomous innovation is then more localized within the process of production. Moreover, concerning the availability of capabilities, three cases can be observed. Capabilities may exist in-house, they may be available outside the firm or they must be created *ex nihilo*.

With these definitions in mind, the following results are obtained. Langlois and Robertson (1995b) argue that when a major entrepreneurial opportunity requires a systemic change that an existing decentralized network is ill-equipped to handle, especially in terms of capabilities, the required business institution may be large-scale vertical integration. Conversely, when markets offer a high level of capabilities relevant to an entrepreneurial opportunity, and especially when that opportunity permits innovation to proceed in an autonomous rather than in a systemic fashion, the result may be economic growth within a vertically and horizontally specialized structure.[5] More recently, Teece (1996) has also investigated the link between innovation and business institutions by crossing the type of innovation (autonomous or systemic) with the availability of capabilities (in-house, outside, *ex nihilo* created). He exhibits different types of institutions that are prevalent in different situations. The 'Silicon Valley type' prevails when there is autonomous innovation and in-house capabilities, but also when there is systemic innovation and creation of capabilities. The 'virtual type', in which outsourcing prevails, corresponds to a situation of autonomous innovation and outside capabilities. The 'alliance (equity) type' appears when systemic innovation and outside capabilities are present. The 'multi-product integrated type' prevails in a situation of systemic innovation and in-house capabilities. Finally, in the case of autonomous innovation and creation of capabilities, both the 'Silicon Valley type' and the 'alliance (equity) type' are possible.

These two last contributions have similar purposes. Firstly, they develop a new explanation of business institutions, different from traditional ones where opportunism, hidden information and hidden action practices prevail. Secondly, they consider that the emerging type of business institutions is intrinsically linked with the problem of coordination firms have to solve.

In our framework the algorithm intuitively shows that business institutions, because of the elements of control they provide, can be implemented to avoid coordination failures. The algorithm also suggests that the nature of business institutions depends on the extent of the coordination failures, in the sense that the thresholds may be variable and that the elements of control have to be sufficient to maintain the system within these thresholds. We will develop the argumentation by showing that the nature of agreements (informal market relation, formal cooperation, integration and so on) vary with the extent of the coordination problem of both competitive and complementary investments, this extent being expressed in terms of the delays defined above. In fact, what we are trying to do is to reintroduce the strategic dimension that, together with the capabilities dimension, governs the coordination problem.

3.2. The Coordination Problem and the Role of Institutions

The core of our argumentation is that the occurrence of a coordination failure is strictly conditioned by the very presence of the two delays related to information transmission and investment gestation. The role of business institutions within industrial coordination will be demonstrated only when these two delays are simultaneously taken into account. However, we will start the argument by supposing that one of the two delays is missing. This step is necessary to exhibit the conventional way to cope with the problem, which is to alternate information or production issues. Within this first step, we will see that the coordination of investments plans is in fact resolved spontaneously through market relations. Institutions are supposed to be necessary only to compensate market failures, as in traditional theories of the firm (second step). In that case, there exist decision rules implemented by firms, based on optimization programmes intended to guide the choice among given forms of business institutions. The third and last step of the argumentation will be dedicated to analysing how the coordination of both complementary and competitive investments will be attained. In this case decision rules depend upon the respective lengths of the two delays, conveying in a more determinate manner different types of coordination and thus of business institutions, including eventually market relations.

3.2.1. Information and production as alternative issues

If one of the two delays is missing, corrective measures concerning erroneous plans can be implemented either immediately or in a planned way. The ability to reappraise wrong choices through time implies the avoidance of any cumulative phenomenon, that is the avoidance of any failure in the coordination of complementary and competitive investments.

We will assume first that the information transmission period is null. This means that every decision maker within firm F has direct informational access to the actions of other firms. In other words, firm F is able to acquire both private and tacit information about other firms, this information being either complete or incomplete. For instance, decision makers within firm F may observe with certainty – or assign a probability distribution to – the productive and strategic potentialities of rivals, as well as the evolution of their demand. In this case, if firm F is engaged in an irreversible investment which may imply an excess of supply on the market, it still has the opportunity to devise an optimal adjustment plan in order to reduce its undesired stocks through time. Because of its privileged access to information, firm F can choose the time periods and more generally the solutions that are best adapted to clear out the stocks.

Now let us assume that the investment gestation period is equal to zero. In this case the decision makers within firm F systematically give preference to flexible investment despite the fact that the resulting supply does not always meet the market demand. Excess demand or supply phenomena may appear but cannot persist. When information is given at the end of the delay, it can be freely used by firm F to implement some corrective procedures on its flexible investment strategies.

This argumentation needs some comments. It appears that coordination failures do not exist when only one delay is considered. The coordination problem is resolved by itself, as time passes, and without the need of a specific action of firm F (except stock inventories and flexible strategies adaptation).[6] The elimination of one of the two delays does not lead to uninteresting situations. There may exist real situations in which firms are quasi perfectly informed or in which they only engage in flexible strategies. However, economists must have something to say about the situations where firms are ignorant about both market knowledge and productive knowledge. These cases should be embodied in a more general framework which should be studied as a priority. However, this is not a dominant practice in the literature, especially in conventional theories of the firm.

3.2.2. Conventional theories of the firm: a classification

Most standard theories of the firm only take into account either one delay or the other, but never both of them simultaneously. These models can be divided into two categories.

The first category brings together models where the investment gestation delay exists, while the information transmission period is null. Game-theoretic models dedicated to problems of irreversible investment (Roberts and Weitzman, 1981; Bernanke, 1983; Dixit, 1992) fall into this first category. Basic games explain the situation where firm F has to develop an irreversible investment, while the environment (the 'nature') acts upon the profitability of this investment either in a good or a bad way. Firm F has to engage costs related to this investment at time 0, while receipts will only be perceived at time 1. If the project is profitable, then it is immediately implemented. Profitability has to be defined at time 0 on the basis of a given decision rule. The commitment to an irreversible investment is then reduced to a point in time, the moment the decision maker of firm F examines the rule to calculate the profitability of its project. In these models, there is no information transmission period. The profitability of investment is derived from a given decision rule based on an intertemporal optimization method. Even if another player is introduced, a player different from Nature, its total potential actions are registered in a well-defined decision tree. The implementation of the intertemporal optimization method is conditioned by the timeless acquisition and the rational treatment of the relevant information.[7] Transaction cost analysis (Williamson, 1985) pertains also to this first category. Specific assets have an interesting characteristic implying that expenses which are engaged to obtain these assets cannot be reallocated to another use without additive costs. Firm F can work out organizational relations with its partners in order to manage this lock-in period for the best, namely through vertical integration or at least long-term contracts. However, the process of choice of the optimal governance structure is implemented according to the principle of 'institutional comparative analysis' which implies, firstly, the efficiency calculation of each institutional form and, secondly, their comparisons two by two in order to exhibit the optimal governance structure. Irreversibility problems implied by assets specificity are then solved by a particular governance structure which is derived from a cost-minimization decision rule. As before, the definition of such a decision rule depends on immediate access to information. These models, like the preceding ones, neglect the information transmission period.

The second category is composed of models in which the information transmission period is considered as positive while the investment gestation delay is null. The property rights approach (Grossman and Hart, 1986; Hart, 1988; Hart and Moore, 1988, 1990) is certainly one of the most typical cases of this category. In this analysis, information is delayed through time. This is why firms decide in the first period to conclude a contract which is not (and cannot be) optimal, but allows them nevertheless to cope with strong uncertainty for a time. According to the contract, one single firm (firm F) is endowed with all the residual rights, just as in a pure integration case. As the second period begins, uncertainty is resolved. The delay of information transmission is then brought to completion and optimal choices are revealed. The uninformed initial contract of vertical integration can immediately and without cost be transformed into an informed and optimal ex post contract. According to the available information, firms have the ability to reappraise their choices without being limited by the slightest irreversibility constraint of some investment which could have been engaged in the first period.

3.2.3. Coordination failures and business institutions

As we have seen in the two preceding paragraphs, if the theory takes into account only one delay, the coordination problem is resolved more or less spontaneously, the role of business institutions being reduced to the compensation of market failures. In fact, a real coordination failure only appears when the two delays are considered simultaneously. Here we will assume that the two delays are present even if we allow one or both of them to be equal to zero. This assumption will be used to design the specific role of each kind of business institution, the market itself being considered as an alternative among others.

When firm F is engaged in a reversible investment programme, the investment gestation delay can be considered as null. Firm F is then endowed with a perfect flexibility of action the performance of which depends exclusively on the availability of information. The objective of this firm is to maintain continuous access to new information in order to be able to adjust the investment programme in the right way. The main problem of the firm is then to secure a suitable potentiality of reaction of its own that must be sufficiently rapid to benefit from the acquisition of new information. In this case formal relations like cooperation or integration are not necessary to resolve the coordination problem. In fact, by their organizational and informational network characteristics, these formal relations could be useful for firm F to acquire information. But, at the same time, the requirement of a perfect adaptation capability of the firm would be hindered by the very fact of participating in this network, the working of which is conditioned by behavioural constraints of its participants. Indeed, market relations seem to be the institutional form that is best adapted to resolve coordination when the delay of investment gestation is equal to zero.

Market relations are also appropriate when the delay of information transmission is assumed to be null. All pieces of information are already known at the time the irreversible investment is implemented (costs, receipts, time of their receipts and so on). As in the preceding case, the elaboration of formal relations is not justified because the coordination problem tends to be resolved by itself, either immediately or in a planned way.

Formal organizations are then only needed when a real coordination failure may appear, that is when firm F faces both information transmission and investment gestation periods. In this situation, the competitors of firm F are prompted to implement well-defined flexible strategies that may question the profitability of the firm and hence its viability. The strategies implemented by rivals are likely to be successful because firm F is locked into its irreversible project and cannot work out defensive plans. Furthermore, unknown events may lead to some additional negative effects. Firm F therefore has to set up suitable actions beforehand so that durable and cumulative disequilibria do not emerge. These actions are intended, first, to acquire information about external strategies which does not appear spontaneously and, second, to make possible the development of the innovation, especially by ensuring the interdependency and the sequentiality of the different stages. These are continuity and constraint requisites which can only be ensured by implementing business institutions.

In fact, when innovation is systemic, this implies that both the information transmission period and the investment gestation period are very long. This means, respectively, (a) that firm F has to create information about the strategies that other firms can implement, and (b) that firm F has to develop at the same time means of coordination of the whole development stages of the innovative process, especially by creating new capabilities. In this case, pure integration seems to better solve the coordination problem of complementary and competitive investments.

If an autonomous innovation is implemented, both delays are shorter. This means that (a) firm F has to improve its knowledge about the strategies of the other firms, and (b) firm F has to coordinate only some stages of the innovation process by making available adapted capabilities internally and externally. Cooperation between firms will then be appropriate.

Finally, if either one or the other delay is very short, indeed even null, innovation is absent. This means that (a) firm F has perfect information on the strategies of other firms, and (b) firm F does not implement an irreversible investment: informal market relations will suffice to resolve the coordination problem.

These results are consistent with Langlois and Robertson (1995b) and with Teece (1996). However, a more complete view of the interactions between firms within the process of competition is proposed because the two delays refer to the capabilities and also to the strategies implemented by the firms. In particular, this view has a competition policy significance that can be sketched briefly. For instance, all agreements should be questioned by competitive authorities if either one or the other delay is very short of null, that is when partners enjoy an informational advantage about market behaviour or when they plan to commit purely flexible investments. The elaboration of an integration should be examined in detail if the lengths of the two delays are short. On the other hand, however, the authorities should accept and even encourage the setting up of cooperation agreements (indeed, even pure integration) as soon as time periods for the acquisition of information and the gestation of investments are found to be long (indeed, even very long). Nevertheless, once the two delays have expired – and then once the common project is brought to completion – the agreement is no longer justified and has to be cancelled.

4. CONCLUDING REMARKS

The first comment is that adding a productive dimension to an already defined problem of informational coordination is simply a matter of increasing the complexity of the analytical framework. Considering the productive dimension gives an opportunity to be more specific about the different types of coordination problems. The informational searching process taken as a mere object of study leads economists to describe only temporary disequilibria. This can also be said when only the investment gestation delay is analysed. Conversely, examining how to create the informational basis that is required in order to develop to completion an irreversible project opens the door to coordination problems which are not immediately resolved. To be maintained within a viability corridor, these coordination failures call for specific business institutions.

The second comment is that considering the productive dimension also allows us to appreciate the causal relation that may exist between the nature of the coordination problem and the institutional form to be implemented. When authors study the informational coordination problem itself, they integrate institutions whose function is to compensate for information processing failures: that is, to reduce information costs and align incentives. As soon as informational problems are linked to productive coordination concerns, business institutions are thereby endowed with a more general function, informational processing being just part of it. The function of business institutions is to make industrial coordination feasible, that is to maintain the viability of an industrial system where firms have local information sets and different productive projects, the distinct stages of which have to be coordinated in a specific manner. The above analysis permits us to distinguish the different institutional forms according to their individual functions.

The last comment is that, within the framework we have proposed, the economic system does work, not despite informational and productive imperfections, but on the contrary because of them. Price fixing, product differentiation, reputation and organizational arrangements are indeed implementable measures that may create the continuity and constraint conditions that are required to develop future projects.

NOTES

1. This sentence is underlined by Böhm (1995, p.166).
2. Walras's *'tâtonnement'* process is one way to meet the first requirement (the other way being Edgeworth's *'recontracting'*). However, this iterative search procedure for determining equilibrium prices in a system of interdependent demand and supply equations

fails as soon as delays or costs of transactions come into the picture. Expressed in the terms of computable economics (cf. Leijonhufvud, 1993, p.8), the statement that 'there is no auctioneer' (Leijonhufvud, 1968, p.76) implies that 'there is no central processor' able to solve the coordination problem. The allocation of resources computation is made by markets and agents acting as parallel computers. 'The array of markets runs algorithms that iterate on the basis of effective excess demands' (ibid.). When the sign of some elements of the excess demand vector differs from the one of the corresponding notional elements, the 'parallel' and the 'centralized' computers do not give the same answer.

3. This algorithm is stated only on general terms. It is mainly a pattern rather than a model of computational analysis.
4. See Leijonhufvud (1968, p.70, fn.5) who, referring to Richardson's 1959 paper, chose to stick to a perfect primary information hypothesis.
5. Within this framework, there is an important and pioneering attempt to integrate the demand side and not only the supply side. For example, in the case of systemic innovation, the product ('appliance') brings together in a single standardized package components that provide all the desired attributes. Vertical integration is in this case the adequate organizational form. In the case of an autonomous innovation, the product is a modular system which is acquired bit by bit, allowing consumers to construct themselves the package that meets their individual preferences for attributes. This framework thus tries to provide a consistent analysis of institutions and innovation, the latter being analysed through its firm and final customers sides.
6. In fact, this leads back to Hayek's case of spontaneous coordination with exogenous institutions.
7. It is noteworthy that, under these conditions, the notion of irreversible investment is questionable. At the time the engagement is made, the ability to synchronize costs and receipts is already expected and planned by the decision rule (at time 0). If these means were indeed not expected at that time, the investment would not be implemented just because it would not be profitable. We shall note that this interpretation does not fit with the sunk costs definition in which the synchronisation has to be worked out through time by the firm itself.

REFERENCES

Baumol, W. (1993), *Entrepreneurship, Management and the Structure of Payoffs*, Cambridge, Mass., MIT Press.

Bernanke, B. (1983), 'Irreversibility, Uncertainty and Cyclical Investments', *Quarterly Journal of Economics*, **98** (1), 85–106.

Böhm, S. (1995), 'Hayek and Knowledge: Some Question Marks', in M. Colonna, H. Hagemann and O. Hamouda (eds), *The Economics of Hayek*, vol. II, Aldershot, UK and Brookfield, US: Edward Elgar.

Caldwell, B. (1995), 'Four Theses on Hayek', in M. Colonna, H. Hagemann and O. Hamouda (eds.), *The Economics of Hayek*, vol. II, Aldershot, UK and Brookfield, US: Edward Elgar.

Chandler, A. (1977), *The Visible Hand: the Managerial Revolution in American Business*, Cambridge, Mass.: MIT Press.

Chandler, A. (1990), *Scale and Scope: the Dynamics of Industrial Capitalism*, Cambridge, Mass.: MIT Press.

Clower, R. and A. Leijonhufvud (1975), 'The Coodination of Economic Activities: A Keynesian Perspective', *American Economic Review*, **65** (2), 182–88.

Dixit, A. (1992), 'Investment and Hysteresis', *Journal of Economic Perspectives*, **6** (1), 107–32.

Ege, R. (1992), 'Emergence du Marché Concurrentiel et Evolutionnisme chez Hayek', *Revue Economique*, **43** (6), 1007–36.

Fisher, F. (1989), 'Games Economists Play: A Noncooperative View', *Rand Journal of Economics*, **20** (1), 113–24.

Foss, N. (1995), 'The Economic Thought of an Austrian Marshallian: George Barclay Richardson', *Journal of Economic Studies*, **22** (1), 23–44.

Grossman, S. and O. Hart (1986), 'The Costs and Benefits of Ownership: a Theory of Vertical and Lateral Integration', *Journal of Political Economy*, **94** (4), 691–719.

Hart, O. (1988), 'Incomplete Contracts and the Theory of the Firm', *Journal of Law, Economics and Organization*, **4** (1), 119–39.

Hart, O. and J. Moore (1988), 'Incomplete Contracts and Renegociation', *Econometrica*, **56** (4), 755–85.

Hart, O. and J. Moore (1990), 'Property Rights and the Nature of the Firm', *Journal of Political Economy*, **98** (6), 119–58.

Hayek, F. (1937), 'Economics and Knowledge', *Economica* (N.S.); reprinted in *Individualism and Economic Order* (1948), Chicago: University of Chicago Press.

Hayek, F. (1945), 'The Use of Knowledge in Society', *American Economic Review*, **35** (4).

Hayek, F. (1946), 'The Meaning of Competition', Stafford Little Lecture, Princeton University; reprinted in *Individualism and Economic Order* (1948), Chicago: University of Chicago Press.

Hayek, F. (1978), 'Competition as a Discovery Procedure', *New Studies in Philosophy, Politics, Economics and the History of Ideas*, Chicago: University of Chicago Press.

Holmström, B. and J. Tirole (1989), 'The Theory of the Firm', in R. Schmalensee and R. Willig (eds), *Handbook of Industrial Organization*, Amsterdam: North Holland.

Kirzner, I. (1982), 'Uncertainty, Discovery and Human Action', in I. Kirzner (ed.), *Method, Process and Austrian Economics: Essays in Honor of Ludwig von Mises*, Lexington, Mass.: D.C. Heath.

Kirzner, I. (1984), 'Prices, the Communication of Knowledge and the Discovery Process', in K.R. Leiube and A.H. Zlabinger (eds), *The Political Economy of Freedom, Essays in Honour of F.A. Hayek*, Berlin and New York: Philosophia Verlag.

Langlois, R. and P. Robertson (1995a), 'Innovation, Networks and Vertical Integration', *Research Policy*, **24**, 543–62.

Langlois, R. and P. Robertson (1995b), *Firms, Markets and Economic Change: a Dynamic Theory of Business Institutions*, London: Routledge.

Lazonick, W. (1991), *Business Organisation and the Myth of the Market Economy*, Cambridge, Mass.: Cambridge University Press.

Leijonhufvud, A. (1968), *On Keynesian Economics and the Economics of Keynes*, New York: Oxford University Press.

Leijonhufvud, A. (1993), 'Towards a Not-Too-Rational Macroeconomics', *Southern Economic Journal*, **60** (1), 1–13.

Loasby, B. (1989), *The Mind and Method of the Economist*, Aldershot, UK and Brookfield, US: Edward Elgar.

Loasby, B. (1990), 'Firms, Markets and the Principle of Continuity', in J.K. Whitaker (ed.), *Centenary Essays on Alfred Marshall*, Cambridge, Mass.: Cambridge University Press.

Loasby, B. (1994), 'Organisational Capabilities and Interfirm Relations', *Metroeconomica*, **45** (3), 248–65.

Marshall, A. (1920), *Principles of Economics*, 8th edn (1979), London: Macmillan.
Piore, M. and C. Sabel (1984), *The Second Industry Divide: Possibilities for Prosperity*, New York: Basic Books.
Richardson, G. (1959), 'Equilibrium, Expectations, and Information', *Economic Journal*, **69**, 223–37.
Richardson, G. (1960), *Information and Investment, A Study in Working of Competitive Economy*, Cambridge, Mass.: Cambridge University Press.
Roberts, K. and M. Weitzman (1981), 'Funding Criteria for Research Development and Exploration Projects', *Econometrica*, **49** (5), 1261–88.
Teece, D. (1986), 'Profiting from Technological Innovation: Implications for Integration, Collaboration, Licensing and Public Policy', *Research Policy*, **15**, 285–305.
Teece, D. (1996), 'Firm Organization, Industrial Structure and Technological Innovation', *Journal of Economic Behavior and Organization*, **31**, 193–224.
Williamson, O. (1985), *The Economic Institutions of Capitalism: Firms, Markets, Relational Contracting*, New York: The Free Press.

8. Merger control law in the European Union

Michel Glais

1. INTRODUCTION

The European Council Regulation on the control of concentration was adopted in December 1989 and came into effect in September 1990. So far, a large number of projects have been submitted. Only a few of them have been declared incompatible with the Common Market. In some cases, the parties have been obliged to propose some undertakings in order to remove the doubts concerning the proposed concentration. The relatively high number of projects submitted to the ruling of the Community authorities can largely be explained by the wide fields covered by the merger regulation, since the control applies both to standard merger operations between two or more independent firms and to takeovers of independent firms by all possible legal means (acquisition of interest, purchase of assets, contract or other). The reality of the control is then recorded according to the degree of a determining influence which the purchase can bring to bear on the activity of the firm involved. Owing to the delay with which the European regulation on the control of concentrations has been adopted, Community authorities have benefited at the same time from the recent advances in the field of economic knowledge and from the experience acquired by national authorities having introduced merger control in their competition law.

In the following survey, a summary of the main theoretical proposals offered by economic analysis will stress the structuralist nature of the European merger regulation. An analysis of the large number of decisions pronounced over the last ten years highlights the fact that, while implementing the regulation in accordance with its general philosophy, the European Commission has sometimes taken into account some considerations of European industrial policy not to reject some mergers however questionable they may be from a strict implementation of the competition rule.

2. THE STRUCTURALIST FOUNDATIONS OF THE EUROPEAN MERGER REGULATION

The objectives assigned to an antitrust policy are well-known. The authorities in charge of this policy have to make sure that the firms' behaviour does not hinder the most efficient sharing out of the productive resources. They are also expected to give the most efficient suppliers opportunities to create new techniques or products more attractive to customers.

Preserving an effective competition thanks to a sufficient diffusion of economic power is the third target the competition policy is supposed to aim at. This objective may sometimes be in conflict with the research of a dynamic efficiency demanding pools of technical knowledge, specific assets and financial facilities sometimes only obtainable thanks to a merger strategy. The scientific community does not have the same view about the grading of these three objectives. The draft of the text of the merger control regulation clearly reflects the wish of European authorities to opt in favour of the structuralist thesis putting forward the immediate interest of consumers to the detriment of an economic analysis more favourable to regulations founded on an economic assessment rather than on a competition assessment of a merger project. The way of delimiting the relevant market, the first step in any analysis of the effects of a merger project on the free process of competition, upholds the structuralist choice adopted by the European authorities.

2.1. Economic Analysis of a Merger Effect on Competition: a Summary

Two main streams of economic thinking conflict over the way to evaluate the merger's effects on economic welfare. According to the oldest one, the structuralist school, what must be taken into account is the impact of a merger's project on the consumers' surplus. According to the other stream (Chicago School), the question is, on the contrary, to know whether the improvement in global welfare (including producers' surplus) overcomes the possible drawbacks in regard to the sufficient diffusion of economic power. Following this proposal, a merger's project could be accepted by the competition authorities, even if it bears a risk of a short-term reduction in the consumers' surplus, provided the overall surplus will clearly be higher than it was before. Anyway, add the defenders of this thesis, many consumers are also shareholders, anxious for an increase in the profits of the firms in which they have invested, and may consider the overall surplus increase as a good target to be pursued by the authorities.

In such a framework of analysis, the problem to solve, however, is determining whether the efficiency gains expected from a merger's project outweigh the loss of welfare (deadweight loss) in the case of a post-merger situation leading to a fall in the industry output and to a price increase.

A new entity born from a merger is supposed to secure an anti-competition market power either by raising its price or by excluding competitors from the market ('Stiglerian' or 'Bainian' market power)[1], the first method being most often mentioned in the theoretical literature on the basis of the use of Lerner's Index. A firm i will get a post-merger market if:

$$L_i = \frac{P_i - C_i}{P_i} > 0$$

where P_i is its price and C_i its marginal cost.

According to Landes and Posner (1981), L_i can be written in a more manageable way for antitrust authorities:

$$L_i = \frac{S_i}{|E_m{}^d| + E^s{}_j\ (1 - S_i)} = \frac{H\alpha}{|E_m{}^d|}$$

where

S_i is market share of i,

$|E_m{}^d|$ is absolute value of price-elasticity of the market demand,

$E^s{}_j$ is supply-elasticity of competitors $j = 1 \ldots n$,

H is Herfindahl–Hirschman Index,

α is a specific parameter used to specify the present suppliers' behaviour: $\alpha =$ 0 when they are price takers; 1 in case of Cournot behaviour and $1/H$ in a pure cartel.

According to the Landes and Posner' equation, the market power of the new entity resulting from a merger will be high if (a) its market share is high, (b) the price-elasticity of the market demand is weak, and (c) the supply elasticity of competitors is also weak.

Moreover, the equilibrium margin between prices and marginal costs will be a decreasing function of the number of symmetric competitors and an increasing function of the market share of each of them.

Usually, a Cournot behaviour is supposed to be adopted in economic models devoted to the analysis of a merger's effects on the market equilibrium. The product offered is considered as homogeneous and supplied according to quadratic costs. When a merger project is analysed in the structuralist view (the target being to preserve the immediate interest of consumers), an inverse relationship between the consumers' surplus and an increase in the rate of concentration is often verified with such models. After the merger, a decrease in its production should be profitable to the new entity, the question being how to know whether or not the other competitors will increase their own outputs to offset it sufficiently.

If the merger does not lead to synergies and new learning, the result will clearly be a new equilibrium, with lower aggregate output and higher price. For instance, with constant and equal marginal costs, the new entity will reduce its output and the aggregate output will be lower. The consumers' surplus will be reduced. The importance of the decrease in aggregate output will depend on the number of the non-parties to the concentration, on how the quantity offered will be shared out between them and on the shape of their marginal cost functions (Willig, 1991, p.297): 'The impact on aggregate output will be less, the more diffusely spread the total output of the non-parties . . . The flatter their marginal costs, the more elastic their output response to the merger will be and the less the merger will raise price and profitability increase market power for the parties'.

The case of firms equally efficient in the market is, however, quite peculiar. Very often, in a Cournot equilibrium, the competitors' marginal costs are different and, moreover, a merger may lead to a decrease in the new entity's marginal cost. However, as proved by Farrell and Shapiro (1990), the decrease in the new entity's marginal cost must, very often, be significant in order to get a price decrease. The larger the required reduction in marginal cost, the greater the pre-merger mark-ups of the parties to the merger.[2] Mark-ups being proportional to the pre-merger market shares, decreases in marginal costs coming from economies of scale or new learning will have to be all the greater as the pre-merger market shares of the parties were higher and as the price-elasticity of the market demand is weaker.

Furthermore, the possible price decrease will be obtained only if the market participants continue to adopt a Cournot behaviour. The price decrease may not happen if, after the merger, the behaviour is collusive.

However, if, in accordance with the second stream of thinking, the analysis takes into account the effect of the merger project on the aggregate welfare (sum of consumers' and producers' surplus), a merger leading to a price increase could be authorized in certain cases, highlighted by Farrell and Shapiro (1990).

Instead of trying to estimate the overall effects of a merger by comparing the pre- and post-merger's resources allocations, the method proposed by Farrell and Shapiro aims to analyse the effect of a merger on the joint welfare of consumers and non-participating firms (net external welfare). According to their analysis, a merger leading to a price increase can also enhance the economic welfare if:

$$S_I < \sum_{i \in 0} \lambda_i s_i$$

where

S_I is market shares of the merging firm,
0 is the set of non-merging firm i,
s_i is the market share of each firm i,
λ_i is a measure of the output of each firm i.

According to Farrell and Shapiro, a lot of mergers should then be approved. Moreover, their analysis stresses the following fact:

> In Cournot and similar theories of oligopoly, with homogeneous goods, the presence of small firms with little market power is not desirable. Their output, produced at a marginal cost that almost consumes its gross social benefit, also displaces or discourages output at (larger) firms with lower marginal costs. Consequently it often enhances economic welfare to close down small or inefficient firms or, failing that, to encourage them to merge so they would produce less output. (Ibid., p.361)

In spite of the real interest of this analysis, practical use of it might not be so easy. Information needed (particularly in order to appreciate the 'λ') would not be as easy to collect as is claimed by the two authors. Built on the hypothesis of a Cournot behaviour adopted by the competitors, the Farrell and Shapiro model is specifically adapted to industries endowed with specific characteristics (homogeneous product, importance of production capacity and so on). Moreover, if, in the post-merger situation, the other competitors are few and hold a substantial part of the industry output, if the market is mature (with a long-run stability of the market demand), a risk of collusion could be feared. The application of Farrell and Shapiro's analysis should be complemented by expertise concerning a possible conclusion of some restrictive agreements between the post-merger suppliers. Collusion might be likely (and the probabilities higher than in the pre-merger situation) in situations of (a) low price-elasticity of the market demand (case of homogeneous intermediate products with no close substitutes and prices unimportant for the overall costs of the final products), (b) important current demand fluctuations, (c) excess capacity of production with high fixed costs, and (d) entry barriers.

Besides the ability of the merged firms to increase their market price, the risk of exclusion of some present and potential competitors from the market must also be taken into account. Such an exclusion is possible when the parties to the merger are vertically integrated and have got some market power over the supply of a scarce resource, forcing their competitors to take positions on two markets.

2.2. The Main Clauses of the European Merger Regulation

The European control of mergers having been adopted recently, the Community authorities had a lot of information about the implementation of merger regulations introduced in many national competition rules, some of them being strongly structuralist (as in Germany), others more concerned with the introduction of efficiency considerations (as in France).

So it is with full knowledge of these experiments that the European Community has deliberately chosen a very strong structuralist conception of the merger control. According to article 2, paras. 2 and 3 of the Council Regulation, the Commission is invited to address the question of determining whether a merger project could create or strengthen a dominant position as a result of which effective competition would be significantly impeded in the Common Market or in a substantial part of it.

Any attempt to interpret the Community text begins with the following question: is the simple fact of recognizing that a project creates or strengthens a dominant position enough to condemn it, or is it also necessary to demonstrate explicitly its negative effect on the interplay of effective competition?

Lawyers seem to be inclined to adopt the first interpretation in so far as they argue that, according to the decisions of the EC Commission relative to article 86 of the Treaty of Rome (article 82 of the new EC Treaty), a dominant position is precisely defined as a position which significantly hinders the interplay of effective competition. This analysis indeed appears right in the light of how both the Commission and the Court of Justice have, on many occasions, defined the concept of dominant position. Furthermore, in answer to a request from the Court of Milan, it was stated that a dominant position, as laid out by article 86, must 'give the power to impede the maintenance of effective competition over a large portion of the market under consideration, particularly in view of the potential existence and position of producers or distributors selling similar goods' (CJCE 18/02/71, Sirena no 16; CJCE 14/02/78, United Brands).

However, the analysis of the criteria which the regulatory authorities are invited to study within the context of the appraisal procedure, as provided for in article 2, para. 1, raises certain questions. The reference to technical and economic progress makes one wonder to what extent a concentration operation which leads to the creation or strengthening of a dominant position might not be justified through the use of the 'economic balance' method often accepted in the context of the law on collusion (article 81, para. 3, procedure). Furthermore, it is quite interesting to recall that previous regulation projects drawn up by the Commission made explicit reference to this possibility of legitimatization. However, there is little room for ambiguity since the final text states that the evolution of economic and technical progress may be taken into account 'provided that it is to the consumers' advantage and does not form an obstacle to competition' (article 2, para. 1(b)).

Determining to what extent a concentration project may lead to the creation or strengthening of a dominant position is therefore the main object of the appraisal task assigned to the regulatory authorities. Despite the real degree of freedom enjoyed by the authorities in the implementation of this ruling, it appears that, in accordance with the established jurisprudence concerning dominant positions, the European regulatory authority has been invited to put the big firms on probation and to base its action on an economic analysis much closer to the teachings of the structuralist view than to those of the Chicago School.

Undoubtedly less confident of the soundness of the competition process, the drafters of the Community text quite evidently feared the perpetuation of the positions of force momentarily enjoyed by some large firms and, with them, secure or guaranteed income and market situations unfavourable to small firms under threat from the predatory practices which large firms might be tempted to adopt.

Whereas article 86 of the Treaty of Rome condemns only abuses of a dominant position, the merger regulation refuses any external acquisition by a firm (or a group of firms) being able to create or to strengthen a dominant position. Implicitly, this means that European authorities introduce a sort of discrimination between the two growth strategies possibly undertaken by a firm. It is legal to hold a dominant position obtained by internal growth. This will not be the case if this position has been obtained by external growth, as this second strategy is considered less 'fair' than the first.

The report '1992, The New European Economy' (document no 35 CEE, 1988) bears out the reality of these doctrinal bases. Having first evoked the work carried out by Leibenstein and Comanor relative to the x-inefficiency phenomenon, and while recognizing that econometric calculations which established a positive and significant causal relation between high levels of concentration (or the role of entry barriers) and supranormal profitability levels 'are the cause of relative controversies, notably concerning the transitory aspect of phenomena studied according to cross section analysis and the role of efficiency in the considerable profits observed in the concentrated industries' (ibid., p.133), its authors conclude somewhat ambiguously that 'more competitive market structures tend to reduce the gap between price and unit cost' (ibid.).

Liberal economists would not contradict this conclusion unless, of course, it implied the intervention of a supposedly all-powerful authority acting as a sort of 'obstetrician' for those market structures it judged more competitive. According to the Chicago economists, the competitive process is naturally sufficiently robust for it to be given free play. They argue that, since the industrial world is constantly changing, technological change is so rapid in certain sectors that the existence of an apparently dangerous monopoly does not justify the intervention of the regulatory authorities since the danger may fade before the measures taken by the authorities take effect. Even supposing their intervention to be rapid (as is the case for European concentration control), it still would not be justified. According to the historical analysis made by some Chicago economists (Brozen, 1982), it probably often results in more problems (especially regarding economic efficiency), than solutions.

As a definitive support to the theory of the necessary intervention of the European regulatory authorities, the authors of the Community 'economic bible' ('1992, The New European Economy') refer to publications aiming to highlight the rather unfavourable feature – as far as the promotion of innovations is concerned – of market situations judged to be lacking in competitiveness (Jacquemin, 1970; Geroski, 1987; Kamien and Schwartz, 1982). The authors of the 1992 report conclude that 'the beneficial effects of European integration on innovation come via the strengthening of competition rather than via the phenomena pertaining to size' (1992, p.187). This, they believe, leads to the necessity of 'a prior rapid control of mergers likely to substantially reduce competition on the community scale' (ibid., p.149).

Thus it is not surprising to observe that, given this theoretical bedrock, the text of the community ruling should give priority to the support of sufficient diffusion of economic power over the concept of efficiency. Furthermore, within the scope of partial equilibrium methodology which the Commission sets itself, the task of accepting the potentially opposing effects a merger project may have on consumers' and producers' surplus levels is settled in advance, since the evolution of economic and technical progress is only taken into account if 'it is to the advantage of the consumers'. Only those projects likely to increase the consumer surplus (either by leading to price reductions or by encouraging increased demand without price changes) should find grace in the eyes of the Commission. Moreover, the Commission has always made quite clear its concern to ensure the protection and development of small- and medium-sized firms, a stance often borne out by Community competition policy. It is also worth observing that the EC Economic and Social Committee regularly requests that particular attention be paid to these firms. It has gone so far as to deplore the fact that the 'impact of Community competition policy on small- and medium-sized firms is examined in a rather superficial way' and to require that a future report on this important question be published in strict collaboration with the task force dealing with small- and medium-sized firms (notice on 16th report, 17th report on competition policy, annexe point 17, p.279).

The importance of the suppression of non-tariff barriers within the Community is also repeated frequently by the authors of '1992, The New European Economy', (ibid., pp.144, 147) as a development factor for small- and medium-sized firms in sectors where product differentiations are both numerous and of value, and as a market-energizing factor thanks to entry opportunities for new firms and the resulting boost to the industrial base. Finally, condemnation was voiced of dominant firms which adopted improper practices against the interests of smaller partners or competitors (Glais, 1991).

2.3. The Importance of the 'Relevant Market' Delimitation in the Merger Control Procedure

Within the partial equilibrium methodology adopted by every antitrust authority, the delimitation of the relevant market constitutes the first step in an analysis of the effect of a merger project. The market delimitation has been proved to be particularly crucial in a lot of cases coming within the ambit of article 86 of the Treaty of Rome.

Among the whole range of criteria used by the antitrust authorities, the market share value of the firm suspected of an abuse of dominant position is usually very highly ranked. A high market share is, indeed, easier to prove when the relevant market has been narrowly defined. Obviously, structuralist economists are more willing to use narrow definitions than those who are more confident in the robustness of the competition process.

On theoretical grounds, the scope given to a market area will be different depending on whether the antitrust authorities adopt the 'demand side' or the 'demand and supply side' approach. On the basis of Lerner's Index formulation proposed by Landes and Posner, US merger guidelines have opted in favour of the second approach. They propose to incorporate in the calculus of the market global output not only the potential production (or capacity) of the present sellers but also the future output of suppliers able to enter the market quickly without incurring significant sunk costs of entry and exit in response to a 'small but significant and non-transitory' price increase of the group of products which would offer a hypothetical profit-maximizing monopoly.

To the contrary, the European authorities are usually more concerned with the demand side approach. According to a notice adopted by the Commission in 1997: 'A relevant product market comprises all those products and (or) services which are regarded as interchangeable or substitutable by the consumers, by reason of the products' characteristics, their prices or intended uses'.

The supply side substitution will only be taken into account in the market definition 'if its effects are equivalent to those of demand substitution in terms of effectiveness and immediacy'. As Alonso (1994) and Fishwick (1989) point out, the Commission has considered supply side interchangeability only in a few and exceptional cases. In the KNP/BT/VRG case (IV M 291. JOCE L 217 27/08/93), the Commission agreed to the introduction in the same market of solid and corrugated boards, in spite of some differences in their main technical characteristics (corrugated boards did not perform as well as solid boards in an extremely wet environment and did not have the strength of solid boards). However, the Commission considered that the technological developments of corrugated boards permitted an improvement in their water resistance. Moreover, this additional processing narrowed the price differential between the two products. However, it is important to note that the Commission considered more precise enquiries unnecessary, the market share of the parties on each of these markets not raising serious doubts relative to the merger's compatibility with the Common Market.

According to the demand side approach used by the European Commission, three questions have to be asked when defining the group of products comprised in a relevant market. The first concerns what Fishwick (1986) calls the 'functional interchangeability' of the candidate products in the relevant market. The antitrust authority has to decide if a product A has physical or technical properties enabling it to fulfil the same function as the product B supplied by the parties to the merger. In the case of a positive answer, the second question involves analysing their 'reactive interchangeability'. In the case of a modest price increase of B, would the consumers react by buying product A? The third question concerns the presence of barriers to substitution. A will not be considered as belonging to the same market as B if it is too difficult to transfer the purchases from B to A (particularly if the buyers have to spend some money on a new investment to use A or if this close product is not so well distributed as B, forcing the consumers to endure higher transport costs).

Laboratory simulation being impossible in the economic field, the concrete application of this procedure proves to be all the more difficult, since the regulatory authorities must very often make their decisions without always benefiting from sufficient information. If, in some cases, econometric methods have been used (in Nestlé/Perrier and Lonrho/Gencor, for instance), most often it is impossible to collect valuable data for a sufficient period of time.

The practice of the Commission in its market delimitation is, in fact, very close to the proposition of Scheffman and Spiller (1981), operating a difference between 'economic' and 'antitrust' markets and considering that an 'antitrust approach' should be adopted when analysing the effect of a merger project on the free process of competition.[3] The result of such a practice is that very often the Commission has apportioned markets so narrow that they sometimes seemed to owe more to the skills of 'microsurgery' than to sound economic analysis (for instance, in BSN/Euralim, seven markets had been delimited in the field of ready-to-eat meals: IV M445; in Grand Metropolitan/Cinzano, a specific market has been attributed to vermouth beverage: IV M184).

One must, however, recognize that the high market shares of the parties calculated on such narrow markets have not, in all the cases, led the Commission to consider the submitted merger as being incompatible with the Common Market. Very often, the potential competition from firms located either within or outside the Community has been taken into account in accepting the merger. But, in some specific cases, the parties have been obliged to offer some important undertakings and commitments in order to render their project compatible with the merger regulation.

3. THE COMMISSION'S ECONOMIC ANALYSIS OF A MERGER PROJECT

In pointing out the possible emergence of a dominant position following upon a merger operation, the Commission has, of course, used the methodology tested for many years in the field of the article 86 application. The analysis is usually devoted to the question of knowing whether the market equilibrium could be distorted by the fact that the parties to the merger could be granted a dominant position. According to the economic theory, in some cases, the emergence of the possible joint dominance of the new entity and some non-participating firms has been especially analysed by the Commission. In accordance with the structuralism assumed by the European regulation, technical and economic progress upheld by the parties is only taken into consideration when it proves to be to the consumers' advantage. However, the Commission has cleverly used the degree of freedom given by the EC regulation to legalize some projects which could have been disputed by the ayatollahs of the strict structuralist dogma. The existence of potential competition coming from suppliers of products not taken into account in the definition of the relevant market has sometimes been mentioned to prove the absence of a dominant position, in spite of the very important market share the parties will get. Most of the time, it is the existence of potential competition from firms located outside the Community which has been taken into account in deciding the compatibility of the merger's project with the Common Market. In some cases, it may be considered that some arguments of industrial policy have been implicitly taken into account to accept some projects which otherwise could have been contested according to a strict structuralist philosophy. In such case, to legitimate some merger projects, the Commission has often taken into account the existence of potential competition coming from firms geographically located outside the relevant market.

3.1. The Merger Effect on the Market Participants

In the first step of the Commission's approach, the question is to determine whether the submitted project will give the parties the opportunity to benefit from independent behaviour towards its current competitors and customers. The inquiry is conducted according to the *'ceteris paribus'* device, particularly without taking into account the possible potential competition coming from undertakings located outside the relevant market.

According to the structuralist models, the future market shares of the parties is the starting point of the analysis. But, true to its previous jurisprudence and perhaps even more than it used to, the Commission does not mean to base its research solely on an assessment of the market shares of the parties to a merger to decide on the potential creation or strengthening of a dominant position. Neither has it defined thresholds for increased vigilance.

At the very most, it has merely pointed out, prudently and with clear-sightedness, that concentration operations involving firms which together hold a limited market share are not likely to hinder effective competition, and that this is often the case when the sum of their market shares does not go beyond 25 per cent of the community territory or a substantial part of it. But, when the concentration project is supposed to give the new entity a market share over 35–40 per cent, the rest of the output being shared between several small suppliers, the European antitrust authorities start a detailed study of the market structure and of the previous participants' behaviour. Evolution over a sufficient period of time and not only absolute values of market shares are taken into account by the Commission. An increase or simply a mere stabilization of the most important supplier's market position will much reduce his chances of gaining a positive decision concerning one of his acquisition projects on the same relevant market. Without trying to check whether this success is not the result of superior economic performances, the European authorities will infer from the growth (or stabilization) of its market share over a long period of time that this firm holds a market power which allows it to behave, to an appreciable extent, independently of its competitors. In Boeing/McDonnell (IV/M877. JOCE L336. 8/12/97), the European Commission noticed that Airbus, after making inroads into Boeing's position in the 1980s, had not been significantly able to get a higher market share in the 1990s. The Commission considered this would have been nearly sufficient to prove Boeing's dominant position. Indeed, according to models like the Cournot approach, this procedure implicitly rests on the fear that it would be profitable to the parties to restrict their post-merger output (creation of a Stiglerian market power). Such a risk is supposed to be important when the market has reached maturity. The impact that a merger's project may have on the process of sufficient competition may also affect the positions of competitors, suppliers and customers owing to the vertical effects of the concerned projects. This is why the Commission is careful to analyse successively the horizontal, then the vertical effects of the submitted projects.

Moreover, the Commission never fails to examine whether the customers have at their disposal a sufficient countervailing power to contest any post-merger price increase the parties could try to set up. Finally, when the submitted project takes the shape of a conglomerate investment, its impact on the financing of the acquired firm is also taken into account.

The danger of the emergence of a dominant position is considered important when the market has reached maturity. Otherwise, the Commission recognizes that the possession of large market shares on a new developing market is not an unusual occurrence and does not necessarily indicate a weaker competition ('high market shares on a new developing market are not extraordinary and they do not necessarily indicate market power' (Digital–Kienzle M 057 22/02/91)).

The 'time' variable undeniably proves to be crucial when determining the existence of a true dominant position. Indeed, it is generally agreed that there are three stages in the evolution of a market: an exploring stage, an intermediary development stage and a mature stage. The position of force which some firms may enjoy during the first two stages of market evolution is, very often, nothing more than the result of an efficient competitive rivalry, as defined by Schumpeter when he considered that plans designed on a very large scale could not, in many cases, even begin to be carried out unless the planners first counted on the discouragement of competition. So only those large market shares held in sectors having reached maturity should be considered.

In Mitsubishi/UCAR (IV/M024), the target firm owned a market share between 35 per cent and 40 per cent of the production of graphite electrodes and graphite-based specialities. (Its closest competitors only reached between 15 per cent and 25 per cent of the market). This high supply share of graphite electrodes, a product having reached technological maturity, plus the quality of the distribution circuit established by UCAR, may have led one to suppose that this firm was in a dominant position. This conclusion seemed all the more probable since the parties themselves acknowledged that any further entry on the market was extremely hypothetical.

Nevertheless, in this case, the Commission came down in favour of the joint project, not only because Mitsubishi's market share was weak but also because UCAR's competitors had proved their technological efficiency on the market in question and because the uses of the product concerned in different sectors could lead to new applications requiring high R&D expenditure.

Some mergers may also have negative effects because they assume the form of a vertical integration granting them the power of excluding some competitors (Bainian market power) or simply because, even though they may be horizontal, they are liable to affect the balance of power between the new entity and its customers.

The existence of some benefits like 'absolute cost advantages' (to use Bain's classical typology) may be deduced from the holding of a key position within a production branch. The control of rare resources is an evident asset to the holder. In such a case, competitors would be at a cost disadvantage and might even sometimes be victims of exclusionary practices by the new entity. So it is via an assertive method and a very analytical approach that the Commission applies itself to the study of the vertical effects of the operations submitted to its approval. When ICI acquired half of the Tioxide group's capital, the Commission has checked to what extent ICI's market position could be reinforced on the upstream paint market in which this multinational firm was solidly implanted (number one world producer), titanium dioxide being an indispensable raw material for paint manufacture (IV/M029)

A positive decision concerning this joint project was only taken after checking that none of ICI's competitors on the paint market would be supplanted. Indeed, the Commission first asserted the maintenance of a sufficient supply of titanium dioxide available to competitors. It also took into account the fact that no substantial savings on ICI costs accrued through the operation, since the intermediary product concerned only represented a small part of the total cost of the paint production.

The supply of aluminium cans for drink packaging was also highly concentrated on the community territory. VIAG's plan to acquire a majority share of the equities of the five firms making up Continental Can European Packaging (CEE) business did present a serious risk of a reduction in the supply of laminated aluminium available to CEE's competitors, given the strong vertical integration existing in this branch of activity. The decision concerning the compatibility of this concentration project was therefore only acquired once it had been established that, on each market segment, there would remain at least one large supplier, independent of the new joint entity, able to meet the supply demands of CEE's competitors. Furthermore, the analysis of the foreseeable evolution of the demand in aluminium indicated a large increase in the size of the market and led one to suppose that the growth in supply would not be upset by the technical indivisibilities to which aluminium manufacturing was subjected.

For joint projects between companies of a commercial nature, care has always been taken to verify the absence of creation or strengthening of a state of dependence which could be unfairly used by the new entities. In some cases, such as Promodès/Dirsa, la Redoute/Empire (IV/M080) and Otto/Grattan (IV/M070), it was established that the suppliers would not be at the mercy of their commercial customers as a result of too weak a concentration of their sales in the new entities created by the merger. Consequently, the Commission displayed its concern to protect the vertical balance of forces between the industrial and commercial sectors.

The risk of the creation of an important situation of economic dependency has been one of the main reasons for the refusal of the merger intended between Kesko and Tuko, the two leading supermarket chains in Finland (IV/M784. L110. 26/04/97).

In a lot of cases, the economic power of the customers has been put forward as a very important variable able to offset the important increase in the market share the new entity would get from the merger. In the Alcatel/Telettra case, the Commission noticed that Telefonica, the only customer on the Spanish market for telecommunications systems and equipment, had maintained a diversified purchasing policy. It added that it was possible for Telefonica to increase its purchase from other suppliers in order to prevent any dependence on the new entity (IV/M042. JOCE L 122. 17/05/91). In the TKS/ITW Signode/Titan case (IV/M970. JOCE L 316. 25/11/98), the customers were supposed to be sufficiently powerful and very well organized and able to deal with the new entity as an equal. The Commission added that in the steel industry the customers, being also the raw material suppliers to the new entity, knew quite well the principal component of the production cost of the concerned final product (metalling strappings) and were able to contest the willingness of the parties to increase their price. On the other hand, the lack of power of some of Boeing's customers has been particularly obvious, as shown by a letter addressed to a Japanese aircraft leasing company on signing an order for Airbus aircraft: 'It could have undesirable implications for the Japan America aerospace industry co-operation' (IV/M877. JOCE L 336. 08/12/97).

In some cases, the impact of the effects of the merger on the financing of the new entity has been taken into account, particularly when the project assumed a conglomerate aspect. The objective of such mergers is not so much to create economic synergies as to get some financial benefits. By investing in several different lines of business, the managers of a conglomerate try to lessen the financial risk of the group or to finance their new acquisition by taking out loans. Conglomerate mergers may reduce competition in a specific industrial sector when the acquired firm is able to benefit from cheap funds from the mother company or from the other components of the conglomerate. In some cases, the Commission worried about such a risk. In the VIAG/Sanofi case (IV M 521), the merger had no direct negative impact on the competition in the relevant markets concerned by the project. However, considering the conglomerate aspect of the merger, the Commission wondered about its impact on the financing of the business concerned. It was only after it was established that the acquired firm would not benefit from more financial resources than before (see also the Del Monte/Royal Foods/Anglo American case) that the project was accepted.

In Boeing/McDonnell, the Commission also noticed that, thanks to the acquisition, Boeing would significantly increase its ability to cope with the economic cycles (revenues achieved in the defence and space sector being more stable than those generated in the commercial sectors). It added that it would increase the scope of cross-subsidization of Boeing's sales in commercial aircraft in the market segment where it meets specific competition. It was proved that, in the past, Boeing had already used the strategy of cross-subsidies to prevent Douglas from launching a new aircraft.

3.2. Post-Merger Joint Dominant Position

As pointed out by economic analysis, the market participants may change their business behaviour after a merger. Instead of sticking to a Cournot behaviour or some other independent strategies, they may shift to a less competitive strategy (conscious parallelism or tacit collusion). In some cases, the Commission has been worried about the possible emergence of a joint exploitation of a dominant position if the merger's project was adopted without some important and structural adjustments. Such a risk is evoked when the market structures take on specific features, such as homogeneous products offered by few suppliers producing in similar costs conditions, a high degree of price parallelism being observed over a long period previous to the submitted merger, high transparency concerning the other market variables, and so on.

The Nestlé/Perrier case (IV/M190. JOCE L 356. 05/12/92) was the first in which the Commission concluded that the projected merger would lead to a duopolistic dominant position on the French bottled water market. It considered that, in such a case, this duopoly would significantly impede competition and would be very likely to cause considerable harm to the consumers. After the merger, the rate of concentration would have been very high (Nestlé and Danone holding more than 82 per cent of the total French water market, nearly 95 per cent of all still mineral waters).

The Commission also proved that these main suppliers had developed instruments allowing them to control and monitor each other's behaviour (particularly as a result of the implementation of a mechanism of regular exchanges of information on the quantities sold each month, broken down by major brands). The Commission considered that such a device would permit immediate detection of any deviation by any single major brand from the expected performance. It added that, after the merger, these exchanges of information would be less indispensable, given the monopolistic nature of the market and the resulting increased transparency of the market itself.

The emergence of a joint dominant position was also highly probable on the worldwide platinum market in the Lonrho/Gencor case. The project would have led to a duopolistic market characterized by high transparency (prices are quoted on commodity stock exchanges). Statistics about production and sales are regularly published by some specialized firms. Considering the very low price-elasticity of demand at current price levels, the existence of high entry barriers, the weak purchasing power of the buyers and the parallel behaviour adopted previously by the suppliers, the project would certainly have led to a strong duopolistic position enabling the two suppliers to increase their prices.

In the ABB/Daimler–Benz case (IV M 580. JOCE L 11. 14/01/97), it was rather the ability for the duopolists to exclude the potential competition which was particularly highlighted. In this case, the Commission considered that the creation of a duopoly would increase the structural danger of a joint blocking strategy of the two German suppliers in the market for trams and underground railway vehicles. In this line of business, the know-how in electrical and electronic components is particularly strategic. Only Siemens and ABB/Daimler–Benz would possess it, the foreign competitors being obliged to cooperate with one of them to acquire this know-how. Previous to this merger plan, the Canadian firm Bombardier had been the only foreign supplier to get some orders in the German market, thanks to its cooperation with a Daimler–Benz subsidiary. The possible withdrawal of its cooperation partner would have prevented Bombardier from being an active supplier in this market.

3.3. Potential Competition: a Key Variable

The analysis of the importance of potential competitors from undertakings located either within or outside the Community constitutes a crucial stage in the European procedure. In some cases it appears to give the Commission a real degree of freedom when a merger project unambiguously allows the promotion of European economic efficiency, even if the merger project endangers an effective and sufficient competition in the concerned market.

Research into the existence of potential entry barriers is, in this respect, particularly important and the Commission attaches specific consideration to this task. Moreover, the Commission never omits to assess the protective character of these barriers within the framework of a dynamic view of the markets in question. On account of the very likely lack of sufficient potential competition, several projects have been considered incompatible with the Common Market (or only compatible thanks to conditions aiming at altering the original concentration). (Nordic satellite distribution: IV M 490. JOCE L53 02/03/96; Deutsche Telekom/Beta Research: IV M 1027. JOCE L53 27/02/99; Boeing/McDonnell: IV M877. JOCE L336 08/12/97). In these cases, the Commission took into account several indexes to justify its refusal.

Existence of long-term arrangements between the parties has been particularly highlighted. The exclusive arrangements between Boeing and three of the most important airline companies in the world tying them with their supplier for a 20-year period have been considered as strongly reducing the potential competition.

The Commission rightly considered that, even if the airline companies derived some economic benefits from these arrangements, the gains would be likely to be more than offset by 'the rigidity incurred by being locked into a single supplier for so long a period, during which it might be proved to be the case that the competitors' prices become lower, their technology and related services superior'.

In some cases, such as Deutsche Telekom/Beta Research, or Bertelsman/Kirch/Premiere (IV M993 JOCE L53 27/02/99), it has been proved that, when the contract expires, the advance gained by the first mover has been considered too great to give a newcomer any chance to compete efficiently in the acquisition of a new contract. In a field of business like Pay TV, the networks effects are very often too protective of the first entrants' market position when they have previously built a large portfolio of consumers.

Given the market position of 'Premiere', the only pay TV supplier in Germany, competitors' prospects of securing any substantial volume of attractive pay TV broadcasting rights will be small. This is because, to have any hope of acquiring broadcasting rights, it is vital to have access to viewers in the form of an established subscriber basis, since rightholders usually want to see their products widely distributed. As 'Premiere's' subscriber basis can be expected to be large in the coming years, thus a sale of rights to 'Premiere' should secure a considerably higher price than a sale to a newcomer. A new entrant would run considerable financial risk by concluding output deals since he would have to guarantee a minimum subscriber base, without knowing whether he could achieve the guarantee figure (Deutsche Telekom/Beta Research).

Holding some essential facilities also constitutes a particular dissuasive weapon against any entry of a potential competitor. The essential nature of a specific facility is established on the basis of several necessary conditions. All essential facilities share four salient characteristics: 'First, the facility must be unique. Second, it must remain unique while its output is widely distributed. Third, it must be centrally located in the path of users' production. And fourth, it must have the ability to impede or enable the process by which such users do their business' (Gerber, 1988).

In Deutsche Telekom/Beta Research, the Commission noticed that the installation of an alternative technical infrastructure for the transmission of pay TV would require a major investment. However, other potential suppliers would not be prepared to make this investment, through lack of opportunities for market penetration. The Commission added that all potential conditional access operators would be dependent on Beta Research's licensing policy. According to the Commission, it would be hardly possible for competitors to get any licence agreement, the licenser being controlled mainly by firms having their own interest as programme suppliers.

In 'Nordic Satellite Distribution', while recognizing that the new infrastructure as described by the parties could be highly efficient and beneficial to consumers, the Commission decided not to accept the merger project. That infrastructure was not considered as open and accessible for all the interested parties. Therefore it was likely that the operation would lead to less variety in the offer to Nordic TV in the future.

In contrast, considering entry to the Spanish market for telecommunications systems and equipment easy to be, the Commission did not oppose Alcatel's takeover project of Telettra. In this case, it was particularly careful to highlight the contestable nature of the Spanish market. The existence of a substantial potential competition was inferred from: (a) the low technical costs involved in the product adaptation with which producers, absent in the Spanish market, would have to comply, (b) the not indispensable character of manufacturing in Spain, and (c) the low transport costs relative to the equipment values, even for American or Japanese suppliers. The market shares of the two concentration candidates were, however, considerable (line transmission equipment: Alcatel, 41 per cent, Telettra, 41 per cent; hyperfrequency equipment: Alcatel, 18 per cent, Telettra, 65 per cent) But, in accordance with the Lerner's Index, as formulated by Landes and Posner, the existence of this potential competition in the more or less short term, plus the buying power of the main customer (in a monopsony position) were enough to carry the decision, on condition that vertical links between the two parties and their single client be terminated. The same doctrine was applied in the ICI/Tioxide decision. ICI's acquisition of this important titanium dioxide manufacturer (the second supplier on the world scale) could have instigated fears of the emergence of a dominant position in so far as it had access to considerable financial resources from its purchaser. However, the Commission considered that such a risk was weak, given that not only were there six competitors in the European Market, but there was also a possibility of penetration by Du Pont (world leader) and by a large Japanese firm (within five years).

Having ascertained that the market for civilian-use helicopters was a world market, considering the absence of specific entry barriers to most national markets, the Commission also decided to give the go-ahead to the joint operation between Aérospatiale and Messerschmitt–Bölkow–Blohm, despite the large market share to which the new entity would have access. Indeed, it took account of the position of strength held by the American industry benefiting from the military research programme which bore no comparison to Aérospatiale's situation, and counted on the development of competition from the other side of the Atlantic following projects to cut military spending.

There has sometimes been taken into account the potential competition coming from suppliers of products not belonging to the relevant market but involved in close lines of business and able to enter the supply of the relevant product in response to a 'small but significant and non-transitory increase in price', within one year, without the need to commit significant investment in new facilities. In the Pepsico/Kas case, the Commission admitted that Pepsico's relatively high market share in the lemon-lime market in Portugal substantially overstates the competitive significance of the notified acquisition: 'Taking into account the existence of a certain degree of supply side substituability, often carbonated soft drink producers currently active in the Spanish and Portuguese area could enter the lemon-lime market, in this way preventing Pepsico from impeding effective competition'. (See also the TKS/ITW Signode/Titan cases in which the Commission agreed to the presence of a close product as a factor increasing the price-elasticity of the relevant product demand). Apparently much more surprising has been the positive decision adopted by the Commission in some cases of mergers submitted in the steel industry. The 'Mannesman/Vallourec/Ilva' case of concentration in the market for seamless stainless steel tubes is a perfect example of the difficulty that sometimes arises when the long-term objectives of industrial policy have to be reconciled with those of competition policy which, in the case of concentrations, seeks to oppose regroupings likely to create or to strengthen dominant positions in the relevant market. Even though, in this case, the Commission gave the go-ahead for the planned joint venture between the three firms in question at just the right time, the final decision threatened to be a negative one. A majority of the Advisory Committee on Concentration had, in fact, voted against the plan, and the favourable decision was carried with a very small majority within the Commission.

It is true that the creation of this concentration joint venture was such as to alter considerably the conditions of supply on the relevant market. With a share of the Community market estimated at 36 per cent, the new entity was faced with only one other operator of similar size (Sandvik, with a market share of 33 per cent), the remaining demand being shared between a number of smaller firms, the largest of which only holding 13 per cent of the market. As in the Nestlé/Perrier case, there was a risk (even a greater one) of creating a joint dominant position between the two leading operators which appeared especially important as the price-elasticity of the demand on the market was low, the products very homogeneous, and there was a high degree of price transparency. So it appeared that none of the groups concerned would enjoy a significant structural cost advantage to offset the substantial gains that would result from engaging in anti-competition parallel behaviour. Therefore, it was by taking into account a sufficient degree of contestability in the market, if not at the time, then at least in the near future, that a positive decision was finally taken. Indeed, the Commission considered that a substantial increase in prices in the Community market would be likely to accelerate the entry of competitors from Japan and the countries of Eastern Europe. In so far as the capacity reductions to be achieved through state aid had become less and less frequent, it is clear that the process of concentration between the operators on the market would have to be speeded up, since the actual economies of scale in the sector required plants to operate at levels close to their optimal levels of capacity. However, it was not evident that the Community Merger Control Regulation and its accompanying 'competition assessment' technique were suitable to promote regrouping of firms in what is already an oligopolistic market. Thanks to the text of article 2 para. 1, making provisions to take into account potential competition from firms outside the Community, it was not difficult to find potential suppliers.

In another case (Krupp/Thyssen/Riva/Falk/Tadfin/AST: IV M484. JOCE L251, 19/10/95), the new entity born of the planned project would win an important market share. In accordance with the Cournot model, the large unemployed production capacities of the competitors have been considered sufficient to prevent the parties making any attempt to raise their prices. (See also the Mannesman/Hoech case (IV M222), in which the Commission accepted the joint venture in spite of the strong evidence that the parties might achieve, upon completion of the concentration, 'Liberty of action that would not be immediately fully controlled by existing competitors'. As in the other decisions, it was considered that the incentives and opportunities for market entry were high enough not only for West European competitors, but also for the East European producers of steel tubes).

4. CONCLUSION

Despite the relatively conservative foundations of the European merger control law, clearly some way behind new advances in modern economic thinking, the decisions adopted by the Commission do not, on the whole, lay themselves open to much criticism. The Commission has proved itself to be able to make good use of the areas of freedom allowed by the Regulation text to outline jurisprudence which conforms to the expectations of those who attach importance to taking account of the impact of a merger project on economic efficiency. Among the numerous projects submitted, only a few have been refused. Thanks to the opportunity offered by article 8 para. 2 of the regulation, in a lot of questionable projects, the structural undertakings proposed by the parties have been considered as sufficient to pronounce their compatibility within the Common Market.

NOTES

1. According to the typology proposed by Krattenmaker *et al.* (1987). The interest of this differenciation is in highlighting the fact that the exclusion of competitors does not necessarily entail the power to increase prices.
2. With m_1, m_2 the pre-merger profit margins of the parties, and C^M the post-merger marginal cost of the new entity,

$$C^M < P\left(1 - \frac{m_1 + m_2}{|E_m^d|}\right)$$

3. While antitrust markets consist of the smallest relevant group of producers possessing potential market power, economic markets are based on arbitrage. For example, if producers' groups L and F are in the same economic market, an attempt by L to raise prices will result in arbitrage eliminating the divergence in the two groups' prices and will usually increase F's sales. In such a situation, the existence of F weakens any market power that would be possessed by L if F's output were held fixed. However, the existence of F does not in itself necessarily eliminate L's market power. Arbitrage tempers but does not necessarily eliminate L's market power (1987, p.127).

REFERENCES

'1992, The New European Economy', Report no 35 CEE (1988).

Alonso, J. (1994), 'Market Definition in the Community Control Policy', *European Competition Law Review*, **4**, 195–208

Brozen, Y. (1982), *Concentration Mergers and Public Policy*, London: Macmillan.
Concurrence et intégration: 'Politique Communautaire de Contrôle des Concentrations' (1994), *Economie Européenne*, **57**.
Farrel, J. and C. Shapiro (1990), 'Profitable Horizontal Mergers and Welfare', reprinted in L. Phlips (ed.), *Applied Industrial Economics* (1998), Cambridge Mass., Cambridge University Press.
Fishwick, F. (1986), 'Definition of the Relevant Market in Community Competition Policy', Working paper DG IV 16764/86.
Fishwick, F. (1989), 'Definition of Monopoly Power in the Antitrust Policies in the United Kingdom and the European Community', *Antitrust Bulletin*, **3**, Fall, 451–88.
Gerber, D. (1988), 'Rethinking the Monopolist's Duty to Deal: A Legal and Economic Critique of the Doctrine of 'Essential Facilities''', *Virginia Law Review*, **74**, 1069–1113.
Geroski, P. (1987), *Competition and Innovation*, EC Report.
Glais, M. (1991), 'La Jurisprudence Récente (article 85 et 86) de la Commission Européenne à l'Epreuve de la Théorie Economique', *Revue d'Economie Industrielle,* **56**, 101–17.
Jacquemin, A. (1970), *Economie Industrielle Européenne*, Paris, Dunod.
Kamien, M. and N. Schwartz (1982), *Market Structure and Innovations*, Cambridge, Mass.: Cambridge University Press.
Krattenmaker, T., W. Landes and S. Salop (1987), 'Monopoly Power and Market Power in Antitrust', *Georgetown Law Journal*, **76**, 587–615.
Landes, W. and R. Posner (1981), 'Market Power in Antitrust Cases', *Harvard Law Review*, **94**, 937–96.
Scheffman, D. and P. Spiller (1987), 'Geographic Market Power under the U.S. Department of Justice Merger Guidelines', *Journal of Law and Economics*, **30** (1), 123–47.
Willig, R. (1991), 'Merger Analysis, Industrial Organization Theory and Merger Guidelines', *Brookings Papers*: *Microeconomics*, 281–312.

Index